D0598183

NO LONGER PROPERTY
SEATTLE PUBLIC LIBRARY

Received on:

AUG 1 4 2013

Green Lake Libra

GREAT MOMENTS
of the U.S. OPEN

GREAT MOMENTS
of the U.S. OPEN

UNITED STATES GOLF ASSOCIATION

by ROBERT WILLIAMS & MICHAEL TROSTEL

with Supervising Editor RAND JERRIS

Photography by JOHN MUMMERT

Foreword by JACK NICKLAUS

FIREFLY BOOKS

The USGA dedicates this book to the thousands of men and women who volunteer their time in support of our national championship. It is their passion and dedication that makes the U.S. Open possible.

A FIREFLY BOOK

Published by Firefly Books Ltd. 2013

Copyright © 2013 Firefly Books Ltd.
Text copyright © 2013 United States Golf Association
All images © courtesy of USGA Archives unless otherwise noted below or on page 213.

All rights reserved. No part of this publication may be reproduced, stored in a retrieval system, or transmitted in any form or by any means, electronic, mechanical, photocopying, recording or otherwise, without the prior written permission of the Publisher.

First printing

Published in the United States by
Firefly Books (U.S.) Inc.
P.O. Box 1338, Ellicott Station
Buffalo, New York 14205

Published in Canada by
Firefly Books Ltd.
50 Staples Avenue, Unit 1
Richmond Hill, Ontario L4B 0A7

Cover and interior design: Peter Ross/Counterpunch Inc.
Creative Direction/Editor: Steve Cameron
Front cover: USGA/John Mummert
Back cover: USGA/J.D. Cuban (Stewart); USGA/John Mummert (Woods)
Back flap: USGA/John Mummert

Printed in China

The publisher gratefully acknowledges the financial support for our publishing program by the Government of Canada through the Canada Book Fund as administered by the Department of Canadian Heritage.

Publisher Cataloging-in-Publication Data (U.S.)
Williams, Robert.
    Great moments of the U.S. Open/Robert Williams, Michael Trostel ; supervising editor Rand Jerris ; photographs by John Mummert ; foreword by Jack Nicklaus.

[216] p. : ill., photos. (chiefly col.) ; cm.
Includes index.

Summary: A collection of stories chronicling the great moments of the U.S. Open, including essays focusing on the origins of the championship, course design, international growth, near misses, and Francis Ouimet's 1913 victory. The book is illustrated with archival images and artifacts from the United States Golf Association's collection.

ISBN-13: 978-1-77085-188-7
1. U.S. Open (Golf tournament)–History. 2. Golfers–Biography. I. Trostel, Michael. II. Jerris, Rand. III. Mummert, John. IV. Nicklaus, Jack. V. Title.
796.35266 dc23   GV970.3.U69W45 2013

Library and Archives Canada Cataloguing in Publication
Williams, Robert, 1969–
    Great moments of the U.S. Open/Robert Williams, Michael Trostel ; supervising editor, Rand Jerris ; photographs by John Mummert ; foreword by Jack Nicklaus. Includes index.
Includes photographs from the USGA Museum.

ISBN 978-1-77085-188-7
1. U.S. Open (Golf Tournament)–History–Anecdotes. 2. Golfers–United States–History. 3. Golfers–United States–History–Pictorial works. 4. Golf–United States–History. I. Trostel, Michael, 1983– II. USGA Museum III. Title.
GV970.3.U69W44 2013   796.35266   C2012-907854-9

Previous spread: An American flag is reflected in the U.S. Open Championship Trophy.

Contents

Foreword

BY JACK NICKLAUS

Putting records aside, I love the major championships. I always did as a player, and I still do as a fan. When I look at the game of golf from a touring professional's perspective, I believe the most significant part of the game, and what I believe most careers should be based on, are the majors. They are the measuring stick. They are the lasting championships. They are the ones people remember. The ones that live on to be passed down through generations.

While they are all meaningful, I have always considered the U.S. Open the most important major championship. The U.S. Open represents our national championship, and because I am an American, there is a special connection to that major and an enormous sense of satisfaction when one is fortunate to win.

In addition, I have always loved USGA championships. I have played in a total of 71, and since I was a junior, they have always been the ultimate and complete examinations of a golfer. I always felt that the USGA did the best job of preparing a golf course that will test you completely. A U.S. Open typically challenges every shot a golfer has in their bag. There are courses that demand length, but all of them require accuracy. A U.S. Open requires shotmaking and shot placement on greens, and, of course, it tests your putting ability. Most importantly, it tests your mental ability – from course management to patience to performing under pressure. I feel very proud of the championships I have won, thus I always looked forward to playing USGA championships – none more so than the U.S. Open.

Every competitive golfer realizes that a victory is a four-day process and the cumulative result of several hundred shots. But every major champion can typically point to a seminal moment – one shot, one swing, one putt – that was critical in their ultimate victory. When I look back on my four U.S. Open victories, there are such moments that were vital to victory and remain unforgettable to this day. Some came with a 1-iron in hand, others with a putter in hand. All ended with joyous fists to the sky.

From a very young age, I dreamed of winning the U.S. Open. Never could I have scripted that my first professional victory as a 22-year-old rookie in 1962 would also be my first U.S. Open and major championship win and that it would play out in the backyard of my long-time friend and rival Arnold Palmer. To get to the 18-hole playoff against Arnold, I needed to convert a crucial up and down from thick greenside rough for par on number 17. I faced a difficult, lightning-fast 4- or 5-footer to save par. To eliminate the break, I decided to ram the putt in the hole, with the risk being that I could face a bogey putt of double the length. After a couple of deep breaths, I fired. My long-time idol, Bob Jones, later wrote in a letter to me that while watching the U.S. Open on TV at home, he almost jumped out of his chair when the putt went in.

It was in 1967, during my second U.S. Open victory and my first of two at Baltusrol, that I got my hands on the famous "White Fang" putter that served me so well that year and helped me to a final-round 65 and a U.S. Open scoring record. Yet the one moment or swing I remember most from that championship came on the final hole. I was playing with Arnold, and we came to the 18th with me holding on to a four-shot lead. If I birdied the par-5 finishing hole, I would break Ben Hogan's 72-hole record of 276. But I faced a 238-yard third shot that played more like 260 because it was uphill, all carry and against the wind. I put everything I had into a 1-iron and put the ball to 22 feet. I made the putt and secured the win and the record. The next time I went to Baltusrol, I dropped a ball at the exact same spot and couldn't even reach the green with a driver.

I have said many times that if I had only one round of golf to play, it would likely be at Pebble Beach. My love affair with the windswept, oceanside links of Pebble Beach began with my win there in the 1961 U.S. Amateur. It blossomed in 1972 with the third of my U.S. Open victories. The win was memorable in and of itself, but on the 71st hole I hit one of the most unforgettable shots of my career. It was at the famed 17th hole, the long par 3 that borders the Pacific and, particularly on this day, plays into the teeth of an angry wind. I had a three-shot lead with two holes to play, and with 219 yards to the pin, went with my trusty 1-iron. On my backswing, I actually felt myself closing the clubface and working too much inside my target line – all spelling a hook. My tempo, however, was probably never as good as it was that week, and I was able to correct my swing on the way down. The ball flew low and true, and although I couldn't see the result, the crowd's roar told me what I needed to hear. The ball had taken a couple of hops, hit the flagstick and stopped 6 inches from the hole.

My return to Baltusrol in 1980 for a U.S. Open Championship was a special one for many reasons. A difficult season in 1979 led to a revamping of my swing in early 1980, and at 40 years old, I was certain I had my skeptics. But a 63 in the opening round tied the 18-hole U.S. Open scoring record and sent a message to many, including myself. My 68 in the final round helped me lower my own 72-hole U.S. Open scoring record, and I remember the warm

Jack Nicklaus

embrace of the fans that day, who kept chanting, "Jack's back! Jack's back!" Yet the day and my fourth U.S. Open title were not sealed until the 17th hole. Isao Aoki had pushed me all day, and he was looking at a 5-footer on 17 for birdie. I hit a sand wedge to 22 feet, made the critical birdie and, to this day, can't forget the rush of emotions that overwhelmed me. The look on my face after I rolled in that putt remains one of my wife Barbara's favorite images.

Throughout golf history, we have read countless tales of memorable moments played out on the closing holes – usually the 18th green – of a major, and there's no doubt I have been fortunate in my career to have a few. But when I look back on my USGA championship career, I can't discount several moments that happened on the first tee that served as important bookends to a championship legacy I cherish.

I think back to when I was just 13 years old and playing in my first national championship, the U.S. Junior Amateur at Southern Hills in Oklahoma. I was the youngest in the field, and I remember nonchalantly stepping on the first tee of my first

match about 30 seconds before it was to begin. On the tee was Joe Dey, then the executive director of the USGA, who would later become a close friend, confidant and mentor. He was joined by Colonel Lee S. Reed, a Kentucky gentleman dressed in all white, goateed and in many ways looking like Colonel Sanders. The Colonel looked at me, and with Joe's nod of approval, said, "Mr. Nicklaus, half a minute more getting here and you would be on the second tee, one down."

Needless to say, I have never been late for a tee time since.

Fast-forward 47 years, and at age 60, I found myself standing on the first tee of the 2000 U.S. Open at Pebble Beach. I knew the week would be an emotional one as I played in my 44th and final U.S. Open. The emotions were amplified when I was asked to take the spot of the defending U.S. Open champion, Payne Stewart, which was left vacant by his tragic passing in October 1999. When they asked for a moment of silence on the first tee to honor Payne's memory, the emotions welled up inside me and I had to reach for a towel to wipe my eyes. I regrouped but eventually experienced my own misty-eyed moment on the 18th green when I said my final goodbye to U.S. Open championship golf.

The moment was a confluence of many things – the finality, the warm-hearted applause by the gallery lining the 18th, my son Jack II on the bag and my wife and other family members awaiting me behind the green. I had reached the par-5 green in two shots, but through teary eyes ended up three-putting. Any other time, I would have walked away angry. This time, it just gave me one or two more strokes and a few extra minutes to say goodbye to an old friend – the U.S. Open.

Good golfing,

JACK NICKLAUS

Jack Nicklaus poses with trophies, from left, the U.S. Open Championship Trophy, the Francis D. Ouimet Memorial Trophy (U.S. Senior Open) and the Havemeyer Trophy (U.S. Amateur).

Facing page: The Jack Nicklaus Medal, created in 2012, is the medal now awarded to U.S. Open champions. A copy of the medal, engraved with the years Nicklaus won the national championship, was presented to him during a ceremony at the 2012 U.S. Open.

Introduction

The game of golf is a central component in the lives of many Americans. It can be a bond between parent and child; a respite from the grind of work; a way to unify a school, a city, or even a country; or a much-needed distraction in a time of crisis or grief. The game did not originate in the United States, but it has grown and thrived here in the 20th and 21st centuries, both as a leisure activity played among family, friends and co-workers and as a top-level athletic competition played by the best amateurs and professionals in the world.

On December 22, 1894, representatives from five golf clubs gathered at the Calumet Club in New York City and founded what would become the United States Golf Association (USGA). Their chief objective was to create an institution to steward the game in the United States by governing its rules and conducting national championships. For more than a century, the United States Open Championship (U.S. Open) has identified our national champion and, in the process, forged unforgettable moments in our collective memory. This book celebrates the heroic champions, their inspirational stories and the extraordinary circumstances that created them and, in doing so, made the U.S. Open one of the world's premier sporting events.

While some stories focus on a particular shot, others embrace the significance of an entire championship. It is impossible to encapsulate more than a century of U.S. Open history in a few hundred pages, but we believe the stories shared here embody the spirit of the championship. They are centered on the accomplishments of individual champions and organized around themes related to the defining moments in the game's history, perseverance, underdogs, great comebacks and dominant performances. The book draws together heroes from different eras who share common experiences and emotions.

The stories are brought to life with stunning archival images and artifacts from the USGA's collection. These iconic images reveal how the championship has changed over time, but they also connect the present to a more distant past. There are many aspects of the U.S. Open that have changed since its inception, but the most critical ingredients remain constant. It continues to be golf's toughest test, played on the greatest courses in the country and driven by volunteers and fans who love this great game. Fittingly, it is also the most democratic major championship in the game, so anyone who has the skill, passion and determination can compete for the title of United States Open Champion.

Facing page: A close-up shot of the front of the U.S. Open Championship Trophy, which features a scene of men and women playing golf in the late 19th century.

Origins: The 1895 U.S. Open

BY RAND JERRIS

The inaugural United States Open Championship was a simple affair, a far cry from the grand pageant that has come to mark the game's premier championship. The gallery was sparse. Media interest was minimal. The nine-hole course was measured in feet, rather than in yards. The field would make four trips around the rocky and swampy layout in just one day, October 4, 1895.

Whereas today more than 9,000 hopefuls apply to test their skills against the world's best in golf's toughest test, just 11 men gathered on the first tee of the Newport Golf Club on a blustery fall day for the chance to take home the newly minted sterling trophy and a handsome gold medal. The winner was, in all respects, unremarkable: a 21-year-old assistant professional, playing in just the third competition of his career, who only found himself in the field because he was employed by the host club and three of the leading amateurs scheduled to play had withdrawn. In truth, however, these details matter little, for from these humble origins evolved a championship that has given rise to some of the most celebrated champions and most memorable moments in the game's rich history.

Golf was unknown to most Americans in 1895, even though the game had been played in North America for at least 150 years. The origins of golf in the United States remain uncertain, despite considerable efforts by historians to identify the precise date and place that the game first arrived on American soil. While some have pointed to references to "colf" and "kolven" in documents from Fort Orange (now Albany), New York, dating as far back as 1657, it is likely that these games were early Dutch precursors to golf and not the game known today. A more certain reference dates from 1729, with the recording of golf clubs in the estate of William Burnet, an early governor of Massachusetts. Ship manifests also document the exportation of hundreds of golf clubs and more than a thousand golf balls from Scotland to the Carolinas, Virginia and Maryland beginning in 1743.

Early newspapers confirm that the first golf clubs in this country were established among the early British and Scottish communities in New York City in the 1770s, in Charleston, South Carolina, in the 1780s and in Savannah, Georgia, in the 1790s. But British and Scottish influence in America began to wane, particularly after the War of 1812, and the game seems to have declined after 1820. Golf resurfaced several decades later in such diverse places as Estes Park, Colorado, in 1875, Burlington, Iowa, in 1883, Oakhurst, West Virginia, in 1884 and Foxburg, Pennsylvania, in 1885. Once the game was reestablished in the 1880s, it continued to grow modestly but steadily. By 1894, there were some 50 clubs in the country, most situated near major metropolitan areas on the East Coast. One notable exception was to be found in Chicago, where a prominent businessman named Charles Blair Macdonald established the Chicago Golf Club in 1892, having

Facing page: Horace Rawlins used this mashie during the first U.S. Open, at the Newport Golf Club in Rhode Island. He was presented a gold medal and the U.S. Open Championship Trophy during the award ceremony. Also pictured is a watercolor painting of the moment by artist Leland Gustavson and a map of the original nine-hole course at Newport Golf Club.

Whitney Warren designed the Beaux Arts–style clubhouse at the Newport Golf Club, shown here in 1925.

learned the game while being schooled in St. Andrews, Scotland, in the 1870s.

Thereafter, the game's growth was explosive. "Golf is the reigning fad of the hour," wrote J. Parmly Paret, a prominent lawn tennis player and sportswriter, in the summer of 1895. "Whether its popularity is a matter of one season or is permanent only the future can reveal, but everything points to a prolonged stay by the favorite sport of the 'bonny Scotchman.' Its growth in this country has been little short of marvelous and is really unparalleled in the annals of sport.... It is the old, old story of Dame Fashion's sway. Some of America's foremost society leaders took up golf last year, and it immediately became fashionable. Now everyone is playing it."

By 1894, the game had indeed grown enough in popularity, as well as geography, for the notion of conducting a competition to determine the nation's best golfer to become a reality. Under the leadership of Theodore Havemeyer, the "Sugar Baron of New York," Newport Golf Club in Rhode Island stepped forward to host the best in the country in a 36-hole stroke-play event in September. The leader at the end of the first round, with a score of 89, was the Chicagoan Charlie Macdonald. His early lead came as little surprise. Many – including Macdonald himself – considered him the premier player in the country. In the second round, however, controversy ensued when Macdonald's ball came to rest against a stone wall. He moved his ball away, and officials penalized him two strokes. When he subsequently lost the championship by one stroke to W.G. Lawrence, a member of the host club, Macdonald lost his composure. He berated the tournament committee and condemned the championship as a fiasco.

Tall and broad-shouldered, with a regal bearing and an elegant mustache, Macdonald was a formidable man. He was pompous and arrogant but held considerable influence. He won his argument, and the national championship was replayed weeks later at St. Andrew's Golf Club in Yonkers, New York. Established in 1888 by John Reid, a Scottish industrialist and confidant of Andrew Carnegie, St. Andrew's was the favored local club of the New York crowd. Building on the popularity, and likely the controversy, of the event at Newport, the festivities at St. Andrew's attracted an even stronger field, featuring the finest amateur golfers from Westchester, Long Island, Boston, Washington and Chicago. Once again Macdonald was favored, and he rolled through the field to meet Lawrence Stoddart of St. Andrew's in the final. Feeling tired and unwell from a premature victory celebration the night before, Macdonald heeded poor advice from a friend and consumed a bottle of champagne and a large steak for lunch. He struggled throughout the afternoon match against an opponent that he should have overpowered. He lost the match on the first extra hole, after the two had finished the scheduled 18-hole match all square. To the dismay of those assembled, Macdonald launched a verbal assault against his opponent, the event and the club. No one club, he argued, had the authority to conduct a national championship. Only a legitimate governing body could make such a claim.

In an effort to restore credibility and sensibility to the fledgling game, Henry Tallmadge of the St. Andrew's Golf Club invited representatives from the clubs at Brookline, Newport, Shinnecock Hills and Chicago to join him for a dinner at the Calumet Club in New York City on December 22, 1894. Their singular purpose was to establish a national governing body that would be charged with conducting a proper national championship, played under proper rules. Among the invitees was Macdonald, for Tallmadge and his allies sought to temper the bluster of the egotistical Chicagoan. And so was born the Amateur Golf Association of the United States. The officers of the new Association determined that very evening that the first true Amateur Championship of the United States would be held in Newport in the late summer of 1895. While they were at it, they added a U.S. Open Championship to the agenda as well.

In the months that followed, the mission of the newborn association expanded to include not only championships for men but an amateur championship for women as well. Now calling itself the United States Golf Association, the organization originally scheduled its men's championships for September, but it delayed the festivities for one month due to a scheduling conflict with the America's Cup yacht races, which were also planned for Newport.

"Newport will be the Mecca of all faithful golfers this week, who will gather for the first championship matches under the management of the United States Golf Association."

– Sports editor, *New York Sun*

Excitement for the new championships grew throughout the summer and into the fall. In the days immediately preceding the start of play, confidence surged among the leadership of the USGA, as well as the sports media, that the coming competitions would prove to be extraordinary. "Newport will be the Mecca of all faithful golfers this week, who will gather for the first championship matches under the management of the United States Golf Association," wrote the sports editor of the *New York Sun*. "So many clubs have joined since the first meeting that the USGA is in a position to elevate the amateur and open championships to a place on an equality with similar golfing fixtures in Great Britain." These were high expectations, indeed.

The Amateur Championship was up first, scheduled to begin on the morning of October 1. Theodore Havemeyer, who had been selected as the USGA's first president during that first dinner at the Calumet Club, had donated a spectacular silver trophy, adorned with griffins, laurel wreaths and floral swags. In unseasonably warm conditions, a field of 32 played Newport's nine-hole Rocky Farm course at match play. Doctors, lawyers, clergy and businessmen were in the championship draw. Macdonald, himself named second vice president of the USGA, defeated Charles Sands, 12 and 11, in the 36-hole final two days later to become both the first U.S. Amateur champion and first USGA champion. Again the pre-championship favorite, Macdonald was never seriously challenged in any of his matches. To the delight – and no doubt relief – of players and officials, nobody contested the result.

As play was underway among the amateurs, the strongest professional field assembled to date in the United States also gathered at Newport in anticipation of the Open competition.

One year earlier, concurrent with the contested amateur competition at St. Andrew's, the club had hosted four professionals in an event that was billed as the first national open tournament. It was won by Scottish professional Willie Dunn, but like the two amateur events that year, the results of this open tournament were never officially recognized, as it was not conducted under the auspices of a true national governing body. One year later, however, there was little questioning of the championship that had been called by the USGA. On October 2, the local newspaper, the *Newport News,* reported the entrants for the inaugural U.S. Open competition – Willie Campbell, James Foulis, John Reid, Charlie Macdonald, L.B. Stoddart, John Patrick, A.W. Smith, Samuel Tucker, Willie Norton, Winthrop Rutherford, Willie Dunn and Willie Davis – in total, eight professionals and four amateurs, the latter being Macdonald, Rutherford, Smith and Stoddart.

By the time play commenced on the morning of October 4, the seasonal weather that had blessed the previous days had taken quite a turn. A cold front had blown in overnight, and with it came fierce winds from the northeast that raked the seaside course. Their enthusiasm sapped by the winds, and presumably the tense competition of the previous days, Macdonald, Rutherford and Stoddart withdrew before the opening round, leaving Smith, the reigning Canadian champion, as the only amateur in the field. Two additional professionals, John Harland of the Weston Golf Club in Massachusetts and Horace Rawlins, the young assistant professional at Newport, were persuaded to round out the field.

Willie Dunn, the head professional at Shinnecock Hills Golf Club on Long Island, and Willie Davis, the host professional from Newport, were considered by many the pre-championship favorites, and thus they were the first off the tee in the morning to start the first round's play. Both men started strong out of the gate, posting 3s on the 900-foot first hole. Dunn would go on to card 5s and 6s on the remaining holes, finishing his first trip around the nine-hole course in 43; Davis shot 45. Playing in the group behind was Willie Campbell, the head professional at The Country Club in Brookline, Massachusetts. Of all the players in the field, Campbell had the most distinguished résumé, having

Above: Horace Rawlins, a native of the Isle of Wight in England, immigrated to the United States and won the first U.S. Open Championship while an assistant professional at the Newport Golf Club. **Facing page:** Rawlins received this gold medal in addition to $150 in prize money.

placed second, third, fourth twice, fifth, seventh and ninth in his seven appearances in the British Open Championship between 1883 and 1889. Like Dunn and Davis, Campbell opened with a 3 at the first then took just three strokes to complete the 1,054-foot second hole. He would go on to shoot 41, taking the lead at the end of the first round by two strokes over Dunn. Paired with Campbell, Rawlins started 4-5, took six strokes to complete the fifth hole and seven strokes on the 1,454-foot sixth, the longest hole on the course. Smith, the only amateur in the field, shot a 47.

A collection of some of the early U.S. Open champions: sitting on the ground is Horace Rawlins, winner of the inaugural U.S. Open; directly behind him is Willie Anderson, who became a four-time U.S. Open champion; and Anderson's arm is around Alex Smith, the 1906 and 1910 U.S. Open champion.

As the players moved on to the second nine, the winds continued to stiffen. "Fine play," wrote the *New York Times,* "was quite impossible." One after another, the favorites succumbed to both wind and pressure. The sixth hole was Davis' undoing; he found every bunker and pit between tee and the green en route to posting a 9 and a second-round 49. Dunn also fell off form, losing strokes here and there to post a second-round 46. For Campbell, the winds of the second round brought on inconsistency, for it was reported that his play was simultaneously "the most brilliant of the day as well as the most careless." Rawlins opened his second nine with a 6 and posted a 7 at the

sixth, but he still managed to shoot a 46. His 45-46 for 91 left him two strokes behind Dunn, Campbell and James Foulis, the professional at Macdonald's Chicago Golf Club, who all shared the three-way lead after 18 holes. Willie Norton, the head professional at Lakewood Golf Club in New Jersey, suffered most of all in the wind, shooting nines of 51-58 while complaining of strong pains in his eyes that led him to withdraw after 18 holes.

The field, now reduced to nine professionals and one amateur, broke for lunch then headed out for the afternoon to determine a champion. John Reid, the professional at Philadelphia Country Club, took a 12 on the now-infamous sixth hole and was never heard from again; he would finish in last place at 206. Samuel Tucker, the professional from St. Andrew's, had taken 10 strokes to complete the same sixth hole in the opening round, and while his play steadily improved throughout the day, his closing rounds of 45-43 were not enough to offset his morning rounds of 49-48 and he finished at 185. There was nothing notable on the scorecards of John Harland of the Weston Golf Club or John Patrick of the Tuxedo Golf Club, but the punishing conditions of the day spelled mediocre play, and the two finished the championship at 183.

For the six other players in the field, each of whom would post scores under 180, the afternoon was a dogfight. Davis and Campbell finally found their form and completed their third trip around the nine-hole track in 42 stokes. Dunn, Foulis and the amateur Smith took 44, but it was Rawlins who seemed to benefit most from the lunchtime break. He came out firing with a 3 at the first, 4s at the third, fourth and seventh holes and another 3 at the eighth. His 41 matched the low nine of the championship that Campbell had recorded in the first round.

With the final round now underway, the majority of the spectators followed Dunn, Davis and Campbell, for it was widely believed that the champion would emerge from among these three. Dunn's play in the final round was steady, but his driving was not up to form, and lots of money was lost on him as the afternoon wore on. After a final-round 42, he retired to the clubhouse with a score of 175 that in the end was good enough for a second-place finish. Foulis, the Chicago professional, awed the afternoon galleries with his power off the tee, giving what one reporter called "the finest exhibition of driving ever seen in this country." Despite holing the longest putt of the championship, his putting was otherwise substandard, and he posted a 43 in the final round to finish at 176.

Smith finally showed the form that had made him a champion north of the border, shooting a final-round 42 that also left him at 176, tied for third. Davis, despite a final-round 42, could do no better than 178 for the championship. Meanwhile, Campbell was undone by the shortest hole on the course, the 517-foot third. He flew his tee shot into Price's Neck Road, behind the green, losing his ball. He teed another and pushed this shot to the base of the stone wall that bordered the green, en route to a humiliating 9 that left both him and his gallery defeated. With a final-round 48, he finished at 179, alone in sixth place.

The afternoon, instead, belonged to young Rawlins. He had started slowly in the morning, as if intimidated by the quality of the field and the significance of the moment. But once his nerves had settled, he found a competitive form previously unknown. His game on the whole was well-balanced: "strong in all its elements, yet brilliant in none." His putting was stronger than his driving, but it was his calm demeanor throughout the afternoon that seemed his greatest asset. "He is a good heady player," noted the reporter from the *New York Times*, "with a happy faculty of not getting discouraged when in difficulties. Then he goes at his work with an ease and fearlessness that is most interesting." As news of Rawlins' steady play spread across the course, the galleries abandoned Dunn, Davis and Campbell and turned their attentions to the home club's assistant professional. What they witnessed was, in the words of Laurence Curtis, the USGA's first vice president, the "best [golf] he had ever seen." Rawlins turned in a final-round 41, matching his third-round tally, and finished at 173.

And so it came to pass that Horace Rawlins, the assistant professional at Newport Golf Club, won the inaugural U.S. Open in conditions that the *New York Times* later described as "half a gale." For the victory, his first ever as a professional, Rawlins received $150, a gold medal valued at $50 and custody for one year of the U.S. Open Trophy, crowned by a winsome female figure of victory.

Rawlins, who learned the game as a caddie on the Isle of Wight off the southern coast of England, came to America in January 1895 to serve as an assistant to Willie Davis at Newport. Prior to his victory in the inaugural national championship, he had played in just two professional competitions, one in his native England and one in America. For many years, it was believed that he was, at age 19, the youngest U.S. Open champion in history, until a search of birth records in the late 1960s revealed his true age to be 21. To this day, he remains the only U.S. Open champion to win on a course where he was employed as a professional.

From humble beginnings came greatness – for a newly crowned champion and for a newly minted championship.

DEFINING MOMENTS

"To promote the interests of the game of golf."
– Minutes of the United States Golf Association, December 22, 1894

For more than a century, the U.S. Open has served as golf's toughest test. Its champions have inspired generations of players and have helped lead the game into the 21st century. Its current state is a culmination of defining moments that have both transformed and developed the game. These landmark achievements represent moments of national pride, displays of unmatched skill and the arrival of golf heroes who have forever changed the landscape of golf. This chapter looks back at the pivotal moments that have helped define the game in America and have expanded its reach around the globe.

The U.S. Open Becomes a Major | Harry Vardon 1900

Early U.S. Opens bore little resemblance to their modern counterparts. The first five championships combined attracted fewer than 200 entries, and the champions were all Scottish or English professionals who had immigrated to the United States to serve the growing number of private golf clubs and resorts. Britain, the world's political superpower at the time, was also the game's powerhouse, but their very best had yet to compete in the fledgling American championship.

In 1900, legendary British professional Harry Vardon was enticed by a lucrative offer to embark on a yearlong tour of America. At age 29, he was already a three-time British Open champion, having won the title in 1896, 1898 and 1899, and he was widely considered to be the best player in the world. With the game growing in popularity in the United States, it is easy to understand why Julian Curtiss, the director of renowned sporting goods manufacturer A.G. Spalding & Bros., sponsored Vardon's trip to the United States to promote their new Vardon Flyer golf ball and Harry Vardon golf clubs.

Upon his arrival on February 3, 1900, Vardon was greeted by a country on the move. Recently re-elected President William McKinley oversaw a prosperous and growing economy. Two years earlier, the United States had defeated an Old World power in the Spanish-American War and established itself as a legitimate challenger to Britain's global empire.

Despite the fact that the Vardon Flyer, a golf ball made of gutta percha (a natural latex material made from tree sap), had been rendered obsolete by the new rubber-core Haskell ball before it ever reached American shores, Vardon's tour was an unqualified success. He played in 91 matches from February

This caricature of Harry Vardon by Leo C. Munro, from the March 2, 1900, issue of *Golf Illustrated*, shows "Dollary Vardon," a satirical sketch on Vardon's barnstorming exhibition matches in America.

Facing page: The legendary form of Harry Vardon, circa 1920.

The field of the 1900 U.S. Open.

through early December, losing only 15 times, the majority of which were against professional two-man, better-ball teams. As one contemporary writer explained, the tour confirmed without a doubt that Vardon had "established for himself a position never before held by any other golfer; he had familiarized the world with a game absolutely unapproachable in commanding power combined with extraordinary accuracy in the long game." From the moment Vardon landed in the United States, golf remained a constant presence in the minds of the American press and its readers. It did not take long before his matches were regularly attended by more than one thousand spectators.

In early May, after playing in 22 matches and losing just once, Vardon returned to Britain to defend his British Open title on the Old Course at St. Andrews. His chief rival was John H. Taylor, the English professional who had won the title in 1894 and 1895. Taylor would win the 72-hole championship, taking 309 strokes (79-77-78-75) to Vardon's 317 (79-81-80-77), and the rivalry between the two greatest players in the world was revitalized.

Vardon returned to the United States immediately, picking up his tour at Shinnecock Hills Golf Club on July 3. Appearing unfazed by his loss at

St. Andrews, he destroyed host professional Tom Hutchinson, 12 and 11, shooting the equivalent of 70-71 in their 36-hole match. The tour continued throughout the summer and into the fall, eventually bringing Vardon to Chicago in early October in time for the U.S. Open at Charles Blair Macdonald's Chicago Golf Club.

Taylor arrived in the United States in early August, engaged by Harper & Bros. to write for their monthly magazine, *Golf,* and play in several matches leading up to the U.S. Open. Spalding and Vardon challenged Harper & Bros. and Taylor to a series of head-to-head matches, but the latter declined. They felt that Vardon, having played on American-style courses all year, would have an unfair advantage. Their rematch would have to wait until the U.S. Open.

Vardon and Taylor were among a field of 60 starters, including four of the first five U.S. Open champions: Horace Rawlins, James Foulis, Fred Herd and Willie Smith (Joe Lloyd, the 1897 champion, did not play). It was the strongest field in the young championship's history. "As far as the present quality of the field is concerned," Taylor told the *Chicago Daily Tribune,* "the present open golf championship of the United States will compare favorably with that of the open British event."

Fair conditions marked the opening of the championship on the morning of Thursday, October 4 – temperatures in the 70s with a southerly breeze that would increase throughout the championship. Vardon was paired with defending-champion Willie Smith. Taylor struck first with an opening round 76 to Vardon's 79, surprising a public who expected Vardon to dominate. But Vardon responded to the challenge, posting a 78 in the afternoon's strong winds to Taylor's 82. As predicted, the two men dominated the opening rounds; the average score for the field through the first two rounds of the championship was 88.4.

The leader board at the end of day one showed Vardon at 157 and Taylor at 158. The editor of the *Chicago Tribune,* unaware of the scoring conventions of the game, ran the headline, "Vardon one point ahead of Taylor at end of first day's play." Back East, the headline of the *Washington Post* read, "Vardon by a Stroke." Stimulated by Vardon's tour, and advertised heavily by Spalding as "The Year of Vardon," golf was now a staple of the sports pages.

Vardon made a strong move the following day in the morning round, carding a 76 to Taylor's 79 and increasing his lead to four strokes. His confidence strengthened, Vardon knew that with the windy conditions Taylor would have to play an exceptional round to catch him. With thousands of spectators following their play, Taylor challenged Vardon in the final round, posting a 78 for a total of 315. Vardon arrived at the 422-yard, par-4 final hole needing only a bogey to claim the championship trophy. Finishing in style, he hit a long drive

A box of "Vardon Flyer" golf balls. The Vardon Flyer, the first endorsed golf ball, was made of a natural latex called gutta percha. The Flyer, however, was quickly rendered obsolete by the introduction of the rubber-core Haskell golf ball.

followed by a "beautiful brassey of something over 200 yards that came straight for the flag and stopped on the far edge of the green." He got down in two for a round of 80 and a total of 313. Vardon had crowned his American tour with a two-shot victory in the U.S. Open, affirming his position as the world's best. David Bell, a native of Carnoustie, Scotland, but now employed by the Midlothian Club in Chicago, finished in third, nine strokes back at 322. At 327, and tied for fourth, were defending champion Willie Smith and Scottish-born professional Laurie Auchterlonie, who would go on to win the championship in 1902.

As Vardon would later write in his autobiography, *My Golfing Life,* "I was exceedingly keen to win the American Open Championship, as I thought it would be a fitting climax to the successful tour I had so far experienced." For the first time, the world's best player had won the U.S. Open Championship, and the presence of Vardon and Taylor had raised the American championship to the level of its British counterpart. Vardon would return to play in the U.S. Open in 1913 and 1920, finishing tied for second both times. But his victory in 1900 had changed golf in America. His handsome looks, stellar play and modest style ignited the interests of American media, spectators and sportsmen in the game of golf. Before Vardon's arrival, the British Open and British Amateur were the only major championships in the game. By the time he sailed home from New York Harbor in December 1900, the U.S. Open had joined the list.

Spectators come to see Harry Vardon at the Oakland Golf Club in his first appearance in the United States. Vardon's victory in the 1900 U.S. Open solidified the championship's reputation as a world-class event.

Facing page: A.G. Spalding & Bros. produced a line of equipment endorsed by Harry Vardon, including a set of irons and the Vardon Flyer golf ball. Here, that iron set lines the background, while the cleek Vardon used in the 1900 U.S. Open sits in the foreground.

America's Tragic Hero | Johnny McDermott 1911

John J. McDermott, 1911 and 1912 U.S. Open Champion

Perhaps Walter Hagen summed it up best when he said that Johnny McDermott was the golfer who "opened the gates to American homebreds."

Scottish- and British-born professionals had won the first 16 U.S. Open Championships, but the 19-year-old Philadelphia native often called a "little firecracker" for his confidence and incendiary comments directed at his foreign-born rivals, turned back Britain's best and in 1911 became the first American to win the U.S. Open.

Born August 12, 1891, in West Philadelphia, John Joseph McDermott Jr. was the only son of Margaret and John Joseph McDermott Sr. At the age of nine, John Jr. became a caddie at Aronimink Golf Club and the sport became his life.

As a child, McDermott had a brash personality. Other caddies described him as a bully, but he could also be reclusive. He often practiced alone, setting out a few tin cans in an orchard near Aronimink. If another caddie arrived, McDermott would leave.

McDermott dropped out of high school during his sophomore year to turn professional. He worked at Camden County Country Club and Merchantville Golf Club, both in New Jersey, before settling in as the head professional at Atlantic City Country Club. His sister, Alice, remembered how hard McDermott worked to become a good player. "He would be on the practice field as soon as it was light, about 5 a.m., and hit shots until 8 a.m., when he opened the pro shop," said Alice. "After his day's teaching, he would go out and play. Often, he finished in twilight with somebody holding a lantern."

International players had dominated the U.S. Open since its inception in 1895, which irritated many American professionals, including McDermott, especially since he had nearly won in 1910. Holding a one-stroke lead through 54 holes, McDermott closed with a 75 that left him in a three-way tie with brothers Macdonald and Alex Smith, who had immigrated to the United States from Carnoustie, Scotland. In the following day's playoff, McDermott shot another 75, but he was denied a championship title by Alex Smith's 71.

One day in 1911, McDermott brashly told players at Atlantic City, "The foreigners are through." After making similar remarks another afternoon, he turned to his caddie and said, "You're carrying the clubs of the next U.S. Open champion."

That June, McDermott fulfilled his prophecy.

His quest to become America's first homebred champion appeared to be a lost cause after the first round, however. McDermott recorded three 6s on his scorecard, posting an 81 that left him tied with eight others in 30th place, seven strokes behind leader Alex Ross of Dornoch, Scotland. That afternoon, however, McDermott put himself back in contention, going out in 35 en route to a 72 during a round in which the scoring average was nearly nine strokes higher. His 36-hole total of 153 left him just four behind Ross and Scotsman Fred McLeod.

The weather was ominous on the final day, with dark clouds and heavy downpours prevailing for most of the afternoon. While Ross and McLeod faded in the soggy conditions, fellow Americans Mike Brady and George Simpson, the head professional at nearby Wheaton (Illinois) Golf Club, each posted 72-hole totals of 307. McDermott, playing in the final group, struggled early in the round but birdied the 72nd hole to force a three-way playoff.

McDermott built a four-shot lead over his fellow Americans through nine holes, but three consecutive bogeys on holes 11, 12 and 13 dropped him into a tie with Brady. McDermott pulled ahead on the 15th when Brady missed a 4-foot putt and secured the victory with a routine par on the final hole.

The U.S. Open's first homebred champion was hailed as an American hero.

"To our off-side way of thinking," Grantland Rice wrote, "John was the greatest golfer America has ever produced, amateur or professional, when it came to a combination of nerve, coolness and all-around skill from the tee to the green."

The following year, McDermott backed up his first national championship victory with a win at the 1912 U.S. Open at The Country Club of Buffalo, erasing a three-shot deficit through 54 holes to win by two strokes. In 1913, McDermott finished fifth at the British Open and won several other prominent tournaments in the United States, including the Western Open (then considered a major championship) and the Philadelphia Open. He had a club endorsement deal

Johnny McDermott poses with the U.S. Open Championship Trophy.

Johnny McDermott remains the youngest U.S. Open Champion in history.

Facing page: Johnny McDermott's 1911 U.S. Open Championship medal and the putter he used during the 1912 championship.

and earned as much as $100 a day by playing with wealthy visitors at Florida resorts. His finances seemed strong and his future looked bright.

Then McDermott's life fell apart. Not long after he returned from the British Open, he discovered his investments had gone sour, a fact he hid from his family. Later that year, McDermott won the Shawnee Open, beating a field that included British players Alex Smith and Harry Vardon. The New York newspapers reported that McDermott, in his victory speech, boasted, "We hope our foreign visitors had a good time, but we don't think they did and we are sure they won't win the National Open."

McDermott was mortified at the reaction in the press. He claimed he was misquoted and issued clarifying statements in an attempt to mend the hard feelings. Golf course architect A.W. Tillinghast later said the Englishmen accepted McDermott's apology, "because they realized Johnny was flush with victory, young and comparatively uneducated." But to the inconsolable McDermott, the damage had been done.

McDermott entered the 1914 British Open, but travel mishaps caused him to arrive late and miss his starting time. When officials offered him a later time, he refused, saying it would be unfair to the other players. He booked passage home on the ocean liner *Kaiser Wilhelm II*. Sailing down the fog-shrouded English Channel, the ship was struck by a British grain carrier and a huge tear was ripped in the ship's hull. McDermott joined other passengers scrambling into lifeboats and drifted in the channel for nearly 20 hours before he was rescued.

Years later, his sister Gertrude recalled, "It was like the last straw. Everything had hit him within a year, and it was all bad."

In October, McDermott blacked out as he walked into his pro shop at Atlantic City. He formally resigned on December 1, 1914. Diagnosed with chronic schizophrenia, he was committed to the State Hospital for the Insane at Norristown, Pennsylvania, on June 23, 1916.

McDermott died on August 1, 1971, just months after watching the U.S. Open at Merion and 11 days shy of his 80th birthday.

More than 100 years have passed since McDermott's 1911 U.S. Open victory, but at 19 years, 10 months, he remains the youngest winner in history, and he is one of only six players to win back-to-back U.S. Open titles. His meteoric rise to two-time U.S. Open champion and tragic fall speaks to the strain of competition and the fragility of the psyche.

The Ultimate Professional | Walter Hagen 1914

Walter Hagen, who won 11 major championships including two U.S. Opens (1914 and 1919), had aspirations to be a professional baseball player. Here he can be seen holding the U.S. Open Championship Trophy in 1914.

Just months after he finished in a tie for fourth place at the 1913 U.S. Open, 21-year-old Walter Hagen packed up his belongings and traveled to Tarpon Springs, Florida. The reason for the trip, however, was not golf-related.

The Country Club of Rochester, where Hagen was employed as a golf professional, had closed for the season, and Pat Moran, the manager of the Philadelphia Nationals professional baseball team, had invited him to pitch in some of their exhibition games over the winter.

Hagen returned to Rochester the following spring brimming with confidence. He was convinced the Nationals would offer him a full tryout the next season, and so he prepared to spend the summer of 1914 splitting his duties as golf professional and pitching semi-pro baseball to get ready for the following year. Though he grew up as a caddie and had success in his first U.S. Open appearance, Hagen, convinced his future was in baseball, decided not to enter the 1914 U.S. Open so that he could focus on his pitching. But Ernest Willard, the editor of the *Democrat and Chronicle* newspaper, was so impressed with Hagen's play at The Country Club in 1913 that he offered to pay Hagen's expenses to Midlothian Country Club in Chicago, the site of the 1914 U.S. Open. Hagen thought it over and ultimately accepted.

At Midlothian, Hagen dealt with some erratic tee shots, a heavily partisan crowd that was pulling for hometown hero Charles "Chick" Evans and a stomach ailment so severe he almost had to withdraw. But in the end, Hagen persevered and emerged victorious. The victory was the first of Hagen's 11 major championship titles and jump-started the career of one of golf's great showmen.

Unlike today, when golfers can earn exemptions into the U.S. Open, everyone who entered in 1914 had to go through qualifying, even the defending champion, Francis Ouimet.

Tom McNamara, who had finished runner-up in two of the previous five U.S. Opens, earned the qualifying medal. Evans nearly disappointed his hometown fans, but he was able to salvage pars at the final four holes to qualify for the championship on the number. Evans' struggles were somewhat surprising given that he had recently won the Western Amateur and had reached the semifinals in the U.S. Amateur the previous five years.

Hagen, who qualified in the middle of the pack, had a dinner of lobster and oysters on the eve of the championship. He awoke in the middle of the night with severe stomach pains and was so weak by morning that he considered withdrawing. Though it hurt to take a full swing, Hagen decided to give it a go. His opening-round 68 matched the lowest 18-hole score in championship history to that point – a record that was not eclipsed for more than a decade – and he led the field by one stroke.

Hagen maintained that lead through 36 holes, and a third-round 75 left him two strokes clear of McNamara heading into the final round. McNamara faded with an 83, but a challenge to Hagen's lead came from Evans, who trailed by eight strokes after 36 holes but closed to within one as the players made the turn in the final round.

According to *The American Golfer*, the gallery was openly rooting for Evans, while Hagen, despite leading at the conclusion of each round, had only a handful of followers: "Hagen had a rather small and undemonstrative following. Not far behind was the big gallery following Mr. Evans. Cheers and the noise of hand clapping coming over the course occasionally told Hagen that the amateur was on his track."

Hagen, who teed off 30 minutes before Evans, pulled his tee shot on the 72nd hole into the rough by the ninth green, but he pitched his ball to 8 feet to set up a birdie and post 290. In fact, Hagen birdied the short 277-yard, par-4 18th in each round – a feat that has yet to be repeated by a champion. Evans, who carried only seven clubs during the week, came to the home hole needing a 2 to force a playoff with Hagen. A good drive left him just off the green, but when his chip settled 10 inches from the hole, Hagen had claimed the first victory of his professional career. He was the first start-to-finish winner, without ties, in U.S. Open history – only five players have since matched him.

At the turn of the century, it was unthinkable to make a living as a tournament golfer. Most professionals accepted appointments at northern clubs in the summer and southern resorts during the winter. Professional events, limited

Walter Hagen, who embodied the term "professional," endorsed many products, including clothing, golf clubs, cigarettes and chewing gum. Here, his likeness is shown on a card from Sport Kings Gum, a candy and card company that produced trading cards featuring the most celebrated athletes in sport.

in number, were simple affairs offering little prize money. The situation slowly changed after World War I, when a loosely organized calendar of events developed from coast to coast. The professionals who competed paid their own expenses from the prize money they collected.

Hagen augmented his earnings by playing in more than 1,500 exhibitions during his career, often traveling to places such as the Dakotas, Wyoming and Utah to promote the game. In doing so, he became the first professional golfer, as opposed to golf professional, who made his living exclusively by *playing* golf.

Hagen's victory in the 1914 U.S. Open started the career of one of golf's most colorful champions. Galleries loved him for his talent, his swagger and his showmanship. He enjoyed fine clothes and automobiles. "I never wanted to be a millionaire," he wrote, "I just wanted to live like one."

Hagen, who himself rose from humble origins, fought for the rights of professional golfers, who were treated like second-class citizens for much of the early part of the 20th century. Hagen's temperament and character were instrumental in improving the status of professional golfers. At the 1920 British Open, Hagen hired a luxury car to serve as his private dressing room because professionals were refused entrance to the clubhouse. He hired a chauffeur who parked the expensive car in the club's driveway and ordered a catered lunch to be served to his car and invited all professionals to join him.

Hagen's four British Open victories (1922, 1924, 1928, 1929) spread his fame internationally, and his likeness appeared on cigarette cards produced in Great Britain and Germany, as well as in the United States. In partnership with the L.A. Young Company of Detroit, Hagen became the first American professional to successfully market a set of clubs bearing his name.

Despite his success at stroke play, Hagen's competitive strength was actually in match play. He exuded confidence and played fearlessly, seemingly giving him a psychological advantage over his opponents. This was evidenced by his five PGA Championship titles (1921, 1924, 1925, 1926, 1927), which was contested at match play until 1957.

Yet even with his impressive career totals, which included a second U.S. Open title, at Brae Burn Country Club in Massachusetts in 1919, Hagen was a victim of Bob Jones' impressive run in the 1920s. Of his 11 major championship victories from 1914 to 1929, Hagen did not win any when Jones was in the field.

But it was Hagen's enduring impact on improving the stature of the professional golfer that remains his legacy. His contributions in this field prompted Gene Sarazen to say, "All the professionals...should say a silent thanks to Walter Hagen each time they stretch a check between their fingers. It was Walter who made professional golf what it is."

Walter Hagen, who was the first professional golfer to earn more than $1 million, often arrived at tournaments in a chauffeur-driven limousine.

Facing page: The mashie used by Walter Hagen to win the 1914 and 1919 U.S. Open Championships.

The Grand Slam | Bob Jones 1930

In 1926, after winning both the U.S. Open and British Open, Bob Jones had an inspired idea. He came to believe that it was possible to win the British Amateur, British Open, U.S. Open and U.S. Amateur all in the same year. At the time, elite amateur golf was as important, if not more important, than the professional game. These four events were the game's majors, but no player had ever claimed all four titles in a single season.

Jones would not share his dream with anyone until the spring of 1930, when he confided his lofty goal to his long-time friend and chronicler, O.B. Keeler. By September 27, 1930, this profound idea would have a name, and Jones' dream would become the most iconic achievement in the game's history – the Grand Slam.

Traveling with Keeler and his American teammates, Jones arrived at Royal St. George's Golf Club in Sandwich, England, for the Walker Cup Match in early May. With his partner, Dr. O.F. Willing, he won his foursomes match convincingly, 8 and 7. He then went on to dominate the great British amateur Roger Wethered, winning their singles match, 9 and 8. Jones, a playing captain, led the United States to an eight-point victory.

Although Jones did not make known the full extent of his grand plan, he had told the press that he wanted to win the British Amateur more than any other championship. It was the only major championship he had never won. From 1924 through 1929 he had won three U.S. Opens (1924, 1926, 1929), two British Opens (1926, 1927) and four U.S. Amateurs (1924, 1925, 1927, 1928).

As Keeler suggested, "Golf tournaments are matters of destiny, and the result is all in the book before ever a shot is hit." Jones struggled in all eight

Robert T. Jones Jr. during the final round of the 1930 British Open.

matches he played, but he rose to the occasion each time with a superb shot, reinforcing Keeler's belief in his friend's predestination. His final match against Roger Wethered was a repeat of their Walker Cup encounter, and Jones again dispatched his British rival, 7 and 6. "Honestly, I don't care much what happens now," Jones told Keeler shortly after the victory. "I'd rather have won this tournament than anything else in golf. I am satisfied." Fittingly, he had captured this coveted title on the Old Course at St. Andrews, the spiritual home of golf.

With the first leg of his mission accomplished, Jones went on to Paris to rest before setting his sights on the British Open at Royal Liverpool Golf Club in Hoylake. The strain of championship play had already begun to take its toll. He confided to Keeler just before play began, "I simply don't know where the darned ball is going when I hit it." But again, it would be his determination that would compensate for his inconsistent ball striking. Somehow fending off late charges by a seasoned Macdonald Smith and fellow American Leo Diegel, Jones' will and some good fortune allowed him to claim the Claret Jug. In winning both British titles in the same year, he matched a feat that had been accomplished only once before, by Englishman John Ball in 1890. Still, as Keeler later wrote for *The American Golfer*, "I must give it as my personal and unalterable opinion that Bobby won the British Open playing at very nearly his worst."

Jones sailed to America on the S.S. *Europa* and was met in New York Harbor on July 2 by a group of well-wishers from Atlanta who had sailed out to meet him. He was welcomed with a second ticker-tape parade up Broadway (the first had come in 1926, as Jones was returning from his first victory in the British Open) and a gala reception dinner at the Vanderbilt Hotel.

For Jones, however, the work was only half done. He left the following day for Interlachen Country Club in Minneapolis, Minnesota, the site of the U.S. Open. It would be the strongest field he would face that year. More than 1,200 competitors attempted to qualify for the 156-man field. Seasoned champions like Walter Hagen, Gene Sarazen, Chick Evans, Leo Diegel, Harry Cooper, Tommy Armour and Macdonald Smith eagerly awaited an opportunity to bring an end to Jones' domination, and the stress was building on Jones. Not only did he want to win, but now the world expected nothing less.

It was around this time that George Trevor, the sportswriter for the *New York Sun*, coined the phrase "the impregnable quadrilateral of golf," referring to Jones' improbable assault on the game's four major championships. Interlachen would not make the attempt any easier. It was not an extremely long course at 6,672 yards, but the severe hazards of Donald Ross' 1921 comprehensive redesign and the championship's ankle-high rough placed a premium on accuracy.

Huge crowds follow Bob Jones and George Voight during the 1930 British Amateur Championship at St. Andrews.

Bob Jones teeing off on the first day of match play during the 1930 U.S. Amateur Championship at Merion Cricket Club (East Course). Jones defeated Canadian C. Ross Somerville, 5 and 4, to advance to the second round.

To complicate matters, the July weather was extremely humid and unusually hot, with temperatures soaring well into and beyond the high 90s throughout the championship.

More than 10,000 spectators arrived on the morning of the first round to see history in the making. Half of those fans followed Jones, who teed off just after 10 a.m. with Jock Hutchison. It was 93 degrees, but the mercury reached 108 before they completed their opening round, both having lost considerable weight and dripping with sweat. Despite the unwieldy crowd and the stifling heat, Jones posted an opening-round 71, trailing Armour and Macdonald Smith by one stroke. The sun took its toll on the field; the average opening-round score was 78.5.

The weather cooled off slightly, into the mid 90s, for the second round. Jones remained very much in contention as he arrived at the dogleg-right, 492-yard, par-5 ninth. Embracing the same strategy he had employed in the first round, he decided to play for the green in two, with hopes of making a birdie. He faced a 240-yard approach to a well-bunkered green. He also had to carry 200 yards of water and the wind was against him. The gallery of spectators swarmed in front of him, so much so that the marshals had to clear a lane. He was distracted mid-swing by a pair of girls who ran across the fairway and he caught the ball thin. It started on line like a low-flying bullet, but headed straight for the water. In that moment, destiny would defy gravity. Instead of sinking on impact, the ball skipped on the water's surface and just cleared the far bank. The amazed gallery cheered Jones wildly as he approached his third shot. Seemingly unfazed, Jones pitched his ball near the hole and sank the short putt for a birdie 4. A rumor spread that the ball had been saved by a lily pad.

At the close of the second round, Jones trailed Horton Smith by two strokes. He was tied with Charles Lacey and Harry Cooper, with Macdonald Smith one stroke further back. In the early rounds of stroke-play events like the U.S. Open, Jones preferred the role of contender to that of front-runner. It allowed him to play aggressively, without feeling that he was simply protecting a lead. In the third round, he chose to attack the course, hoping to separate himself from the pack and thereby lessen the pressure he knew would come in the afternoon's final round. With birdies on the fourth, sixth and seventh holes, Jones made the turn at three under par. With birdies at the 11th, 12th and 16th holes, he reached six under par for the round. But even his brilliant play could not withstand the heat, nor the mounting pressure, and he grew weary. He dropped strokes with bogeys on the two final holes, but his 4-under-par 68 still tied the single-round scoring record for the U.S. Open. Jones' masterpiece left him five strokes clear of Cooper with 18 holes to play.

Bob Jones teeing off on the ninth hole at Interlachen Country Club during the first round of the 1930 U.S. Open. Jones shot an opening round 71, while Tommy Armour and Macdonald Smith led the field.

Nearly 16,000 spectators standing 10 and 12 deep strained to watch Jones play the first hole in what would be his final round in a U.S. Open. He was exhausted, and it would take all of his mental strength to cross the finish line. After a routine par at the first, he dropped three strokes on the outward nine.

While Cooper, Horton Smith and others began to fade, Macdonald Smith, the 42-year-old Scottish veteran who had lost the 1910 U.S. Open to his brother Alex Smith in a three-way playoff that also included John McDermott, now found himself within three strokes of the lead. When Jones, who was playing 30 minutes in front of Smith, double-bogeyed the 192-yard, par-3 13th hole, the lead was down to one. What once appeared to be a triumphant march to victory had become a dramatic duel. Jones and Smith battled back and forth on the inward nine, and Jones clung to a one-stroke lead with one hole to play.

The final hole at Interlachen was a demanding 402-yard par 4. Jones hit a massive drive 300 yards up the right side of the fairway. This left an uphill, mid-iron approach to an elevated green with two distinct tiers. His second shot reached the green, but came to rest on the lower tier some 40 feet from the hole. A two-putt for par was not a given. "As I stepped up to the putt, I was quivering in every muscle," Jones later recalled. But destiny would not be denied. The long putt broke several feet to the right before finding the back of the hole for a birdie 3 and a final-round 75. Smith would not catch him. As thousands cheered, the news went out over the first live radio broadcast of the U.S. Open. Jones had won the championship for the fourth time, matching Willie Anderson's record

Bob Jones is accompanied by USGA officers Herbert Jaques and Findlay S. Douglas as well as members of the U.S. Marines during the 1930 U.S. Amateur at Merion.

Facing page: The Grand Slam collection: 1930 U.S. Amateur and Open Championship programs; 1930 U.S. Open Championship scorecard and ticket; Bob and Mary Jones' passport; Calamity Jane II putter, scorecard and golf ball from the final match of the 1930 U.S. Amateur Championship; and all four championship medals from Jones' Grand Slam.

and bringing him one step closer to the improbable. "Jones," Keeler wrote, "is now well within reach of the impregnable quadrilateral."

As the U.S. Amateur was not scheduled until mid-September, Jones was able to rest for two months before realizing his dream at the Merion Cricket Club outside Philadelphia. He won his first four matches handily then routed Eugene V. Homans, 8 and 7, in the 36-hole final. From dream to reality, Jones had conceived and achieved what Keeler would call "the Grand Slam."

Jones shocked the world when he announced his retirement from competitive golf on November 17, 1930, at the age of 28. As the legendary golf writer Herbert Warren Wind would later note, "There were no worlds left to conquer for Bobby Jones." Fittingly, he ended his USGA championship career where it had begun, at Merion Cricket Club at the age of 14 in the 1916 U.S. Amateur. Jones left the competitive game at the peak of his powers, having won 13 major championships in eight years. During this period, he either won or finished second in the U.S. Open each time he played, a record that redefined the word "dominance" in sport. And he had accomplished all of this as an amateur. It is appropriate that the greatest achievement in golf history was accomplished simply for the love of the game.

The Arrival of the Golden Bear | Jack Nicklaus 1962

After Bob Jones shocked the world in 1930 by retiring from competitive golf just two months after completing the Grand Slam, fans began to wonder if they would ever see another champion like him again. The world got a glimpse at the answer 32 years later, when Jack Nicklaus became the first man since Jones to simultaneously hold the U.S. Amateur and U.S. Open titles. It was not necessarily the answer that every golf fan wanted. At the time, Nicklaus' victory was one of the most unpopular in golf history, since it came at the expense of the immensely popular Arnold Palmer.

In a poll of 192 golf writers published in the May 1962 issue of *Golfing*, 93 picked Palmer as the favorite to win the U.S. Open. Only 13 writers picked Nicklaus. Palmer had just won the 1962 Masters and openly discussed his intention to take the modern Grand Slam, by adding victories in the U.S. Open, British Open and PGA Championship. The world of golf was enjoying a love affair with Palmer, who had joined the tour in 1955 and had already recorded 33 victories, including five major championships, before the 1962 U.S. Open began.

Nicklaus turned professional on November 6, 1961. At his first tournament, the 1962 Los Angeles Open, he finished 50th and earned $33.33, which barely covered his caddie's fees. A professional win still eluded Nicklaus when he arrived at Oakmont Country Club for the 1962 U.S. Open, but confidence did not. As he later told *Golf Magazine*, "I felt I should have won [the U.S. Open] the previous two years as an amateur, so I felt 1962 was the year I should win." Nicklaus had finished second to Palmer in 1960 at Cherry Hills Country Club in Denver and tied for fourth with Mike Souchak in 1961 at Oakland Hills Country Club outside Detroit.

Jack Nicklaus during the 1962 U.S. Open at Oakmont Country Club.

Facing page: An aerial photograph shows the contours of Oakmont's 18th hole (center) and the 14th green (lower left) during the 1962 U.S. Open.

Spectators cross a bridge spanning the Pennsylvania Turnpike to follow the action at Oakmont during the 1962 U.S. Open.

Henry Clay Fownes opened Oakmont in 1904 and together with his son William Clark Fownes Jr., the 1910 U.S. Amateur champion, fashioned its design over several decades into one of the most punishing tests in golf. The course had played host to the U.S. Open in 1927 (Tommy Armour, 301), 1935 (Sam Parks, Jr., 299) and 1953 (Ben Hogan, 283) and proved itself to be among the toughest tests in the championship's history. The design featured deep, furrowed bunkers, which made for true hazards; firm, heavily contoured greens that required exacting approaches; and the fastest putting surfaces in golf. All these elements supported the Fownes' philosophy that "a shot poorly played should be a shot irrevocably lost."

If there was any player who felt comfortable at this difficult venue, it was Palmer. Oakmont was almost in his backyard, and the golfing world expected him to win. Only 35 miles from Palmer's home base in Latrobe, Pennsylvania, the challenges and subtleties of Oakmont were well known to him. Feature articles in *Newsweek* and *Sports Illustrated*, written before the championship, validated Palmer's position as the best player in the world and all but proclaimed him the only logical winner.

Practice rounds were canceled on Wednesday due to heavy rains that, fortunately for the players, softened the course. Gene Littler took advantage of the conditions and shot a 69 to take the first-round lead on Thursday. Tour rookie Bobby Nichols and Bob Rosburg were close behind with 70s. Joe Dey, the USGA's executive director, had instituted twosomes for the first time to help speed up play, and he seized the opportunity to put Nicklaus and The King together in a marquee pairing. Palmer started his round slowly, posting a double bogey on the second hole, but he rallied with five consecutive 3s on the back nine to post an even-par 71 and finish tied for fourth with five others, including Gary Player and Billy Maxwell. Nicklaus, showing no sign that he was intimidated by his playing partner, birdied the first three holes en route to a 72 that left him tied for 10th at day's end.

The USGA set attendance records at Oakmont with close to 20,000 spectators each day. Close to half of these followed Palmer and Nicklaus, and almost all could be counted as members of "Arnie's Army." As the championship evolved, calls of support for Palmer were eventually joined by taunts directed at Nicklaus, who dared to challenge The King. Palmer, somehow ignoring the six stitches in his right-hand ring finger from an accident he had sustained on Monday before his first practice round, negotiated Oakmont's challenges beautifully while shooting a second-round 68 for a total of 139 and a tie for the lead with Rosburg. Nicklaus shot a 1-under-par 70 and was three strokes back at the halfway point.

The leader board tracks the action during the 1962 U.S. Open at Oakmont.

The final two rounds were played on Saturday, a marathon day that was then a part of championship golf's toughest test. After 54 holes, the leader board showed Palmer and Nichols at 212, leading Phil Rodgers and Rosburg by one and Player and Nicklaus by two. The highlight of the third round was Palmer's play at the 292-yard, par-4 17th hole. At 1:35 p.m., an extended roar from Arnie's Army announced to the field that Palmer had driven the green and then drained an 18-foot putt for an eagle.

Palmer was in control of the championship until he came to the reachable par-5 ninth hole in the fourth round. Just right of the green in two, he made two poor chips and settled for a bogey 6. He had been four strokes ahead of Nicklaus on the ninth tee, but Nicklaus' birdie at the ninth and 1-under-par 35 on the back nine would erase that margin. Both men had birdie putts of less than 20 feet on the 18th hole to win the championship, and both missed

by inches. After four rounds, the rookie and The King were tied at 283. They would face one another in an 18-hole playoff on Sunday.

Palmer, on the eve of the playoff, told the media, "I want to win this one more than any tournament I've ever played." But he also revealed concern about Nicklaus in the media tent following the fourth round, saying, "I'd rather it was anybody but that big, strong happy dude. I thought I was through with him yesterday. I'd rather be playing somebody else."

The concern was well founded. By the eighth hole of the playoff, Palmer trailed Nicklaus by four strokes. But Palmer rallied with birdies at nine, 11 and 12 to charge back to within one stroke. As Nicklaus later explained, "Most people get flustered when Palmer does this and start bogeying. Don't be an idiot. Remember you have played 12 holes and you're one up, that's all that counts. Just play your own game. Palmer can bogey them too." On the 161-yard, par-3 13th hole, Palmer did just that. His tee shot found the green, but he three-putted from 40 feet.

Nicklaus would maintain the two-stroke advantage throughout the remaining holes. When Palmer failed to capitalize on Nicklaus' wayward drive on the final hole, the championship fell to the Golden Bear. In the end, Nicklaus shot an even-par 71 to Palmer's 74.

Putting was the crucial difference in Nicklaus' victory. Palmer three-putted seven times in the first four rounds and three times in the playoff. Nicklaus three-putted just once in 90 holes – the only man in the field who could claim that statistic.

The victory marked the turning point in Nicklaus' career, from successful amateur and collegiate player to major champion. In the process, it ignited the greatest rivalry in golf, a rivalry born as much out of great respect as of tremendous skill. That respect was clearly evident to all as the combatants shook hands and locked eyes on the 18th green that Sunday. Over the ensuing decades, their sportsmanship would set a new standard for sport.

By no means did Nicklaus' victory dethrone The King. Later that year, Palmer would win the British Open at Royal Troon Golf Club, and he would go on to win 28 more tournaments over the next decade. But the 1962 U.S. Open was the first of Nicklaus' 18 professional major championship titles. It launched the reign of the Golden Bear and set him on a course to become one of the greatest champions the game has ever seen.

Jack Nicklaus holds the championship trophy after winning the 1962 U.S. Open at Oakmont.

Facing page: Arnold Palmer congratulates Jack Nicklaus on winning the 1962 U.S. Open. The two would remain rivals and friends for many years.

International Breakthrough | Gary Player 1965

Gary Player embraces the U.S. Open Championship Trophy following his victory in 1965.

Gary Player walked up the 71st fairway in the 1962 U.S. Open lamenting a lost opportunity. He had put himself in position to win the championship, but a final round of missed chances left him five strokes out of a playoff with Jack Nicklaus and Arnold Palmer. Player confided in the referee walking with his group, "I'm so disappointed not to win the U.S. Open. Had I won, I had planned to give the prize money to charities. But let's keep that a secret. One day I shall win and I'll turn back the prize money to good causes."

Three years later, he was in a position to do exactly that. Player defeated Australia's Kel Nagle, 71 to 74, in an 18-hole playoff at Bellerive Country Club in St. Louis to win the 1965 U.S. Open. During Sunday's final round, Player nearly gave away the championship by squandering a three-stroke lead. After Monday's playoff win, however, Player gave away everything but the title, donating all his winnings to charity, saying, "I am a foreigner here. The American people have treated me so well I wanted to give something back."

American-born golfers had dominated the U.S. Open through the middle decades of the 20th century. Homebred players won every U.S. Open between 1928 and 1964 – a length of time that spanned nearly two generations. With players such as Palmer, Nicklaus and Billy Casper dominating the game's landscape in the early 1960s, it seemed a foregone conclusion that an American would once again claim the title in 1965.

While Palmer and Nicklaus battled for national championships, money titles and America's affections in the 1960s, South Africa's Gary Player took the international game by storm. It has been said that no one in history logged more miles playing golf than Player, who traveled more than 15 million miles while winning titles on six continents.

Player was born in Johannesburg, the youngest of three children. His mother died of cancer when he was just eight and his father was often away from home, working in the gold mines. He compensated for his slight build (5-foot-7 and 150 pounds) with a strict diet and fitness regimen that complemented his natural athleticism and grace. He turned professional at age 17 and in 1959 won the British Open as a 23-year-old, becoming the youngest champion to that point in history. Player went on to win the 1961 Masters and 1962 PGA Championship, along with dozens of other tournaments across the globe in the early 1960s. He came into the 1965 U.S. Open as one of the game's leading players.

Breaking from the custom of holding U.S. Opens at historic venues, the USGA awarded the 1965 championship to a course that was just five years old. Built on rolling Missouri farmland just west of St. Louis, Bellerive was designed by Robert Trent Jones Sr. and featured unusually large and subtly contoured greens. At 7,191 yards, it also established a record as the longest course to host the championship.

For the first time in history, the U.S. Open was played over four days. This new format not only provided increased television revenue and exposure, but it also solved the challenge of having the 60-plus players who had made the cut complete 36 holes on Saturday.

Despite Bellerive's length, long hitters seemed to gain little advantage in the opening round. In fact, Nagle and Deane Beman, two of the shortest hitters in the field, were two of just three competitors to break par on Thursday. Nagle, who shot 68, played fairway woods into four of the par 4s and claimed he would have had a fifth if he had not hit his drive into the rough and been forced to lay up. Beman, the game's leading amateur, used 13 fairway woods for his approach shots but still managed a 1-under 69. Player shot a 70, telling the media after the round that he couldn't "remember ever making finer contact with the ball." Three missed putts from inside 8 feet cost him what could have been a spectacular round.

Player matched his score in the second round to take a one-stroke lead over Nagle and Mason Rudolph. Beman, with rounds of 69-73 for 142, was alone in fourth. Player made one birdie (an 18-footer at the ninth), one bogey and 16 pars in a consistent, if unspectacular, round. The biggest story on day two, however, was the big names that were absent from the leader board. Palmer – who had a victory, two runner-up finishes and a tie for fifth in his previous five U.S. Opens – shot 76-76 for 152 and missed the cut. Likewise, the defending champion, Ken Venturi, was going home after rounds of 81-79. Nicklaus rebounded from an

Gary Player wears his trademark black shirt and slacks during the 1965 U.S. Open.

Gary Player emphatically celebrates a holed putt during the 1965 U.S. Open. For the first time in history, television audiences enjoyed coverage of the championship in color. More than a dozen cameras were used to broadcast the final two rounds.

opening 78 with a 72 to make the cut on the number, but thereafter was never in contention. He got up and down just once in 13 attempts on Thursday and Friday. For the first time in seven years, Palmer and Nicklaus would both finish outside the top five at the U.S. Open.

Many television viewers and network executives were sorely disappointed that the game's two biggest names were out of contention. Eighteen years earlier, in 1947, the U.S. Open, played at St. Louis Country Club, was televised live for the first time. A local television station, KSD-TV, used a single camera placed on top of a station truck parked behind the 18th green to transmit images to the station via telephone wires. In 1965, more than a dozen cameras and a crew of 75 helped to broadcast the final rounds at Bellerive, located a mere seven miles from St. Louis C.C. The 1965 broadcast marked the first time that the U.S. Open was televised in color, which was even more noticeable as two club officials ordered the 17th and 18th greens to be sprayed emerald green to make sure the course looked its best for the cameras.

Another surprise development from the first two rounds was the difficulty of the par-3 sixth hole. It played only 195 yards but was guarded by three bunkers and a small pond at the front right of the green. On Thursday and Friday, the hole yielded only 15 birdies against 14 triple bogeys or worse, including two 8s and a 9 by Canadian pro Bob Panasiuk, who hit two balls in the water and putted another into the pond. By the end of Sunday, the hole played at 247 strokes over par for the week – the most difficult hole to that point in U.S. Open history.

Both Player and Nagle avoided trouble at the treacherous sixth throughout the championship and, through 54 holes, Player led the Australian by two strokes. By the time the competitors made the turn on Sunday, Player had pushed his edge to three. As he waited to hit his approach shot on the 10th hole, Nagle, playing in the group in front of him, drained a 15-foot birdie putt. Slightly rattled, Player missed the green for his first bogey of the day. The two-shot swing trimmed the lead to a single stroke. On the 12th, Nagle struck again. This time it was a 40-foot curler that found the hole. "It was a monster of a putt," said Player to the media after the round. "I really felt that one in my guts." This time, however, Player responded, matching Nagle's heroics with a 6-iron approach to 15 feet and a birdie of his own.

Player again seemed in control of the championship when Nagle double-bogeyed the 15th. His lead was once again three strokes, and he had not made a bogey over the final three holes through the first three rounds of the championship. But within 15 minutes, everything changed. Player's tee shot on the 218-yard 16th hole found the greenside bunker. He was able to blast to 15 feet but three-putted for double bogey. Just minutes later, Nagle converted a 4-foot

Gary Player, the first foreign-born player to win the U.S. Open since Tommy Armour in 1927, kisses the championship trophy – golf's most coveted award.

birdie putt at the par-5 17th to pull even. Nagle parred the 18th, and Player, with the memory of his three-putt at 16 still fresh in his mind, lagged his 28-foot birdie attempt to within inches for a par that set up Monday's 18-hole playoff.

Nagle was not well-known in the United States, as he played most of his golf on the Australasian Tour. In fact, several newspapers referred to him as *Ken* Nagle at various times throughout the championship. Though at 44 years old he was vying to become the oldest U.S. Open champion, Nagle was not the underdog he seemed. He had missed the cut in his two previous U.S. Open appearances but had an impressive record in the British Open, finishing in the top five in six out of seven championships from 1960 to 1966 – including a win in 1960 that denied Arnold Palmer a shot at the Grand Slam.

The playoff, however, was never close. Nagle was wild off the tee and missed four putts of less than 6 feet on the first nine. On the fifth, Nagle hooked his drive off a female spectator's forehead, then had his clubface turned by thick rough and struck another spectator in the leg with his second shot. He settled for a double-bogey 6. Player, meanwhile, was in total control. Wearing the same black shirt he had worn the first four rounds and playing his patented draw, Player birdied three of the first eight holes and led by five strokes at the turn. Nagle parred in from the 11th hole, but the damage had been done. Player became the first foreign-born golfer since Scotland's Tommy Armour in 1927 to win the U.S. Open.

USGA Executive Director Joe Dey was effusive in his praise for Player, writing, "A conspicuous quality of the new U.S. Open champion is his respect for others, for golf and for himself. He is disarmingly sincere … and sometimes he seems too good to be true. Yet he is a strong character of firm convictions, which he articulates well."

True to his promise three years earlier, Player donated his winnings to charity following his victory. He gave $5,000 to cancer research in honor of his mother and returned $20,000 to the USGA to help develop junior golf.

In total, Player won more than 160 tournaments worldwide, including three British Opens, three Masters and two PGA Championships. He is one of just five players to win all four of golf's major championships. Player's international stature coincided with the expansion of professional sports on a worldwide level. International players joined the National Hockey League, the National Basketball Association and Major League Baseball in significant numbers, improving the quality of competition and bringing new styles of play.

Golf also benefited from an influx of foreign players who challenged American golfers to improve their games. Building on Player's accomplishments, Spain's Seve Ballesteros won five major championships and more than 90 tournaments worldwide starting in the mid-1970s, electrifying fans with his dazzling shotmaking skills and flair for the dramatic. In the 1980s and early 1990s, England's Nick Faldo, Germany's Bernhard Langer and Australia's Greg Norman each held the number-one spot in the Official World Golf Ranking and consistently challenged for major championship titles. Perhaps the man whom Player impacted most was fellow South African Ernie Els, who became just the fourth foreign-born U.S. Open champion since the Great Depression when he won in 1994; Els added a second title in 1997.

Player was golf's first truly international champion. He not only helped to raise awareness of the game worldwide through his exceptional play, but he built the groundwork for future generations to enjoy the game by advocating physical fitness and charitable endeavors.

Facing page: Known for his short-game wizardry, Gary Player used this sand wedge and golf ball during the 1965 U.S. Open at Bellerive.

The Chip | Tom Watson 1982

Designed in 1919 by Jack Neville and Douglas Grant and located 110 miles south of San Francisco along the Monterey Peninsula, Pebble Beach Golf Links is one of the world's most iconic courses. Unmatched in its beauty and majesty, Pebble Beach is nearly synonymous with compelling U.S. Open Championships, and some of the game's biggest names have supplied the heroics. There was Jack Nicklaus' 1-iron to the 17th green in 1972, Tom Kite's chip-in at the seventh in 1992, Tiger Woods' 15-stroke victory in 2000 and Graeme McDowell's snapping of a 40-year European winless streak in 2010. But of all the remarkable moments in U.S. Open history, perhaps none is better remembered than Tom Watson's heroics at the 17th in 1982.

He stepped to the tee tied for the lead with Nicklaus, who, playing three groups ahead, had just parred the 72nd hole to post a 4-under 284. Though Watson had supplanted Nicklaus as the best player in the game and had even beaten him in head-to-head duels before, Watson had never been able to break through at the championship he coveted most: the U.S. Open. He had finished in the top 10 in six of the previous eight championships, but victory had eluded him. He led through 54 holes at Winged Foot in 1974 but closed with a 79 to finish tied for fifth. The following year at Medinah, Watson built a three-shot lead through 36 holes only to shoot 78-77 on the weekend to finish in a tie for ninth. In 1980, he began the final round one stroke behind Nicklaus and Isao Aoki at Baltusrol but failed to hole crucial putts down the stretch and finished third.

In the five years leading up to the 1982 championship, Watson had won 27 PGA Tour events, including two Masters and three British Open titles, but he admitted, "I must win the U.S. Open to be considered one of the great players."

President Gerald R. Ford presents the U.S. Open Championship Trophy to Tom Watson at the conclusion of the 1982 championship at Pebble Beach.

Facing page: Tom Watson is all smiles after sinking his final putt of the 1982 U.S. Open.

Tom Watson, who had dreamt of winning the U.S. Open since he was 10 years old, was known for his quick but smooth swing tempo.

When he was a boy, Watson's father, Raymond, had quizzed him on the names of the U.S. Open winners. Before long, they had become as familiar to him as the names of the members of his own family. "I was aware of the U.S. Open probably before I got out of diapers because my dad was a historian about the tournament," recalled Watson. "Ever since I was 10 years old I had dreamed of winning the title."

Through 14 holes on Thursday, it appeared that Watson was headed for another major disappointment. A bogey at the par-5 14th dropped him to three over par and put him in danger of slipping out of contention early. But consecutive birdies at 15, 16 and 17 salvaged his round and kept him within striking distance with an even-par 72. Though his ball striking was even worse in the second round, Watson putted superbly, sinking two bogey putts of over 20 feet to match his opening-round score. "I shot a 77 and scored a 72," said Watson, who hit only five of 14 fairways on Friday. "I really drove the ball poorly the first two days and got away with murder." Watson made some slight adjustments before his third round to correct what he perceived as too upright of a swing. The result was a 4-under-par 68 that vaulted him from five strokes behind into a share of the lead through 54 holes.

From the beginning of the round on Sunday, Watson's playing partner, Bill Rogers, sensed that the Kansas City native was supremely confident. "He knew it was his time and place," said Rogers, the defending British Open champion. "When I saw him pull [out his] driver on the fourth hole I knew he was serious. He drove it right in front of the green. He wanted to win."

Though he missed a few iron shots on Sunday, Watson hit every fairway with monotonous repetition until he finally misfired on 16. Holding a one-stroke lead on Nicklaus, Watson's drive found the right fairway bunker, which had been deepened by former USGA president Sandy Tatum shortly before the championship started. Due to the elevated lip of the bunker, Watson was forced to blast out sideways. Playing his third from a downslope on the fairway, Watson's sand wedge skipped to the back of the green, some 60 feet away. Facing a long, treacherous par putt that was downhill and broke more than 10 feet to his right, Watson coaxed the putt to within a foot. "That putt more than anything, even the ones I made, kept me in the tournament," said Watson.

Watson was now tied with Nicklaus, and the stage was set for one of the most dramatic finishes in U.S. Open history. At 209 yards, Pebble Beach's par-3 17th was playing as the most difficult hole during the final round. Watson had already birdied it twice during the week, but Sunday's back-left hole location made it a longer, more challenging hole than it had played the previous three days. The large, hourglass-shaped green has two distinct levels separated by a steep ridge and is protected by bunkers, rocks and the Pacific Ocean. After watching Rogers hit a 4-wood onto the middle of the green, Watson carefully selected a 2-iron and took dead aim.

As a college student at nearby Stanford, Watson had already played this shot hundreds of times, though in markedly different circumstances. He would drive up to Pebble Beach on Saturday mornings, tee off before anyone else was on the course and pretend he was battling Nicklaus for the U.S. Open title. Now, that was the reality.

Watson had, in fact, gone toe to toe with Nicklaus in previous major championships with positive results. Watson held off a hard-charging Nicklaus at the 1977 Masters, combating the Golden Bear's final-round 66 with a 67 of his own to win by two strokes. Later that summer in the British Open, Watson and Nicklaus engaged in one of the greatest duels of all time at Turnberry. Both players opened with rounds of 68-70-65, and on the final day Watson birdied the 17th and 18th to shoot 65, edging Nicklaus by one. Hubert Green finished in third place, 10 strokes behind Nicklaus. Rivalries such as Hogan-Snead in the 1950s, Palmer-Nicklaus in the 1960s and Nicklaus-Watson in the late 1970s and early 1980s did more than engage the public's interest in the game; they also motivated the players to elevate their games. Unlike others who wilted in the shadow of the Golden Bear, Watson was invigorated by the challenge and seemed to play his best when pushed by Nicklaus.

Both had impressive records at Pebble Beach. Watson had already won two Bing Crosby National Pro-Am titles there, while Nicklaus, 10 years his senior, had won the Crosby three times in addition to victories in the 1961 U.S. Amateur and 1972 U.S. Open. Ten years earlier, on the same 17th hole where Watson now stood, Nicklaus had hit a 1-iron that bounced once, hit the flagstick and came to rest six inches from the hole, setting up a decisive birdie that sealed the third of his four U.S. Open titles.

Now Watson, seeking his own cherished moment, drew back the club and fired toward the target. The ball started right on line, but as it flew closer, Watson watched helplessly as it drifted left, bounced once and chased through the green into deep greenside rough. Watson had short-sided himself and faced a delicate, downhill pitch to a hole that was just 20 feet away. Standing nearby, Rogers believed that if Watson could get the chip to within 10 feet it would be considered a very good shot. Nicklaus, watching on a television monitor in the scoring tent, suddenly liked his chances. "I thought it was over," said Nicklaus. "I thought I had won the tournament."

Tom Watson is congratulated by long-time caddie Bruce Edwards on the 18th green at Pebble Beach.

Above and facing page: One of the U.S. Open's greatest moments: Captured in sequence, Tom Watson holes a chip from the deep rough behind the 17th green at Pebble Beach to take a one-shot lead over Jack Nicklaus with one hole left to play.

The one thing Watson had working in his favor was that he had drawn a good lie. He was also prepared for the moment. "I had practiced that shot for hours, days, months, years," said Watson. "It's a shot you have to know if you're going to do well in the U.S. Open where there's high grass around the greens." After studying the shot, Bruce Edwards, Watson's caddie, turned to him and told him to get it close. "Get it close?" asked Watson. "Hell, I'm going to make it." As in so many cases, dramatic moments take years to build but only seconds to resolve. He slipped the leading edge of his sand wedge underneath the ball and lofted it barely onto the putting surface. "When it hit the green I knew it was going in," said Watson. As the ball curved toward the hole, he chased after it. Just as predicted, the ball struck the flagstick and dropped in for a birdie 2. Watson burst into a spontaneous dance and pointed at Edwards as if to say, "I told you so."

Watson had summoned the shot of his career at the most crucial juncture of the championship. "All great players make great shots when they need them," said Nicklaus. "I thought the shot was impossible," said Rogers. "He just hit a perfect golf shot." Having turned a sure bogey into a birdie, Watson reached the 72nd hole with a one-stroke lead. At 540 yards with the Carmel Bay

hugging the left side all the way from the tee to the green, the 18th hole is no sure par. But Watson played it beautifully, hitting a 3-wood to the center of the fairway, a 7-iron lay up and a 9-iron to the middle of the green. He even rolled in the 20-foot birdie putt for good measure, giving himself a two-stroke victory. Nicklaus greeted Watson at the green and was the first to congratulate him, shaking his head as he said, "You're something else."

Once again, Nicklaus and Watson had pushed each other to new heights. By capturing his coveted title, Watson denied Nicklaus what would have been a record fifth U.S. Open victory. Nicklaus has called it his most heartbreaking defeat. They would both win more majors – two British Open titles for Watson and the 1986 Masters for Nicklaus – but the 1982 U.S. Open was the last of a series of peerless head-to-head duels.

Watson's chip immortalized him as one of golf's legendary champions and is a shot that ranks among the best in the game's history, along with Gene Sarazen's double eagle at the 1935 Masters, Arnold Palmer driving the first green at Cherry Hills in 1960 and, of course, Nicklaus' 1-iron at Pebble Beach in 1972. Watson later wrote in *Golf Digest*, "It was the greatest shot of my life and it won the championship I most wanted to win."

Golf's Biggest Stage: U.S. Open Courses

BY MIKE DAVIS WITH HUNKI YUN

The U.S. Open is my favorite week of the year. There is no emotion that rivals the excitement and anticipation of conducting a national championship for 156 players – ranging from the best professionals in the world to amateurs fulfilling lifelong dreams by qualifying for golf's biggest stage. The exhilaration is so great that I hardly need to sleep that week, which is fortunate because I usually start my day on the course at 3 a.m. and don't leave until midnight. My job, in the years preceding the championship and throughout the week it is played, is to ensure that the course selected for the U.S. Open provides the most complete challenge for the best players in the world.

While the players are undoubtedly the biggest headliners, the U.S. Open course certainly shares the marquee. Unlike championships in other sports, the field of play at the U.S. Open is more than a stage. Rather, it is a performer itself, playing a major role in determining the outcome. Competitors have to negotiate the unique challenges presented by each venue, ranging from the ocean winds at Pebble Beach to the bewildering contours of the greens at Pinehurst No. 2. For golf fans, just the mention of courses like Shinnecock Hills, Winged Foot and Olympic are as evocative as names of champions like Bob Jones, Jack Nicklaus and Tiger Woods.

During the 117-year history of the U.S. Open, 50 facilities have hosted the national championship. These courses are among golf's greatest, toughest tests, and they have been the scenes of some of the most memorable moments in golf history. For the United States Golf Association, the selection and preparation of a course for the U.S. Open is one of our most important tasks.

While the architectural excellence of the course remains at the core of a U.S. Open site, we have to consider numerous other factors when choosing a course. Over the next few pages, I will offer a glimpse into the thinking that goes into how we at the USGA select courses to host our national championship.

The goal of the U.S. Open is to identify the best player on a great golf course under difficult conditions. So the architecture of the course and how it tests the world's best players are of paramount importance. A U.S. Open course needs to challenge competitors' physical skills, offer strategic options and instill doubt – even fear – in their minds. These basic criteria considerably reduce the pool of candidates for a U.S. Open course; of the 16,000 or so courses in the United States, fewer than 100 probably achieve these aims effectively.

Most of these layouts are included on lists that magazines and other cognoscenti publish that rank the greatest courses in the country. All U.S. Open courses are great courses, and many were

Facing page: Pebble Beach Golf Links, the site of five U.S. Open Championships and some of the most memorable U.S. Open moments. The approach to the eighth green is played over a yawning chasm of Monterey Bay.

The 16th hole of Shinnecock Hills Golf Club in Southampton, New York, which was part of a new layout completed on the club's eastern Long Island location in the 1930s. The clubhouse, designed by Stanford White in 1892, has remained unchanged.

designed during the first few decades of the 20th century, an era commonly known as the Golden Age of golf course architecture.

These courses are a direct link to golf's past. Golden Age sites such as Bethpage State Park, Merion Golf Club, Oakmont Country Club, The Olympic Club, Pebble Beach Golf Links, Pinehurst Resort and Winged Foot Golf Club enable today's golfers to walk the same fairways on which champions such as Lee Trevino, Tom Watson and Payne Stewart experienced some of their greatest moments.

These courses are marked by interesting, varied topography. The holes are routed to use the site's landforms and flow together to form a cohesive playing experience. Individual holes challenge players both mentally and physically and offer multiple playing options from tee to green. Strategic green complexes test both approach shots and short-game ability. Undulating putting surfaces demand proper interpretation of slope and speed.

Great courses have set the stage for some of golf's most memorable shots, such as Jones' midiron, the equivalent of a modern 2-iron, at Inwood Country Club's 18th hole to seal his first U.S. Open in 1923, Arnold Palmer's drive at Cherry Hills Country Club's first hole that ignited his final-round 65 in the 1960 U.S. Open and Rory McIlroy's 6-iron on the 10th hole at Congressional Country Club that nearly went in the hole for an ace and placed an exclamation point on his record-breaking performance in the 2011 U.S. Open.

Good design also punishes poor shots and can decide the outcome of the U.S. Open. During the final round of the 1939 U.S. Open at Philadelphia Country Club, a well-placed bunker on the 18th hole caught Sam Snead's wayward drive. Mistakenly believing he needed birdie to tie for the lead, Snead played too aggressively and made a triple bogey. Similarly, miscues by Colin Montgomerie and Phil Mickelson on the demanding final hole at Winged Foot during the 2006 U.S. Open led to double bogeys that left them one stroke behind winner Geoff Ogilvy.

While the principles of great design listed earlier have not changed, the standards of the best players in the world, as well as the logistical demands of the national championship, have evolved. Some Golden Age courses have expanded over the years to remain as challenging now as they were nearly a century ago.

Although many people consider great layouts to be masterpieces, courses differ from classic works of art in that they have evolved over the years. U.S. Open layouts have seen a variety of

Above: The Church Pew bunker at Oakmont Country Club – an eight-time host of the U.S. Open Championship – is the course's signature architectural feature. Following spread, from left: The fourth hole at Chambers Bay in University Place, Washington. Right: The new look of Pinehurst No. 2, following the recent renovation by Ben Crenshaw and Bill Coore.

changes, from cosmetic touch-ups to complete redesigns. No course has gone untouched. At Oakmont, the removal of thousands of trees transformed the look of the course between the 1994 and 2007 U.S. Opens. Pebble Beach installed a new fifth hole prior to the 2000 U.S. Open. In 2014, we will see a Pinehurst No. 2 layout that has been transformed since 2005; architects Ben Crenshaw and Bill Coore have replaced much of the rough with sandy waste areas that frame the fairways, making the course much more treacherous for those hitting errant tee shots.

Renovations are not a recent phenomenon. In the 1930s, Shinnecock Hills, which held the 1896 U.S. Open, built a completely new layout at its eastern Long Island location. So the course that will host the 2018 U.S. Open has little in common with the layout that was the site of the second national championship. The only constant has been the Stanford White-designed clubhouse, which dates to 1892.

Others have not been able to accommodate the modern U.S. Open. Myopia Hunt Club, which hosted the U.S. Open four times between 1898 and 1908, remains enjoyable and very challenging for everyday golfers. However, the course is neither long enough nor demanding enough to be a viable championship venue.

As older courses have dropped out of consideration, we are always looking for new U.S. Open sites. Since 1999, we have debuted three courses: Pinehurst No. 2, Bethpage Black and Torrey Pines South. Over the next few years, we will be introducing two new courses. In 2015, the U.S. Open will be heading to Chambers Bay, a municipal layout built on a former gravel pit south of Seattle. The treeless landscape and firm, fast conditions resemble a links course, and many viewers may believe they are watching a British Open rather than a U.S. Open. Two years later, another public course, Erin Hills, in the rolling farmland northwest of Milwaukee, will host a similarly natural, firm and fast championship.

Both courses opened in the 21st century and exemplify the evolution of U.S. Open courses. While Golden Age designs remain the best expressions of the architectural standards required for the national championships, newer layouts offer exciting prospects for upcoming championships. Whether the course was designed more than a century ago or opened in recent years, great design is as timeless as the appeal of the U.S. Open itself.

Above: The fourth hole on the Black Course at Bethpage State Park in Farmingdale, New York. The USGA's commitment to supporting public golf is so strong that six of the 10 U.S. Open sites between 2008 and 2017 are open to the public, including Bethpage. **Facing page:** The 18th hole at Merion Golf Club in Ardmore, Pennsylvania, site of the 2013 U.S. Open.

The U.S. Open has long held a reputation for being played nearly exclusively on parkland courses in the Northeast and Upper Midwest. Certainly, there is some truth to this generalization – after all, those regions are where golf first developed in this country. Moreover, the climate in those areas is more favorable for setting up the course to U.S. Open standards in early summer.

Traditionally, the U.S. Open has been played on bentgrass greens, which thrive in cooler climates and allow us to maintain the speed, firmness and smoothness necessary to test the world's top golfers. Unfortunately, bentgrass cannot handle warm climates, one reason why northern courses hold an advantage in hosting the U.S. Open. Still, the USGA has taken the U.S. Open to Texas three times, North Carolina twice and Georgia once. Looking to the future, recent advances in bermudagrass that will allow it to be cut and maintained short enough for U.S. Open standards could influence site selection.

It is important to move the U.S. Open around the country, and we are excited to soon visit Washington's Chambers Bay and Wisconsin's Erin Hills – two states to which we have not previously taken the championship. And as thrilled as we are that

Washington and Wisconsin will be joining the U.S. Open family, we are just as happy that Chambers Bay and Erin Hills are public courses. For too long the U.S. Open was synonymous with private golf. Even when the U.S. Open was played at public-access courses, they were at prestigious resorts, like Pebble Beach and Pinehurst.

It was a momentous occasion when Bethpage State Park, owned and operated by New York State, hosted the 2002 U.S. Open. The USGA's commitment to supporting public golf is so strong that six of the 10 U.S. Open sites between 2008 and 2017 are open to the public. As the governing body for golf in America – a country in which the vast majority of the courses are public – the USGA has displayed long-overdue recognition and support of everyday golfers, who make up the game's valuable core, with these U.S. Open sites.

Conversely, two clubs that I'm often asked about that haven't hosted the U.S. Open, and likely won't in the near future, are two of the best and most famous courses in America: Pine Valley Golf Club in southern New Jersey and the Cypress Point Club on California's Monterey Peninsula. While there is no doubt that both deserve their lofty rankings and the nearly universal awe

they generate among golfers, neither club has invited the USGA to consider it for the U.S. Open. This invitation is a crucial aspect of the selection process. The U.S. Open is a very large and public event, and it is understandable that many private clubs do not wish to host the championship.

Even if a club with a great course is interested in hosting, we still have to consider the logistics. The site needs to be large enough to accommodate more than 50,000 people – spectators, volunteers, staff, media – as well as grandstands, concession areas, operational compounds, television equipment, transportation staging areas and spectator services.

We then study the surrounding area, looking at variables such as population base, potential traffic concerns, the number of hotel rooms and the parking availability for as many as 20,000 cars. The USGA works closely with municipalities to conduct the U.S. Open, and the support of the local community – both the public and private sectors – is crucial for ensuring a successful event.

Those are a lot of requirements, which is why the pool of potential U.S. Open courses is small. Add other factors like geography, climate, agronomy and history, and the number of viable sites shrinks further.

These factors seem to be at odds with the selection of Merion Golf Club as the host of the 2013 U.S. Open. For many reasons, Merion is a surprising choice for today's U.S. Open. It is small, and the neighborhood around the course presents many challenges in constructing the infrastructure needed to conduct the championship. There are also some who question whether the East Course, opened in 1912, is long enough to test today's competitors. However, we are holding the U.S. Open there because the short but stern layout demands good decision-making and precise execution from the best players in the world. The 2013 U.S. Open is Merion's 18th USGA championship, the most of any club, and that long history is also worth celebrating.

From a business and operational perspective, Merion's small size, which will mean fewer spectators and less revenue, represents a substantial financial risk for the USGA. But Merion is a unique example that illustrates that the quality of a golf course is the most important factor in choosing a U.S. Open site.

––––––––

Bob Jones, the winner of four U.S. Opens, once wrote: "There are two distinct kinds of golf – just plain golf and tournament golf." He penned these lines in reference to the preparation

The ninth hole at Winged Foot Golf Club's West Course in Mamaroneck, New York.

a golfer must undertake for tournament play. But the same could be said of the golf courses selected for the U.S. Open and the preparation that they must undertake to become ready for competition.

Once a host course is selected, we perform years of groundwork preparation leading up to the championship. I have been setting up championship golf courses for more than 20 years, and my team and I examine each hole, starting at the green and going back toward the tee.

We spend a lot of time studying the contours of the putting surface, as well as its surroundings. In addition to noting potential hole locations, we look at the entire green complex, especially as it relates to how the architect intended the hole to be played. If the hole is short, an elevated green protected by deep bunkers in front would be appropriate, as the approach shot would be high, be able to clear the hazards and land softly on the putting surface.

However, the same green complex would be incompatible with a longer hole. If a longer approach shot – hit on a lower trajectory – cleared the hazard, it would bounce and roll, potentially

over the green. The green of a long hole would need space to accommodate a shot's bounce and roll.

We then turn our attention to the landing zone for drives. Once we determine where we want competitors to play from, we study the existing obstacles – trees, bunkers, doglegs – that the player must avoid in order to set up a desirable approach shot. We want to reward good shots and penalize poor execution or decision-making. If the landing area does not accomplish this goal, we may consider adding or subtracting a feature.

Finally, we ask ourselves which club – driver, fairway wood, hybrid – we would like players to hit from the tee. If the existing teeing ground is insufficient for this purpose, we may add a teeing ground if space is available. The tricky part is that we have to visualize the way the game will be played several years into the future and adjust accordingly.

This adjustment has always been the case in the U.S. Open as the game, especially as played by the most accomplished players, is constantly evolving. When Chicago Golf Club hosted the 1900 U.S. Open, the layout measured 6,032 yards. Eleven years later, when the championship returned, the course had been lengthened to 6,605 yards. Now, 2017 site Erin Hills can stretch to nearly 8,000 yards.

Contrary to what some think, we don't tweak a golf course with the aim of producing a specific total yardage or winning score. We look at the holes individually, make each the best that we can and then add up the yardages at the end.

As the date of the championship gets closer, we start filling in the details, including fairway widths, grass heights and even the type of sand in the bunkers. During this process, there are two factors very much at the forefront of our thinking.

The first is precise awareness of the game's top players. That includes qualities such as how far their drives carry in the air, how high they hit a 6-iron shot from the fairway, how much spin they impart on the ball on a 40-yard pitch and how they move the clubhead through wet bluegrass rough.

This knowledge is essential to a good setup. With regard to the firmness of a green, for example, there is a delicate line between a setup in which a ball hit from a clean lie with a 7-iron hits the putting surface, takes two bounces and stops, and one in which the first bounce eliminates much of the spin and the ball rolls over the green. The latter does not achieve the goal of rewarding good shots and penalizing poor ones.

The second factor in our setup thinking is a thorough understanding of the course's architectural traits. Conceivably, we could implement a blanket setup of narrow fairways, high rough and firm greens. However, those conditions would obscure the architecture of the site.

We would like to highlight the unique features of each course. Oakmont's most important trait, for example, is its fast greens, so we'll spend a lot of time making sure players are adequately tested by hole locations. Pinehurst recently underwent a restoration in which the rough was replaced by sandy, scrubby areas that bring in a huge element of chance in terms of producing a variety of lies. Due to this, the 2014 U.S. Open at Pinehurst will feature wide fairways and very little rough.

Whether it's encouraging a less-than-ideal lie that still dangles the prospect of going for the green after a mediocre drive, instead of laying up, or moving up a teeing ground on a par 4 to present the possibility of driving the green, good setup produces as much a mental test as a physical one.

If a player makes the decision to try the riskier shot and executes, there is a reward. If he tries and doesn't execute, there is a penalty. The idea is to introduce more birdies and double bogeys instead of peppering the leader board with pars and bogeys. These swings make for more exciting, more interesting golf that engages both players and spectators.

For all the differences that each course presents, the one common quality that we strive to achieve for every U.S. Open site is firm, fast conditions. This is what separates the U.S. Open from other tournament setups. We want players to have to think about what happens after the ball lands. We want them to negotiate the contours of the fairways, the areas around the greens and the putting surfaces themselves and to think about how gravity will affect the shot once the ball is rolling.

At most golf tournaments, players hit shots through the air on a direct line from point A to point B; the U.S. Open's fast, firm conditions ask them to get from A to B using point C, which requires control over every aspect of the ball – carry distance, accuracy, trajectory and spin.

The third hole of The Olympic Club's Lake Course in San Francisco, California.

That is why the U.S. Open is so hard to win, and I am always amazed by the skill of the competitors. Although the course and setup are important, the U.S. Open is ultimately about how the players handle the conditions, the pressure and their own games.

We have had some memorable U.S. Open finishes in recent years. In 2006, the championship was decided by how the contenders handled the final hole at Winged Foot. And few will soon forget the putt made by Woods on the 72nd hole of the 2008 U.S. Open at Torrey Pines to force a playoff, which he won. The tension and anticipation surrounding the 18th green prior to his putt was nearly unbearable.

Despite the years of work prior to each championship, nobody at the USGA can take credit for those finishes; after all, the players hit the shots that created the excitement and etched the lasting memories. But if we pick a great course and set up the course appropriately, we certainly can foster the drama and excitement that our national championship deserves.

PERSEVERANCE

"You must do the thing you think you cannot do."
– Eleanor Roosevelt

The U.S. Open is a relentless test that provides many easy roads to failure and only a few perilous paths to success. To become a national champion, one must survive the travails of human drama encompassing man versus nature, man versus man and, perhaps most importantly, man versus himself. While facing adversity, some players not only prevailed, but summoned the inner strength to elevate their games to another level. Dealing with hardships that seemed insurmountable, they endured extreme weather, sickness, physical pain and eroding confidence to become national champions. Celebrated in the following pages are those players who, when all evidence suggested otherwise, ignored reason in pursuit of excellence.

The Longest Open | Billy Burke 1931

On the best of weeks, the U.S. Open is a grueling examination of golf. It is a mental and physical grind, bringing the world's best players together to compete on the nation's most celebrated and challenging courses. Perhaps no championship was a better example of "Golf's Toughest Test" than the 1931 edition at Inverness Club in Toledo, Ohio. In sweltering heat and oppressive humidity, Billy Burke outdueled George Von Elm in a contest that required 144 holes – the equivalent of playing *two* regulation-length championships in just five days.

After 72 holes, Burke and Von Elm were tied at 292. A 36-hole playoff on the following day didn't resolve the matter, as both players ended the day knotted at 149. Finally, over the course of the second 36-hole playoff, Burke shook free of Von Elm, beating him by a single stroke in the longest U.S. Open ever contested.

Burke, a professional at Round Hill Club in Greenwich, Connecticut, and a former iron foundry worker, was actually playing his third consecutive week of pressure-packed golf. Two weeks before winning the 1931 U.S. Open, he had played his way onto the United States Ryder Cup team by surviving 72 holes of qualification. The following week, Burke won both his Ryder Cup matches as part of the winning side at Scioto Country Club in Columbus, Ohio.

But Burke's hot play wasn't garnering headlines coming into the championship. For the first time since 1919, the U.S. Open field did not include Bob Jones. Jones had retired shortly after winning the Grand Slam in 1930, leaving at the top of his game. Several publications mourned the loss of Jones from the U.S. Open. *Golf Illustrated* reported that there was "much lessened popular interest

Former ironworker Billy Burke holds the U.S. Open Championship Trophy after his victory in 1931.

Facing page: Billy Burke holds his finish during the final round of regulation play during the 1931 U.S. Open. Burke endured extreme heat and 144 holes to win his first, and only, major championship.

More than 5,000 spectators surround the 18th green to watch Billy Burke defeat George Von Elm at the 1931 U.S. Open.

Facing page: Billy Burke plays from the long rough at Inverness Club during the 1931 U.S. Open.

in the event due to the absence of Bobby Jones." *Vanity Fair* wrote that it finally gave other professionals a chance because they didn't have to face "the mental hazard of the Great One, somewhere on the links performing his miracles." In *The American Golfer*, Grantland Rice wrote, "Many felt that with Bobby Jones missing the U.S. Open championship at Inverness, it would be a somewhat dull and drab affair."

But after witnessing the duel between Burke and Von Elm, Rice changed his tune, writing, "It turned out to be the most sensational Open ever played in the 500-year history of golf. Golf made good again to prove that the game must always stand above the player, to prove again that anything can happen, and that it follows no set laws."

Inverness was set up tight, with some members of the media saying it had the narrowest fairways they had ever seen at the U.S. Open. The heat and humidity reached oppressive levels as the mercury topped 105 degrees during each day of the championship. Ice packs and cold towels were distributed to the players and their caddies to keep them cool. O.B. Keeler wrote that, "George Von Elm in the terrible grind lost nine pounds in five days, while Burke, outwardly at least placid and content, had gained two pounds – a circumstance

George Von Elm congratulates Billy Burke on the 18th green at Inverness Club after the completion of what remains the longest U.S. Open in history.

which, if accurate, gives rise to wonder as to his diet." In part because of the heat, 1931 was the last year in which the U.S. Open was held in July. All U.S. Opens since have been contested in June.

The low round of the championship was shot by Von Elm on the second day of competition; his back-nine 32 for a 2-under 69 gave him the lead by one over Burke and Eddie Williams. After a third-round 73, Von Elm opened the final round with a two-shot lead on Burke. Little did the duo know, they weren't even halfway finished. Through 63 holes, the championship was seemingly in Von Elm's hands. A 38 or better on Inverness' inward nine meant the title would be his. Only four players had won both the U.S. Amateur and the U.S. Open. Von Elm, the 1926 U.S. Amateur champion, was vying to match the accomplishments of Francis Ouimet, Jerry Travers, Chick Evans and Bob Jones.

But bogeys on the 12th, 14th, 15th and 16th meant that Von Elm needed to birdie the final hole just to tie Burke, who had already posted 292. He did – hitting the narrow fairway of the short par 4, pitching to within 8 feet and sinking the putt to force a playoff.

Von Elm was no stranger to going extra holes in a USGA championship. The year before, at the 1930 U.S. Amateur at Merion (East Course), Von Elm lost to Maurice McCarthy in 28 holes – the longest 18-hole match in USGA history, a record that has since been matched but not broken.

In a back-and-forth playoff at Inverness, conducted over 36 holes, Burke built a four-shot lead through 16 holes, but momentum swung to Von Elm when he made up six shots in three holes, birdieing the 24th, 25th and 26th while Burke bogeyed. Burke made up single shots at the 28th, 32nd and 33rd to take a one-stroke lead, but as he had done the previous day, Von Elm birdied the final hole to tie Burke and force another 36-hole playoff.

Burke started his morning round the next day bogey-double bogey and quickly trailed Von Elm by three strokes. At lunch, Von Elm still led by a stroke, but on the opening nine of the afternoon round, Burke played some of his best golf of the championship, recording three birdies to go out in 34. He seized the lead for good when Von Elm bogeyed the 32nd hole and held on to win the championship by a single stroke.

Two main factors helped Burke win the championship. First, Von Elm putted poorly throughout the second day of the playoff. Despite hitting most greens in regulation, the Utah native needed 72 putts over the final 36 holes. Von Elm missed three putts from within 3 feet, including a crucial putt from 18 inches on the 34th hole that left him two strokes behind with just two holes to play. The second factor was Burke's exquisite play at the 492-yard, par-5 ninth hole. Burke, who was not a long hitter, carded five birdies and an eagle in the eight times he played the hole.

Jones, a spectator for the first time in more than a decade, wrote an article in *The American Golfer*, touting Burke's play in the double-playoff as "one of the greatest things I have ever known in golf." He wrote that it "not only proves that he knows how to hit a golf ball, but also that he is supplied with an unlimited amount of courage, stamina, nerve control and the ability to keep his concentration unbroken."

While Burke and Von Elm can be lauded for their efforts in 1931, they would only combine for two more top-10 finishes in the U.S. Open for the remainder of their careers. The story of this U.S. Open was its length – 144 holes over five days. The following January, USGA President Herbert Ramsay presided over a vote of the USGA's executive committee to revert back to the 18-hole play-off system that had been in place from 1895 to 1928. The U.S. Open playoff has remained at 18 holes since 1932, though in 1953 it was resolved that the champion would be determined by sudden-death if the participants were still tied at the end of 18 holes. The playoff has followed that format since.

Billy Burke dumps a bucket of water on Wiffy Cox during the 1931 U.S. Open. Temperatures exceeded 100 degrees throughout the championship.

H.H. Ramsay, president of the United States Golf Association, is shown presenting the U.S. Open Championship Trophy to Billy Burke (center) while George Von Elm looks on.

Mind Over Matter | Olin Dutra 1934

Olin Dutra, a native of Monterey, California, would persevere through a severe stomach ailment, losing almost 20 pounds, during the 1934 U.S. Open.

By 1934, the U.S. Open was firmly established as one of the nation's premier sporting events. Of the 150 players in the field, the only ones exempt from qualifying included the top-30 finishers from the 1933 U.S. Open, the 19 members of the Walker Cup teams from the United States and Great Britain, and 10 special invitations issued to foreign professionals. The other 1,004 entrants that year attempted to qualify for the remaining 91 spots at one of 22 sectional-qualifying locations around the country. Since the retirement of Bob Jones in 1930, no player had come to dominate the game. The 1934 U.S. Open would provide yet another opportunity for an extremely talented player to rise from the long shadow of Jones to claim the spotlight.

Olin Dutra first qualified for the U.S. Open in 1930 at Interlachen Country Club, where he finished 25th just as Jones was claiming the third leg of his historic Grand Slam. Dutra improved to 21st in 1931 and truly contended in 1932 and 1933, finishing seventh on both occasions. Born in Monterey in 1901 into a Portuguese immigrant family of meager means, he grew up caddieing with his brother, Mortie, as well as Al Espinosa and his brothers at Del Monte Golf Course and later at Pebble Beach. Mortie and Olin would both go on to become professional golfers, and Olin would eventually become the head professional at the exclusive Brentwood Country Club in Los Angeles.

Olin won numerous regional events in California, including the Southern California PGA Championship in 1930 and 1931 (he would eventually claim this title a total of six times), but he had yet to capture significant national attention. He did in 1932, when he captured the PGA Championship, played at match play during this period, winning his five matches in dramatic fashion and playing

196 holes (including two qualifying rounds) in the stroke-play equivalent of 19 under par. Despite this impressive victory, most of his peers did not view him as a threat to win the U.S. Open. One unnamed colleague was quoted as saying, "He has the shots, but lacks the will to win."

Dutra understood his limitations and knew that shotmaking was not one of them. Rather, it was his mental attitude that had held him back in his pursuit of the national championship when he had been in contention in 1932 and 1933. In the winter of 1934, he wrote to his friend and accomplished professional Leo Diegel, "I have been working on a system to develop self-confidence. You know I have the shots to win. Now my inferiority complex is banished. The old chin is out. You boys had better look out for yourselves at Merion. I am going to fight."

With his self-doubt now seemingly under control, Dutra set out from California for the U.S. Open at Merion Cricket Club. During a stop in Detroit to meet Mortie, who was also playing in the U.S. Open, Olin contracted amoebic dysentery, brought on by food poisoning, and was briefly hospitalized. Well enough to be released but still very sick, he contemplated withdrawing from the championship. His brother convinced him otherwise, and together they made their way to Merion. By the time they arrived, Dutra had lost 15 of his 230 pounds. He may have conquered his mental demons, but this physical one would plague him throughout the championship.

When play began on June 7, no one was picking Dutra as a favorite to win. The press was focused on Gene Sarazen, Johnny Goodman, Paul Runyan, Craig Wood, Bobby Cruickshank, Horton Smith, Harry Cooper, Tommy Armour and the great Walter Hagen. So it was not surprising when Dutra posted a score of 76 to trail the first-round leaders Wiffy Cox, Cruickshank and Charles Lacey by five strokes. Under doctor's orders, he was eating sugar cubes to maintain his energy

The gallery watches Olin Dutra and Gene Sarazen during the 1934 U.S. Open at Merion Cricket Club (East Course). Here, Sarazen is seen blasting out of a greenside bunker. Olin Dutra's eventual victory is perhaps one of the most inspirational tales in the history of the game.

Miniature club made from the driver used by Olin Dutra during the 1934 U.S. Open Championship.

Left to right: Olin Dutra, USGA President Herbert Jaques and Olin Dutra's caddie, Harry Gibson, during the trophy presentation at the 1934 U.S. Open at Merion.

Facing page: Olin Dutra, seen here in an advertisement for Beech-Nut chewing gum, used this Spalding golf ball and 1-iron during the 1934 U.S. Open at Merion.

and drinking plenty of water to ward off dehydration. He would improve to a 74 in the second round for a total of 150, tied for 18th place, as Cruickshank posted another 71 for a total of 142 and a two-stroke lead over Gene Sarazen.

Given the severity of his illness, it was impressive that Dutra as much as survived the 36-hole cut. But with his newfound self-confidence, he set his sights a bit higher in the third round. The wind had picked up at Merion and was markedly affecting play. Dutra had grown up playing in the windy conditions of Monterey, which were also common at his home club of Brentwood. Such experience, combined with his ability to drive the ball accurately and long, gave him an advantage over the field, which he would capitalize on in the third round, posting a 1-over-par 71. Cruickshank would falter with a 77, and Sarazen's 73 would leave him with just a three-stroke lead over Dutra heading into the final round.

Sarazen, playing with Horton Smith, began his final round at 2:50 in the afternoon and completed his first nine holes in 38 strokes (two over par). Dutra, playing with fellow Californian and accomplished amateur Lawson Little in the final pairing at 3:05, matched Sarazen's 38 on the outward nine. Dutra was still three strokes back with nine holes to play. The turning point of the championship would come moments later, as Dutra took advantage of the short 335-yard, par-4 10th hole by almost driving the green for an easy birdie, while Sarazen hooked his drive into a ditch on the 11th hole and struggled to make a triple-bogey 7. Dutra was now ahead by one.

Sarazen would double bogey the 12th and battle back with birdies at the 13th and 18th holes to post a final-round score of 76 for a total of 294. Dutra, conquering his physical and mental demons, held steady on the inward nine and needed only a bogey 5 on the final hole to best Sarazen by one stroke. The 18th hole at Merion is long and difficult – a 458-yard par 4 with a narrow driving zone and a difficult approach, often played from a downhill lie to an elevated and well-protected green. After a long, straight drive that found the fairway, Dutra hit his spoon (the equivalent of a modern 3-wood) to the edge of the green. Mortie yelled from the crowd, "Take it easy, Olin," after Dutra had played his first putt to 4 feet. No time for heroics, he lagged his second putt to the lip of the hole and tapped in for a 72 and a total of 293 to win the U.S. Open by a single stroke over Sarazen.

Winning the U.S. Open is a stressful and strenuous achievement, even for players in the best of health. It requires a unique inner strength, focused determination and the sheer will to win. Despite physical agony and a weakened body, Olin Dutra found this transcendent spirit within himself and claimed greatness. His remarkable victory in 1934 remains one of the most heroic and inspirational moments in the championship's long and rich history.

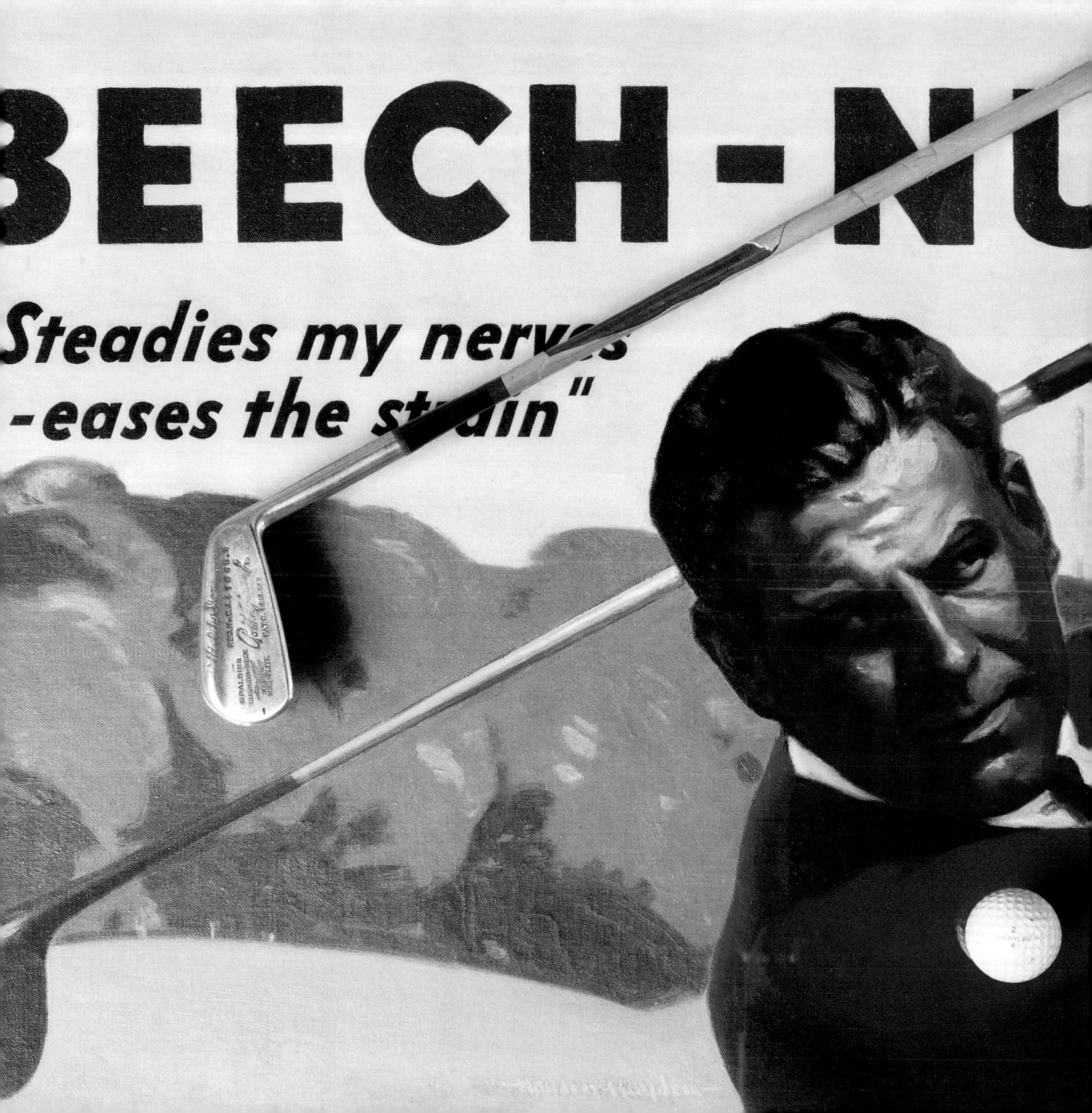
BEECH-NU
Steadies my nerv
-eases the st ain"

Battered but Not Beaten | Ken Venturi 1964

Ken Venturi gives a victory speech at the 1964 U.S. Open at Congressional. Venturi would later spend 35 years providing color commentary for CBS Sports.

As Ken Venturi staggered down the 72nd fairway at Congressional Country Club in Bethesda, Maryland, it became clear that the 1964 U.S. Open was a case study in survival and perseverance. With oppressive heat and humidity, it would not only prove to be one of the hottest contests in the championship's history, it would also lead to a change in the championship's format. Partly due to the physically demanding conditions under which Venturi won, the USGA voted to play the 72-hole championship over four days instead of three starting in 1965. Despite discussion of reverting back to a 36-hole final day in the late 1960s, the format of the U.S. Open has remained at 72 holes over four days ever since.

For the third consecutive year, Arnold Palmer was in contention heading into Saturday's final rounds. After his heroic comeback victory in 1960 at Denver's Cherry Hills Country Club, Palmer had shared the lead at Pennsylvania's Oakmont Country Club in 1962 before losing to Jack Nicklaus in a playoff. In 1963, at The Country Club in Brookline, Massachusetts, he held a share of the lead through 36 holes before falling to Julius Boros in a playoff. At Congressional, Palmer opened with near-flawless rounds of 68 and 69. He trailed only Tommy Jacobs – who made a 60-foot birdie putt on the 18th hole to shoot 64 on Friday – and was four strokes clear of anyone else in the field, setting up what many thought would be his second U.S. Open title.

Venturi was six strokes behind through two rounds – in the mix but not capturing any newspaper headlines. He grew up in San Francisco and developed his game at Harding Park Golf Course on the edge of the city. Venturi lost in the championship final to Mason Rudolph in the inaugural U.S. Junior Amateur in 1948 and was a pupil of Byron Nelson in the early 1950s. While still

an amateur, Venturi finished runner-up in the 1956 Masters. He held a four-shot lead through 54 holes but closed with an 80 to finish one stroke behind Jack Burke Jr. Between 1956 and 1960, Venturi won 10 tournaments on the PGA Tour and finished in the top 10 in seven of the 13 major championships he played.

But after another runner-up finish in the 1960 Masters, Venturi suffered a string of injuries. In 1961 he hurt his back, and in 1962 he injured his wrist in an automobile accident. He had not qualified for the previous three U.S. Opens and nearly missed in 1964 as well. Venturi got through the local qualifier at Memphis, but he struggled in his sectional at Detroit. He opened with a 77 and, after playing the front nine of his second round in two over, nearly withdrew. He regrouped to shoot 70 for a total of 147 to qualify.

When Venturi, now 33, came to Congressional for the 1964 U.S. Open, he had not won in almost four years. His game had begun to round into shape with top-10 finishes in Pensacola, Westchester and Grand Blanc earlier in the year, but he was not viewed as a credible threat to win the championship by most fans or media members.

Ken Venturi plays out of a bunker on the 72nd hole during the 1964 U.S. Open. Venturi grew up in San Francisco, developing his game at Harding Park Golf Course. He was a finalist in the 1948 U.S. Junior Amateur Championship and one of Byron Nelson's prized students.

Ken Venturi drives on the 10th tee at the 1964 U.S. Open. Players and spectators endured temperatures of more than 100 degrees and high humidity during the championship.

After opening rounds of 72 and 70 left him in a tie for fourth with Charlie Sifford, Venturi began his Saturday morning round on fire. He birdied the first, fourth, fifth, eighth and ninth holes to turn in 30. After adding another birdie at the 12th, Venturi held the lead, but the heat and humidity were taking a toll on him. He managed to par the next four holes, but he missed short putts on the 17th and 18th holes to relinquish the lead to Jacobs. Palmer faded out of contention with a 75 on Saturday morning and was never a factor in the final round.

In the locker room, Venturi was feeling weak and had the chills. He did not eat between rounds and was given iced tea with lemon and salt tablets to restore his strength. Dr. John Everett, a physician and member of Congressional, examined him and determined that, while his pulse was still normal, Venturi had lost a lot of fluid from his body. After a brief nap, Venturi decided to play on despite the rising temperatures. Everett followed him around the course with ice packs throughout the final round.

Facing page: MacGregor driver and Royal golf ball used by Ken Venturi during the 1964 U.S. Open.

While Venturi pressed on, taking 12 additional salt tablets during the round, it was Jacobs who struggled. The man who could seemingly do no wrong in rounds of 64 and 70 ballooned to a 76 in the final round. Venturi parred the first five holes and, after bogeying the 456-yard, par-4 sixth, responded with birdies at the par-5 ninth and par-4 13th. After the 15th hole, Venturi cut his pace in half to conserve energy. He told Joe Dey, executive director of the USGA, "You can penalize me two strokes if you want to, but I'm slowing down." With Jacobs fading, Venturi hit his 1-iron to within 15 feet of the hole at the par-3 16th. After a two-putt par, Venturi later said, "Then all I had to do was finish."

As he holed the final putt, Venturi dropped his putter and raised his arms toward the sky, saying, "My God, I've won the U.S. Open." His playing partner, Raymond Floyd, playing in his first U.S. Open, picked Venturi's ball out of the hole and handed it to him with tears in his eyes. In the post-round press conference, Venturi received a standing ovation from the press corps. As he reached the steps to take him up to the podium, Venturi said, "I've never been so tired, but this is going to be the happiest climb of my life."

He shared a letter that he had received on the eve of the championship from his parish priest, Rev. Francis Murray, who wrote, "For you to become the 1964 U.S. Open champion … the effect would be both a blessing and a tonic to so many people who desperately need encouragement and a reason for hope.… If you should win, Ken, you would prove, I believe, to millions everywhere that they too can be victorious over doubt, misfortune and despair."

His triumph at Congressional netted Venturi a $17,500 check – a fortune to someone who had spent the last few years asking old friends for sponsor's exemptions because his game had slipped due to injury. For at least a week, he had put the injuries behind him, silenced the naysayers and summoned all his strength to will a victory at the 1964 U.S. Open.

The four-stroke victory over Jacobs would be the only major championship Venturi would win. After wins at Hartford and Akron later that year, he was diagnosed with carpal tunnel syndrome in both wrists. He won once more on Tour, in 1966 at Harding Park, but was forced to retire after the 1967 season.

Facing page: After years of frustration and injuries, and a week of intense heat and humidity, relief and happiness overtake Ken Venturi after he putts out to win the 1964 U.S. Open, for his only major championship.

Heart of a Champion | Payne Stewart 1999

Payne Stewart arrived at the golf course on Sunday as a man on a mission. He was looking to avenge his previous year's excruciating loss to Lee Janzen at The Olympic Club, but it was something else that diverted Stewart on his way to the practice range before the final round of the 1999 U.S. Open – the quest for a pair of scissors.

The cool and misty conditions at Pinehurst Resort's Course No. 2 sent many players scrambling for umbrellas and rain gear. But in warming up, Stewart felt that his jacket was too bulky and stopped by the golf shop to borrow a pair of scissors so that he could shorten the sleeves from the wrist to the elbow. After hitting a few warm-up shots, Stewart determined that his impromptu alteration was not sufficient. He sent his caddie, Mike Hicks, to find another pair of scissors so that he could do some additional tailoring. When all was said and done, Stewart had created a makeshift rain vest for himself that was an iconic image of the championship by day's end.

For the second consecutive year, Stewart held the lead through 54 holes at the U.S. Open, but like his jacket, the final round was anything but clean-cut. Though Tiger Woods, with just one major championship title to his name, was not yet *Tiger Woods*, the list of contenders was very strong. It included the world's top-ranked player, David Duval, who had already shot 59 and won four times in 1999; Phil Mickelson, who was five years away from his first major championship but had already amassed 13 PGA Tour victories; and Vijay Singh, the reigning PGA champion.

Stewart's overall record in the U.S. Open was exemplary. From 1984 to 1998, he had won once, finished runner-up twice and logged three other top-10

Payne Stewart hits an iron from the fairway during the second round of the 1999 U.S. Open.

Facing page: Payne Stewart celebrates after sinking his par putt on the 18th green to win the 1999 U.S. Open. Sculptor Zenos Frudakis immortalized Stewart's fist pump, and a statue of this moment now stands near the 18th green of Course No. 2.

finishes in 15 starts. Despite his excellent record, which included a playoff victory over Scott Simpson at Hazeltine in 1991, the defeat at the hands of Janzen, who came from five back on the final day at Olympic, stuck in his craw. "After the U.S. Open in 1998 everybody told him 'That was a great try, you came so close,'" said Tracey Stewart, Payne's wife. "He hated that. He wanted to be number one."

Having missed the cut in Memphis the previous week, Stewart arrived at Pinehurst a few days early and began working with his coach, Chuck Cook, five days before the first round. They walked the course together, with Stewart carrying an 8-iron, 9-iron and wedge and hitting a variety of shots from all conceivable areas. Mickelson, on the other hand, did not arrive until Tuesday evening and was only able to play one practice round. He was detained at a doctor's appointment with his wife, Amy, who was eight-and-a-half months pregnant with the couple's first child. Throughout the week, Mickelson's caddie carried a pager and he vowed to leave the course, no matter his standing, and return home to Scottsdale, Arizona, if the baby was on its way. "We could only think of one scenario in the whole entire world that would make this difficult," said Amy Mickelson. "I go into labor and Phil's going to win the U.S. Open."

As the week unfolded, it appeared that both might be distinct possibilities. Mickelson was just one stroke behind Stewart to start the final round, with Woods, Duval and Singh giving chase. Playing in the second-to-last group, Woods fired the first shot. While Stewart and Mickelson were walking off the first tee, a huge roar came from the green ahead, where Woods had rolled in a birdie to move into a share of second place with Mickelson. Duval followed suit with birdies at the second and third holes to join them at even par. Singh started consistently with seven consecutive pars, but he converted birdies on holes eight and 10 to move to even par as well. Of the leaders, only Duval fell out of contention with a bogey-bogey-double bogey stretch late on the outward nine. Stewart retained his one-stroke advantage as both he and Mickelson posted 1-under 34s on the first nine, but bogeys at the 10th, 12th and 15th, against a birdie at the 13th, left Stewart one stroke behind the left-hander on the 16th tee.

"I felt, with three holes to go, like I was in control … because I was leading and it's a very difficult course to make birdies on," said Mickelson. The 16th had yielded the fewest birdies of any hole all week and, at 489 yards, was the longest par 4 in U.S. Open history to that point. Playing ahead, Singh had made his first bogey of the final round on the 16th to drop back to one over par, two behind Mickelson, but Woods made an unlikely birdie, punctuated by a fist pump and roar from the gallery, to move back to even par for the championship. Mickelson missed the fairway, chipped back into play and hit a solid 7-iron to 8 feet. Stewart was just off the green in two but, trailing by a stroke, played an

Official Stroke Card
99th United States Open Championship®
Questions as to the Rules of Golf shall be referred to the USGA Rules Committee

Competitor _____ Payne Stewart _____

Round ___ 4 ___ Date ___ June 20, 1999 ___

For USGA Use
Previous Total __209__
This Round __70__
New Total __279__
Verified: 18th ___ Pr. ____ Pub. ____

HOLES	1	2	3	4	5	6	7	8	9	OUT	10	11	12	13	14	15	16	17	18	IN	TOTAL
YARDS	404	447	335	566	482	222	398	485	179	3,518	610	453	447	383	436	202	489	191	446	3,657	7,175
PAR	4	4	4	5	4	3	4	4	3	35	5	4	4	4	4	3	4	3	4	35	70
	3	5	3	5	4	3	4	4	3	34	6	4	5	3	4	4	4	2	4	36	70

Marker's Signature

Competitor's Signature _Payne Stewart_

Payne Stewart's official fourth-round scorecard from the 1999 U.S. Open.

---

aggressive pitch that he caught thin and chased to the back of the green.

"I remember thinking on 16 after Payne bladed his chip past the hole that Tiger was the guy that was going to possibly catch me," said Mickelson. But Stewart had other ideas. He lined up his putt, took a deep breath and remembered the tip that his wife, Tracey, had given him the previous night – keep your head still. "Given what he was looking at, 25 feet, breaking two ways, downhill at the end, I thought it was about as tough a putt as a guy could have," said Jim Mackay, Mickelson's caddie. Stewart didn't blink. The ball rolled toward the hole and plunged into the center. Stewart moved to the hole with a confident gait and retrieved his ball, acknowledging the raucous crowd behind him.

Mickelson was next. He was universally acclaimed as having one of the best short games on Tour, but this time he faltered. His 8-foot attempt to match Stewart's par was pulled to the right for his only bogey of the day. "That was the turning point," said Mickelson. "Now what anyone else ahead of me is doing is irrelevant because I've got my hands full with Payne."

Now tied, the pair strode to the 191-yard, downhill, par-3 17th. Woods had just lipped out an 8-foot par putt to drop back to one over par. Stewart and Hicks debated club selection, finally opting for a smooth 6-iron over a hard 7-iron. It was a good choice. The shot never left the flagstick, settling 5 feet from the hole. With the pressure on, Mickelson nearly topped it with a superlative effort of his own. His high, soaring 7-iron landed softly and rolled to within 8 feet. The best U.S. Open finish in more than a decade was getting even better. "I remember walking off the [17th] tee thinking how lucky I was to be there," said Mackay. "I was having the time of my life." But Mickelson's putter let him down again, as his bid to move back into red figures rolled past the edge. Now with a chance to regain the lead, Stewart didn't hesitate. He poured his short putt in the center, holing his second clutch putt in as many holes.

Above and facing page: Payne Stewart, in his self-modified rain vest and signature plus fours, celebrates making his 15-foot par putt to defeat Phil Mickelson for his second U.S. Open Championship title.

Woods and Singh had to settle for pars at the 18th, leaving Stewart and Mickelson to battle for the championship title. Stewart missed the fairway and drew a bad lie in the right rough. "When I got up there, I had no chance to even think about the green," said Stewart. Instead, he took a wedge and pitched back into the fairway. "I didn't compound the situation by making two mistakes in a row," said Stewart. "I took my medicine [and] put the ball out where I could at least give myself a chance to get the ball up and down." From the fairway, Mickelson played his approach safely to the front of the green, 35 feet from the hole. After Stewart played a lob wedge to 15 feet and Mickelson lagged his birdie putt to tap-in range, the stage was set for one of the most dramatic conclusions in U.S. Open history.

Before the championship, Stewart had told the media, "Pressure is something that you have to learn to deal with. I think that comes over time spent out here putting yourself in that situation. I think I'm prepared for that now, being able to handle the situation when it presents itself." Now, here he was on the 72nd hole of the championship, a year removed from an excruciating loss, with a chance at redemption and a putt to win the U.S. Open. He picked his line – inside right – and made the stroke. "When I looked up it was about two feet from the hole and it was breaking right in the center," said Stewart. "I couldn't believe it."

As the putt dropped, Stewart pumped his fist forward and took one giant step toward the hole, his shrieks of joy drowned out by the unrestrained gallery. Hicks ran to Stewart, and the two shared a long, emotional embrace. "The putt on 18 was the most exciting thing I've seen in 20 years caddieing," explained

Hicks. It capped off one of the greatest displays of putting in major championship history. Stewart needed just 24 putts in the final round, including clutch one-putts on each of his final three holes. "Payne was in such a zone that whole week," said Hicks. "He didn't get into that frame of mind often, but when he did it was special to watch."

It would be the first of several runner-up finishes for Mickelson in the U.S. Open. But walking off the 72nd hole, Stewart approached Mickelson and helped put everything in perspective. Stewart grabbed his face and told him, "I'm so happy for you. You're going to be a father!" "I just thought that was really cool – very classy," said Mickelson. It would also happen much quicker than anyone could have expected. The morning after he flew home, Amy went into labor. Just 26 hours after suffering a crushing loss, Amanda Brynn Mickelson was born. Phil Mickelson was a father.

Payne Stewart's second U.S. Open victory is a memory frozen in time. Triumph turned to tragedy four months later, when Stewart's airplane depressurized on a flight from Orlando to Dallas, killing Stewart, two pilots and three other passengers. It was a sudden loss that left the golf community stunned. To Mickelson, there was only one memory of Stewart that he felt defined the man. "That last hole is the way I choose to remember him as a player, a person [and] a father." A statue of Stewart in his victory pose – leaning forward with his arm outstretched and leg extended – next to the 18th green at Pinehurst No. 2 now commemorates his accomplishment, serving as a reminder of the fragility of life and the extraordinary champion that was Payne Stewart.

Delivering in the Clutch | Tiger Woods 2008

Tiger Woods with the U.S. Open Championship Trophy after his playoff victory in 2008 at Torrey Pines.

The limp became more pronounced as the championship wore on. He winced on nearly every follow-through and bent over in pain after even his best shots. Yet there he stood, alone atop the leader board after 91 holes, when he had had every reason throughout the week to throw in the towel. Tiger Woods' gritty performance at the 2008 U.S. Open drew comparisons to Ben Hogan's courageous comeback in 1950 at Merion. But this moment was uniquely Tiger's, complete with miraculous recovery shots, clutch putts and fist pumps that electrified the galleries at Torrey Pines.

This U.S. Open victory was nothing like Woods' first, a dominating performance eight years earlier, some 450 miles up the California coast at Pebble Beach, where he blew away the field by a record 15 strokes. He was still the world's best player, having spent 500 consecutive weeks in the top spot of the Official World Golf Ranking, but health-wise, Woods was decidedly less than 100 percent. The 2008 U.S. Open marked his first competitive round – and first time walking 18 holes – since the final round of the Masters in April. Two days after the conclusion of that tournament, Woods had arthroscopic surgery on his left knee to repair torn cartilage. He also suffered a double stress fracture of his left tibia during rehabilitation, a fact he shared only with his inner circle until weeks after his triumph at Torrey Pines. Throughout the entire championship, Woods maintained a stubborn stoicism about the injury, telling the media only that his leg was sore and that he was undergoing treatment between rounds.

The championship itself could not have started any worse for Woods. Paired with the second- and third-ranked players in the world, Phil Mickelson and Adam Scott, Woods pulled his drive into the heavy rough to the left of the fairway bunker on the opening hole. He pitched back to the fairway, knocked his wedge over the green, chipped to 5 feet and missed the putt, settling for a double-bogey 6. Despite his early struggles, Woods managed to card a 1-over-par 72 and shared 19th place after the first round. "To make two double bogeys and a three-putt and only be four back, that's a great position to be in, because I know I can clean that up tomorrow," said Woods.

Yet Woods was still struggling through nine holes on Friday. Starting his round on the 10th hole, he made an eagle and four bogeys and was in danger of dropping out of contention as he made the turn at three over par for the championship. To compound his problems, Woods blocked his drive to the right on the first hole, and his ball came to rest on a trampled area near a cart path. Opting not to take a free drop because it would have put him behind a tree, he hoisted an 8-iron from 157 yards to 10 feet and converted the birdie putt. The sequence initiated a stretch in which Woods birdied four of five holes to move back into red figures. Another birdie at the par-5 ninth, his closing hole, gave him a 5-under-par 30 on his second nine, moving him into a share of second place.

Saturday started off much the same way as Friday for Woods. A double bogey at the first followed by bogeys at the fourth and 12th left him one over par for the championship. But Woods wasn't the only player having trouble. Hometown favorite Phil Mickelson, who did not carry a driver in his bag during the week, had short-game issues at the par-5 13th. Just short of the green in two, Mickelson needed four pitches to hold the green and three putts for a quadruple-bogey 9 en route to a 76.

As Woods was in trouble yet again on the 17th, Lee Westwood was giving an interview in the media center. Having posted a 1-under-par 70, Westwood held a two-stroke lead over Woods and was fielding questions about how he planned to hold off Woods on the final day. Then it happened, swift and sudden, in a matter of 15 minutes. An unlikely chip-in for birdie at the 17th and a 35-foot putt for eagle on the 18th vaulted Woods into the lead. Westwood would now have to overtake Woods if he wanted to claim the title.

Playing in the last group for the sixth time in the last eight majors, Woods' start to the fourth round was just as rocky as those of the previous three days. A double bogey at the first and a bogey at the second sent him tumbling back to even par. He moved back into red figures with birdies at holes nine and 11, but he offset his gains with bogeys at the 13th and 15th. As the day wore on, it became clear that the three main contenders for the prize were Woods, Westwood and Rocco Mediate, a good-natured journeyman with five PGA Tour victories who, playing in the second-to-last group, had posted a 1-under-par total of 283.

Tiger Woods and Rocco Mediate share a lighthearted moment during their playoff for the 2008 U.S. Open.

Tiger Woods cringes after his tee shot on the second hole during the final round of the 2008 U.S. Open.

Never in his 13 previous major championship victories had Woods relinquished a 54-hole lead, but that's what he faced if he did not birdie the 72nd hole, a reachable par 5 of 527 yards with a pond protecting the front-left portion of the green. Trailing Mediate by one, Woods pulled his drive into the left fairway bunker, negating any chance of reaching the green in two. From a clean lie in the sand, Woods blocked a 9-iron into the second cut of right rough, leaving himself a difficult approach. With 101 yards to the hole, he chose to hit a hard 60-degree wedge to the hole location that was tucked just 6 yards from the front and 6 yards from the right edge of the green. He executed beautifully, and his ball came to rest within 12 feet of the hole.

After Westwood came up just short on a 20-foot birdie putt that would have tied Mediate, all the attention turned to Woods. Stalking the hole from all angles, he determined his putt needed to be played two and a half balls outside the right edge. He told himself to stay committed and to make a smooth and solid stroke. And for the third consecutive evening, Woods produced a finish that left thousands around Torrey Pines and millions of television viewers across the country in awe. "I hit it exactly where I wanted it to and it went in," said Woods, who celebrated one of the biggest putts of his career with a guttural scream and pulsating fist pumps. If it had been anyone else, the gallery's reaction might have been disbelief or amazement, yet with Woods it was another of the "I-told-you-he'd-make-it" moments on which he had built his career. "I don't think there was a person on the planet who was watching who didn't think he was going to make it," said 1996 runner-up Tom Lehman. "You expect it every time," said 2006 champion Geoff Ogilvy. "It's never surprising." Woods had once again delivered when it mattered most.

Despite the raucous celebration, the championship still needed to be settled on Monday. Woods and Mediate arrived at Torrey Pines wearing the same color combination – black pants and a red shirt – but the similarities ended there. At age 32, Woods was squarely in the prime of his career. Despite his injured leg, he was unquestionably the game's best player and had a superlative record in both the U.S. Open, with victories in 2000 and 2002, and in playoffs, compiling a 10-1 record on the PGA Tour. Mediate was his perfect foil. At age 45, he was on the back nine of his career. He was ranked 157th in the world, and it had been more than six years since his last Tour victory. Mediate had needed a birdie on the first extra hole of a playoff at the Columbus, Ohio, sectional qualifier just to earn a spot in the field of the 2008 U.S. Open.

After an almost playful start to the playoff, in which Mediate had the crowd roaring on the first tee by reciting lines from *Caddyshack*, Woods opened up a three-stroke advantage through 10 holes and appeared poised to run away

Tiger Woods plays his tee shot on the 14th hole during the final round of the 2008 U.S. Open.

with the championship. "It could have been over pretty quick," said Mediate, "and … all of a sudden I pick up three, four shots and in a few holes I'm one up." Woods bogeyed the par-3 11th when his tee shot found the front-left bunker, and he followed it with another bogey on the 505-yard, par-4 12th. After both players birdied the par-5 13th, Mediate followed with a birdie at the drivable 269-yard, par-4 14th to tie Woods. On the 15th, with Woods in a good position, just 18 feet from the hole, Mediate dropped a 35-foot birdie putt for his third consecutive birdie to take his first lead since the fourth hole. "I thought I was going to win after that putt went in on 15," said Mediate, after the round.

The players traded pars on 16 and 17, and once again the championship came down to the 18th with Woods trailing by a single stroke. This time it was less dramatic, yet equally effective, for Woods, who hit the green in two with a 4-iron from 217 yards and two-putted from 40 feet for birdie. Mediate, who elected to play the 18th as a three-shot hole, faced a putt from 15 feet to win. "I said to myself, 'You've waited your whole life for this putt, just don't lag it,'"

Above and facing page: Tiger Woods celebrates his birdie putt on the 18th hole at Torrey Pines with a spectacular fist pump. The putt forced a playoff with Rocco Mediate.

said Mediate. He gave it plenty of pace but missed the line. The playoff moved to sudden death for just the third time in the championship's history.

On the first extra playoff hole, the seventh at Torrey Pines, Mediate pulled his drive into the fairway bunker and bounced his approach off a cart path, and his ball came to rest against a grandstand. After a free drop, he pitched to 30 feet. Woods, who hit the green in regulation, lagged his birdie putt to within inches. He tapped in and walked over to the green's right edge to watch. When Mediate's par attempt missed, Woods had won his third U.S. Open and ninth USGA championship. "I think this is probably the best ever," said Woods, putting the victory ahead of his record-breaking 1997 Masters and 2000 U.S. Open wins. "He's just so hard to beat," said Mediate. "He is who he is. There's nothing else to say."

From David Duval and Ernie Els to Phil Mickelson and Vijay Singh, many leading players of the decade played the role of rival to Woods. It was in this championship, however, that Woods overcame his greatest challenger – himself. He had accomplished the unthinkable on what turned out to be a broken leg. "It's about dealing with things and getting out there and giving it your best shot," said Woods. "There [are] never any excuses. You just go play. That's the beauty of it – enjoying the opportunity to compete whether you're 100 percent or not." Eight days later, he underwent reconstructive surgery on his left knee and did not play another tournament in 2008. His gutsy performance at Torrey Pines didn't break records like many of his other major-championship wins, but it could stand as the victory that best defines his career.

America's First Golf Hero

BY RHONDA GLENN

The 20th of September was a damp, dreary day at The Country Club, a citadel of golf in Brookline, Massachusetts, along the western rim of the old city of Boston. Water dripped from the massive trees lining the fairways, and golf balls plugged in the sodden turf. The rambling clubhouse, with its graceful porches and dormer windows, towered over the course like a gloomy sentinel. On this dank Saturday, Francis Ouimet made the United States finally fall in love with golf.

Ouimet was a shy and unlikely hero. In the years to come, he would discuss his great victory with reluctance, seldom with the press and never with his family. "He never discussed golf," said Barbara McLean, Ouimet's daughter. "Not to my knowledge. Not in my presence. He never discussed golf. It was, 'What did you do in school today?'"

In 1913, the modest, gangly youth with the long face was in the eye of a perfect storm: Before World War I, British golfers were dominating the golf scene and the American game had yet to pick up a head of steam. Of the 17 U.S. Open champions dating back to 1895, a dozen were born in Scotland and three in England. Only Johnny McDermott, a native of Philadelphia, had managed to crack the British stranglehold. In 1911, McDermott had been the first American to win the national championship. He had repeated in 1912.

McDermott, however, is not among the major characters in this story. Those roles are filled by Ouimet, the impeccable Harry Vardon, Ted Ray and Wilfrid Reid. While McDermott did compete in the 1913 U.S. Open as defending champion, he was showing signs of emotional decline. He was competing on borrowed time. Tragically, he would fall victim to schizophrenia.

In *The U.S. Open: Golf's Ultimate Challenge*, author Robert Sommers called the 1913 championship "the most important and the most cosmopolitan U.S. Open played so far."

There were 160 players entered in the championship, only the second time the field had reached triple digits. Many were working-class American professionals, but a few came from as far away as France and Great Britain. Ouimet had only to walk across the street.

When Francis was four years old, his French-Canadian father and Irish mother had purchased a house in Brookline on Clyde Street, across the street from The Country Club's 17th hole. The Ouimets struggled to make ends meet, and Francis soon began working as a caddie at the club. The youngster taught himself to play golf, using his brother's clubs and golf balls he found on the course. It wasn't long before he was the best high school golfer in Massachusetts. He organized a golf team at Brookline High and was its star player. When his father insisted that Francis quit school and do something useful, he left Brookline High.

Facing page: The putter and four Tom Stewart irons used by Francis Ouimet to win the 1913 U.S. Open.

Francis Ouimet, shown here a few days after winning the 1913 U.S. Open, had caught USGA President Robert Watson's eye, and he issued him a personal invitation to play in the 1913 U.S. Open Championship.

One year later, Ouimet, now 17, wanted to enter the 1910 U.S. Amateur. "To compete in the national amateur championship I had to belong to a recognized golf club … I put in an application for junior membership in the Woodland Golf Club … I was elected to membership in Woodland, paid my dues ($25 he borrowed from his mother), then got busy to find myself a job," Ouimet recalled years later.

Soon after, he landed a position at the sporting goods concern Wright and Ditson. When he turned 20, Ouimet's persistent practice paid off. He won the 1913 Massachusetts Amateur and, in early September, advanced to the second round of match play in the U.S. Amateur at Long Island's Garden City Golf Club.

His play caught the eye of USGA President Robert Watson, who issued him a personal invitation to play in the 1913 U.S. Open. But Ouimet faced a dilemma familiar to amateurs of modest means – he had to return to work. Watson persisted, arrangements were made with Ouimet's employer and the young man entered the U.S. Open.

———

Despite Ouimet's splendid regional reputation, in that field he was nearly anonymous. It showed. On the first tee he was so nervous that he topped his tee shot, which skittered just 40 yards down the fairway. Most spectators tromping around The Country Club that week favored the American defender McDermott, the brilliant Englishman Vardon or the long-hitting Ray, Vardon's countryman. The French player Louis Tellier was another favorite, as was his brother-in-law, English professional Wilfrid Reid.

Vardon was golf's first superstar and the most famous player of his generation. At 43, the then five-time British Open champion possessed a fluid, powerful swing. With Ray, Reid and noted British journalist Bernard Darwin, Vardon was on an American tour sponsored by Lord Northcliffe (Alfred Harmsworth), a blustery English newspaper magnate who owned the *Daily Mail*, the *Daily Mirror* and the *Times of London*. Lord Northcliffe had dispatched Vardon, Reid and Ray overseas to challenge emerging American golf talent. Darwin was sent along to write about it. The 1913 U.S. Open played a central role in Darwin's story.

A solid 5-foot-9, Vardon had enormous hands that enfolded the club perfectly in what became known as the "Vardon grip." With a smooth, upright swing, his ball flight was higher than most, giving his approach shots greater carry and a softer landing. He won almost at will. His peaceable temperament made him a favorite, but it was his competitive reputation and golf swing that truly attracted crowds. He did it so easily.

Ted Ray was seven years younger. He idolized Vardon. Like Vardon, Ray was born on the Isle of Jersey, and he caddied and learned the game at the same course where Vardon had first played. The big, hefty Ray was known for his prodigious power, but he could never crack the famed threesome of Vardon, John Henry Taylor and James Braid, the players who dominated the game for 20 years and whom Darwin called "The Great Triumvirate." In 1912, however, Ray's stock went up when he won the British Open, which brought him attention in the United States.

And then there was Wilfrid Reid. Reid's income came mostly from exhibitions, many with Vardon, who liked the personable young Englishman and had taken him on as a protégé a few years earlier.

"I could not repay [Vardon]," Reid wrote to a friend. "You see, he took me under his wing when I was 18 years old and was actually my golfing father. A priceless gift of God and which I shall never forget."

Vardon had helped Reid land his first job as a professional at La Boulie Golf Club in France, but Reid was a dedicated family man and golf provided only a precarious living. With industry, he played in exhibition matches, held club jobs, gave instruction and designed courses. And, despite his small stature, he was a tenacious competitor in the few tournaments of that day.

Eddie Lowery (left) and Francis Ouimet (right) during the 1913 U.S. Open. Lowery knew he would not be paid for his services as the caddie for an amateur, but the excitement that unfolded during the championship more than made up for the lack of monetary compensation.

In 1913, American enthusiasm for golf was getting a huge boost from the U.S. Open. With the glittering presence of overseas players, an estimated 10,000 spectators turned out for the early rounds. By Saturday, the turnout would double.

After qualifying rounds on Tuesday and Wednesday, 49 players teed it up for the first two rounds on Thursday. The co-leader

– the dapper and sturdy Reid – was a surprise. Reid had previously won the French and Swiss Opens, but nothing of this magnitude. His precise iron shots and fine play over the first 36 holes boosted him to a tie with Vardon at 147, three over par and two strokes ahead of Ray. American professional Macdonald Smith and "Long" Jim Barnes were another stroke behind, followed by Ouimet and newcomer Walter Hagen at 151. Tellier came in at 152.

With Ouimet's name near the top of the leader board, club members scoffed at his caddie, 10-year-old Eddie Lowery. The boy knew he would not be paid for lugging an amateur's clubs, but the excitement of it was more than enough remuneration. The perky, positive lad had skipped school for the privilege and, as the U.S. Open unfolded, somehow managed to remain one step ahead of his distraught mother and the truant officer.

Reid, 28, was excited. If he won, he would receive not only prize money but also an enhanced international reputation that would promote his other golf pursuits. That night, however, any designs Reid had on the championship were obliterated by an incident in the dining room of Boston's Copley Square Hotel.

After play ended, Reid, Ray and other players went to dinner at the hotel. Reid was flying high. Always opinionated, that night he talked even more than usual. It would bring his U.S. Open chances to a violent end.

"My grandfather was a constant heckler," said Reid's grandson, Tony Zmistowski. "He was very opposed to British professional golfers having to pay taxes in the United States and then, when they got back to England, having to pay taxes on what they had won [in the United States]. They were enduring double taxation."

The tax problem was motivating Reid to become a U.S. citizen at the earliest opportunity. In the hotel dining room he kept at Ray, haranguing the big man for not changing his citizenship. Tensions mounted, and Reid even began needling Ray about his Jersey origins. When Ray had had enough, he reached across the table and used his big paw to twice punch the smaller Reid in the face.

"My grandfather, although they were very good friends, mouthed off at him," Zmistowski said. "Ted Ray just hit him in the nose."

Reid flew into Ray, fists swinging, until a headwaiter and other players finally pulled them apart. Ray's punches injured Reid in more ways than one. When he showed up at The Country Club the next day to play the final two rounds, he not only had a large bandage on his nose, he was a shaken man. Reid would shoot 85-86 in the closing rounds, stomping his own dreams of glory to dust.

———

Course conditions had also changed and now matched the mood. "With nerves on edge, the weather turned miserable," Sommers wrote.

Rain had been falling since midnight, and during the third round the ball often plugged in the muddy fairways and wet rough. Scoring suffered on the waterlogged course. Vardon fired a 78 and Ray a 76. Ouimet had a comparatively good 74. After 54 holes, the Massachusetts Amateur champion was tied for the lead with the great Vardon and Ray at 225.

That afternoon, Ray went from bad to worse, finishing with a dispiriting 79 and a 304 total for the 72 holes. The score looked vulnerable. Vardon had teed off behind Ray and finished his round while Ouimet was only on the fifth hole. Vardon, like Ray, had shot a 79, and they were tied at 304.

In the miserable conditions, high scores prevailed, but, without any public scoreboards, none of the players knew what was happening on the course. Ouimet was the only American still in the fight. He needed a 78 to win, a 79 to tie and had gone out in 43. At the short par-3 10th, he frittered away two more strokes, scuffing one shot barely 20 feet and then three-putting from 8 feet. Ouimet would have to play the last eight holes in one under par to tie. He was going in the wrong direction.

"I played rotten, and to make matters worse, Harry went out and did the same thing," he said.

While threading his way through the gallery, Francis overheard a spectator whisper, "It's too bad he's blown up." It was just what the amateur needed. The challenge spurred him to play some of the best golf of his life. By the time he reached the 17th tee, he needed one more birdie to tie.

Francis Ouimet, Harry Vardon and Ted Ray during the playoff on the 18th green of the 1913 U.S. Open. More than 20,000 spectators flooded the confines of The Country Club to witness the playoff.

The famous hole was a 360-yard par 4, a dogleg left that curled around a cluster of fairway bunkers. Ouimet's tee shot found the fairway and Lowery handed him his jigger, the equivalent of today's 4-iron. Ouimet made a smooth swing and knocked his ball to within 15 feet of the flagstick. He later said that he reminded himself to be sure to give the putt a chance. He struck the ball firmly. When it hit the back of the hole and dropped in, he was tied with the English players. All he needed was a par on the home hole to force a playoff.

Ouimet thought he would have a birdie putt to win, but his approach shot checked up short of the green and his chip was only fair, leaving him with a 4-footer for a par to tie. He rolled it in.

The incredible had happened: An American, barely older than a boy, an ex-caddie who lived across the street from the hallowed club, had tied two of the biggest stars in the game for the National Open championship. In modern-day terms, it's as if a British schoolboy were in a playoff for the British Open with Tiger Woods and Phil Mickelson, an unknown amateur going up against two of the most famous players in the world. In America, a nation of novice golfers, it was even bigger than that.

In the 18-hole playoff the following day, pandemonium ruled. More than 20,000 American working men, and a few women, freed from their jobs in factories, shops and offices on Saturday, seethed over the soggy course.

Ouimet awoke, had a light breakfast and then walked across the street to hit some practice shots. McDermott watched him warm up and told him, "You are hitting the ball well. Now go out and pay no attention whatsoever to Vardon and Ray. Play your own game."

Just before 10, Ouimet joined the Englishmen on the first tee. He drew the longest straw and had the honor, nailing a fine drive. Vardon and Ray also hit good tee shots, and off they went. At the turn, the three remained tied at 38.

All three hit the green at the 140-yard 10th, and Ouimet was nearest the hole. When first Vardon then Ray three-putted and Ouimet managed his par, he gained the edge for the first time. They all made pars on the 11th and headed for the 12th tee.

Despite the drizzle and mud, Ouimet was having a day most golfers can only dream about. His drives were long and pure, his approach shots well struck and his putting smooth and precise. "Ouimet had been outdriving Vardon regularly, and on the twelfth he outdrove Ray as well," wrote Herbert

That conclusive birdie putt on the 17th hole, Herbert Warren Wind later wrote, "Perhaps more than any other single shot was the one heard round the world."

Warren Wind in *The Story of American Golf*. Ouimet was the only one to reach the green in two strokes, hitting a superb shot to within 10 feet of the hole. Vardon was short of the green and Ray was down an embankment. They could do no better than bogeys, while Ouimet made a par 4 to take a two-stroke lead.

But Vardon birdied the 13th on a nifty 9-footer to pick up a stroke on the young amateur. Then, on the par-5 14th, Vardon showed the first signs that his game was cracking. When he was hitting the ball well, Vardon preferred to hit a fade. Now he was losing shots to the left. He hooked his drive into the high rough, then hit a shot out and then hooked his approach shot.

Veteran golf reporter Linde Fowler sensed that Vardon was worried and that Ray seemed restless – he could make no headway. Ouimet, however, was so cool that on one hole, when a spectator incredibly cornered him to ask for advice on his own golf game, he patiently answered the questions.

All three players parred the 14th hole. Ray took himself out of it on the next hole when he took two shots to escape a bunker and double-bogeyed. He was now four strokes behind Ouimet and three behind Vardon. With only three holes left to play, Ray was finished, and Ouimet said later that he knew it. Vardon, meanwhile, was rattled. Sensing doom, the self-assured golfer who never smoked on the course lit a cigarette.

Ouimet and Vardon took sure pars on the short 16th. Ray had another bogey. They walked to the 17th tee, the trailing crowd growing more unruly.

Vardon had the honor on the 360-yard, par-4 dogleg left, and he played a brave tee shot that was intended to hug the corner and give him a shorter shot to the green. It was risky and Vardon flinched, hooking the ball into the bunker that guarded the dogleg. From a poor lie, Vardon couldn't go for the green and had to play short. His third shot wasn't close. He bogeyed.

Many times Ouimet had walked the 17th hole as a caddie. He could, in fact, gaze down its fairway from his front porch. The day before he had birdied the hole to seal a spot in a playoff. Now, with two holes to play and a three-stroke lead, he drove to almost the exact spot where he had hit his tee shot on the Friday. Lowery handed Ouimet his mashie, which is the equivalent of a modern-day 5-iron, and he hit one of the best approach shots of his life. He was 18 feet from the hole.

His putter had not let him down all week. Now he had to get down in two to carry a three-stroke lead to the final hole. Ouimet drew back his putter, made a smooth stroke and, sure enough, the ball dropped.

Ouimet never let up. His good drive on the home hole was followed by an iron shot to the green, but his approach putt left him with a good 4-footer for par. Lining up that short putt, for the first time he realized he was going to win, and he began to shiver all over. Steadying himself, he made the winning putt.

"The crowd who had slogged around the course in the drizzle, worn out from playing every shot with Ouimet, still staggered by the boy's nerveless poise and his brilliant golf, reeled around the eighteenth green and the clubhouse in the gayest stupor many of them ever experienced in their lives," wrote Wind.

Spectators hoisted the young American and his caddie to their shoulders. Ouimet spotted fellow golfer Jerry Travers in the crowd and urged him to pass the hat among his followers to collect some cash for the hard-working Lowery. A photograph of Ouimet on the shoulders of gleeful supporters, with young Lowery in the foreground, captures the moment when this country began to look to golf.

"I think it was just this way," Ouimet said years later, "that Vardon and Ray rather expected me to crack, not having the experience for things like this as they had, and when the time went on and I did not crack, but went along with them, I think it had an unfavorable effect on them."

That conclusive birdie putt on the 17th hole, Wind later wrote, "Perhaps more than any other single shot was the one heard round the world."

After completing what is arguably the biggest upset in U.S. Open history with his victory over Harry Vardon and Ted Ray, Francis Ouimet is paraded on the shoulders of his fellow countrymen at The Country Club in Brookline, Massachusetts.

British domination was over. The era of flamboyant American professional Walter Hagen began with his U.S. Open victory the following year. Hagen's supporting cast over the next few years included Americans Travers, Gene Sarazen and Chick Evans. Ted Ray, the towering Englishman who played such a key role in this 1913 championship, would return to win the 1920 U.S. Open, but Ray would be one of only two British players to win the U.S. Open until Tony Jacklin's victory in 1970.

As the years went by, the famous story of the 1913 U.S. Open remained a landmark of the game of golf. Among the leading players in that saga, Ray played in the British Open as late as 1937, when he was 60 years old. He died in London in 1943 at the age of 66, largely unnoticed due to World War II.

Harry Vardon won his sixth British Open in 1914, but, for Vardon, golf never again seemed quite so easy. Fashioning shots to fit American turf, Vardon believed, got him into bad habits. In 1920, at 50, he led the U.S. Open by four strokes with seven holes to play before bad weather and a shaky putter left him tied for second behind Ray. Vardon died in London in 1937. He was 66.

In 1921, eight years after his near-miss in the U.S. Open, Wilfrid Reid became an American citizen.

"My grandfather was so upset because of all that had happened [in 1913]," said Tony Zmistowski. "He came in eighth but he was right up there and in the middle of everything. [Afterward] he said it was wonderful. He liked Francis Ouimet. He liked the whole thing."

Reid went on to serve as the professional at several prestigious clubs in the United States, including Seminole Golf Club, Atlantic City Country Club and the Broadmoor. With his design partner William Connellan, Reid designed Indianwood Golf Club in Michigan, the site of several USGA championships. After retiring to West Palm Beach, Florida, Reid still played golf

Above: Francis Ouimet (center) joins hands with Harry Vardon (left) and Ted Ray (right) after winning the 1913 U.S. Open.

Facing page: The 1913 U.S. Open Championship medal won by Francis Ouimet. Americans had begun to transform the golf landscape.

almost daily. Many mornings, he swam far out into the Atlantic Ocean, circling the Lake Worth Pier before swimming back to shore. He died in 1973 at the age of 90.

Francis Ouimet's life continued to be extraordinary. In 1914 he set sail for Europe, and while his quest to win that year's British Amateur was unsuccessful, he enjoyed the hospitality of Ray, who offered to show him the sights. On this trip, Ouimet enjoyed many convivial evenings in the company of Ray and Vardon. That summer, upon his return to the United States, Ouimet won the 1914 U.S. Amateur. Four years later he married Stella Sullivan. They had two daughters. Ouimet stayed in the sporting goods business and, in 1931, again won the U.S. Amateur. He played on the first eight USA Walker Cup teams and was captain of the next four. In 1951, Ouimet became the first American to be elected captain of the Royal and Ancient Golf Club of St. Andrews, Scotland.

"When he was named captain of the Royal & Ancient, he was overwhelmed with the honor," said Barbara McLean, his daughter. "My sister said he was really taken aback with that."

In late August 1967, Ouimet, now 74, was coming home from work when he felt weak. Gasping, he stopped to lean against a building for support. It was a hot night, and he kept to his plan of going to his daughter's house in Wellesley for dinner. But he wasn't himself, and shortly after dinner he went home. At around 2 a.m., he telephoned his daughter and was quickly taken to a hospital. He had suffered a heart attack and, a week later, on September 2nd, Francis Ouimet died.

His funeral at St. Paul's Church in Wellesley Hills was sparsely attended, said his daughter Barbara. It was, after all, Labor Day weekend, and most of Ouimet's friends were out of town. They would not learn of the great man's death until days later.

What Francis Ouimet did for American golf in that dramatic week 100 years ago cannot be overstated. Most importantly, his feat popularized golf in this country. Over the decade that followed his astonishing victory, the number of American golfers tripled. In the year of the 1913 U.S. Open, 350,000 Americans played golf. One decade later, public golf courses had popped up from coast to coast and two million Americans were playing the game Ouimet loved.

FRANCIS OUIMET
OPEN CHAMPION
CONQUEROR OF THE CHAMPION
H. VARDON
AND
E. RAY
THE COUNTRY CLUB
BROOKLINE, MASS.
SEPTEMBER 19TH 1913

DISMAY IN GREAT BRITAIN

Defeat of Vardon Emphasizes
Decadence in Sports.

London, Sept. 21.—"The Weekly Dispatch," in an editorial headed "Is ...

UNDERDOGS

"What lies behind us and what lies before us are small matters
compared to what lies within us."

– Ralph Waldo Emerson

Why do we cheer for underdogs? Is it because we can relate to them? They are often unpolished and authentic, and in many cases they challenge society's notions of what people can achieve. They also remind us that through hard work and perseverance, we can live out our own visions of greatness. For golfers, the underdog is the embodiment of our childhood dream, where on some deserted practice green we sink our last putt to beat one of the game's best and win the U.S. Open. Underdogs help to inspire the next generation of great players and prove that America's national championship is truly open to all.

Another American Homebred Arrives | Gene Sarazen 1922

Eugenio Saraceni was born on February 27, 1902, in the small town of Harrison, just north of New York City. He was the youngest of two children born to humble Italian immigrants. As the only son, he began to caddie to help support his family, earning 15 cents a bag at the Apawamis Club in nearby Rye. Like many other professionals of the day, he would learn to play the game in the caddie yard, inspired by a caddie-turned-USGA-champion named Francis Ouimet.

His father, a carpenter trained in Rome, took a dim view of golf. When it came time for his 13-year-old son to find a profession, he had Eugenio apprenticed to a carpenter. It looked as if carpentry would be the young Saraceni's future until 1918, when the dusty and unhealthy conditions at an army barracks worksite landed him in the hospital with pneumonia and pleurisy. Gravely ill, he received the last rites before fighting his way back through several painful surgeries. Following his recovery, the doctors told Eugenio that he had better find a job outdoors. He soon took a job as an assistant professional at Westchester Country Club, changing his name to Gene Sarazen. Driven to overcome his humble start in life, Sarazen saw a pathway through the game of golf. His ability to conquer adversity through optimism would lead him to greatness.

Standing 5-foot-5 and weighing 150 pounds, Sarazen was small in stature, but in three short years he would become a serious competitor. He copied Ouimet's interlocking grip and developed solid mechanics and timing that made him a long hitter despite his size. A *Literary Digest* article from 1922 noted, "It was Sarazen's idea to keep plugging away until he had his swing grooved where he could play stroke after stroke in exactly the same way," especially

Gene Sarazen holds the U.S. Open Championship Trophy and the British Open's Claret Jug, both of which he captured in 1932.

Facing page: The 1922 U.S. Open Championship medal won by Gene Sarazen.

Large galleries followed Gene Sarazen on his way to winning the 1922 U.S. Open at Skokie.

under pressure. In 1920, to fill the months between his summer assignments as a club professional, he joined the professional winter circuit.

The turning point in Sarazen's career would come in the winter of 1922, when he beat Leo Diegel by eight strokes in the Southern Open at New Orleans Country Club, earning his first professional victory against a first-rate field. Impressed by this new homebred professional, W.C. Fownes, the 1910 U.S. Amateur champion, offered Sarazen the position of head professional at the Highland Country Club in Pittsburgh. The reason, as Sarazen explained in his book *Thirty Years of Championship Golf*, was that Fownes believed Sarazen could bring the U.S. Open Trophy home to Pittsburgh and increase the region's stature in the game.

Fownes employed Emil T. "Dutch" Loeffler to coach Sarazen in the months leading up to the 1922 U.S. Open, held at Skokie Country Club in Chicago. Loeffler was a friend and fellow professional who was also employed as the greenkeeper at Oakmont Country Club (the club that Fownes and his father, Henry, had created in 1904). Loeffler and Sarazen practiced together that spring. Sponsored by Fownes, they made a trip to Skokie in mid-July to play a few practice rounds before the championship and to prepare a strategy for the specific shots they would need. After the visit, Sarazen wrote to fellow professional Tom Kerrigan, "This course is built right around my game. Bet on me."

Some of golf's brightest players of the era and favorites to win the 1922 U.S. Open, from left to right: Jock Hutchison, Bob MacDonald, Chick Evans and Walter Hagen.

Grantland Rice, the great American sportswriter, was not betting on Sarazen to win the U.S. Open but instead on the world's leading professional, Walter Hagen, who had won the British Open at Royal St. George's earlier that summer. Hagen was 10 years older than the 20-year-old Sarazen and had made a similar homebred journey from the caddie yard to the professional ranks. He had won the U.S. Open in 1914 and 1919, and the press widely considered him the favorite. Rice also identified amateurs Bob Jones and Chick Evans as possible contenders, together with a group of professionals that included defending champion Jim Barnes, Jock Hutchison and Johnny Farrell. Sarazen, although a promising newcomer, did not rank as an obvious challenger.

"The outstanding feature of Skokie is that it is absolutely honest," wrote A.T. Packard in *The American Golfer*. "There is not a blind hole on the course." Redesigned by Donald Ross in 1914, the 6,532-yard, par-70 course placed a premium on accuracy.

Sarazen's practice rounds with Loeffler would prove valuable. After the first 36 holes of play, there were two surprises on the leader board. Sarazen was tied with Hagen at 145. But both were trailing a 43-year-old grandfather named John Black, who had shot a pair of 71s to lead by two strokes. A native of Troon, Scotland, Black had immigrated to America 15 years earlier to serve as a professional at Claremont Country Club in California, but he was little known outside West Coast golf circles.

Still in search of his first USGA championship, Jones was four strokes off the pace at 146 at the halfway point. But he made a move in the third round, posting an even-par 70 to share the lead with William "Wild Bill" Mehlhorn at 216. Black stood one stroke back at 217. Hagen trailed by three at 219, while Sarazen struggled in the third round, posting a 75 for 220. Assuming that both Black and Sarazen would succumb to the final round's pressure, most of the spectators followed Jones and Hagen, until, as Grantland Rice reported in *The American Golfer*, "an ear-splitting racket at the ninth green indicated that Sarazen had gone out in 33." A gallery of more than one thousand spectators swarmed to watch him finish. After bogeying the difficult 440-yard, par-4 10th, Sarazen steadied himself with a par at the 11th and then finished like a champion. With birdies at the 12th and 18th, Sarazen posted a 2-under-par 68 for a total of 288.

Now he had to wait to see if Hagen, Jones or Black could catch him. Hagen's chances faded with poor play on the second nine. Needing to birdie the three closing holes to tie, he came up short. Jones was next, needing to birdie one of the two final holes. He took a gamble at the dogleg, 405-yard, par-4 17th and made a bogey 5. It was now Black's championship to win. He had shot a 1-under 33 on the outward nine and needed a 37 on the back nine to win or a 38 to tie. He had not taken more than 37 strokes on the back side during the first three rounds, but the pressure of the U.S. Open's final round now arrived. Bogeys at the 14th and 15th holes left Black no strokes to spare. The 17th would be Black's undoing. He hit his drive out of bounds en route to posting a double-bogey 6. Needing an eagle on the final hole to tie, Black piqued the spectators' interest when his second shot to the 470-yard par 5 landed just 10 feet from the hole before rolling into a greenside bunker. A well-played bunker shot was close enough to secure a birdie, but it did not fall for the eagle he needed. Sarazen was the U.S. Open champion.

The night before the championship began at Skokie, Sarazen had told Bob Jones and Johnny Farrell, "I've got a hunch that I am going to win this one. I am going to be pretty close in the running for the first two days. My bad round will be my third, but on the last round I'll burn up the course." Sarazen's words proved prophetic. Later that summer, he would confirm his status as a leading professional when he defeated Hagen in a highly publicized 36-hole challenge match and then went on to capture the PGA Championship in August.

Sarazen later wrote of his successful mindset in 1922, "I had no idea at the time how difficult the things I was accomplishing really were." His belief in himself made anything seem possible. In four short years, Gene Sarazen had gone from the caddie yard to national champion and joined Walter Hagen as one of America's premier homebred champions.

Gene Sarazen is credited with designing the modern sand wedge. He used this club to conquer the bunkers during the 1932 British Open Championship at Prince's Golf Club in Sandwich, Kent, England.

Facing page: Gene Sarazen is hoisted to the shoulders of fans while holding the U.S. Open Championship Trophy and an American flag following the closing ceremony of the 1922 U.S. Open.

The Cattle-Car Champion | Johnny Goodman 1933

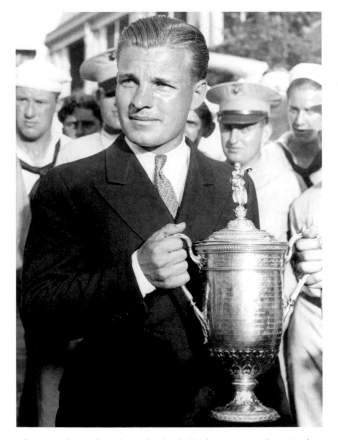

Johnny Goodman of Omaha, Nebraska, holds the U.S. Open Championship Trophy after winning the 1933 U.S. Open by one stroke over Ralph Guldahl at North Shore.

Though few in the golf community might have expected it, Johnny Goodman may have known all along that greatness dwelled within him. Goodman quoted the English poet Lord Byron in his high school yearbook, writing, "I woke up one day and found myself famous."

Byron's words proved prophetic for Goodman. The Omaha native burst onto the national stage when he registered one of the great upsets in golf history by beating Bob Jones in the first round of match play in the 1929 U.S. Amateur, and showed everyone it was no fluke when he won the U.S. Open four years later, at North Shore Country Club in Glenview, Illinois.

With that victory in 1933, Goodman joined Francis Ouimet, Jerry Travers, Chick Evans and Bob Jones as the only amateurs to win the U.S. Open. No amateur has done it since.

The very fact that Johnny Goodman was able to compete for the national championship speaks to the democratic nature of the American game – especially at a time when the country was going through immense hardship. While Goodman's victory over Jones occurred weeks before the Stock Market Crash of 1929, his win at North Shore came at the nadir of the Great Depression. The economic markets remained unstable, banks were failing and unemployment had reached its peak of nearly 25 percent.

In Goodman, Americans found someone with whom they could relate. He was born in 1908 and raised near the slaughterhouses in South Omaha, the fifth of 13 children of Lithuanian immigrants. His father, William, was a butcher but spent most of his time at local barrooms. He abandoned his family when Johnny's mother, Rose, died giving birth in 1924.

Johnny Goodman putts on the ninth hole at North Shore during the final round of the 1933 U.S. Open.

Goodman's introduction to golf was as an 11-year-old caddie at the Omaha Field Club, one of the oldest golf clubs west of the Mississippi. He made 50 cents each loop and learned to play the game by imitating the swings of the players for whom he caddied. By the time he reached high school, Goodman's skills had progressed considerably, but he lacked the funds necessary to travel to national tournaments.

While still a junior at Omaha's South High School, Goodman and two of his friends from the caddie yard rode cattle car trains to St. Louis to play in the Trans-Mississippi Amateur. The boys performed well and were dubbed the "Boxcar Trio" by the press.

Though he claimed his first significant title at the Trans-Mississippi the following year, in 1927, Goodman was not recognized as a major force in amateur golf until he beat Jones in the first round of the U.S. Amateur at Pebble Beach in 1929. He followed that remarkable upset with three consecutive Nebraska Amateur titles from 1929 to 1931, but he entered the 1933 U.S. Open at North Shore largely unnoticed. No newspaper articles mentioned Goodman in their previews of the championship, instead focusing on more prominent

Though temperatures exceeded 100 degrees during the 1933 U.S. Open, thousands of spectators flocked to North Shore to watch Johnny Goodman become the last amateur to win the national championship.

professionals such as Walter Hagen, Tommy Armour, Olin Dutra and the defending champion, Gene Sarazen.

Illinois was experiencing an unprecedented heat wave during the summer of 1933. The stifling conditions were blamed for more than two dozen deaths in the Midwest. Temperatures were near or exceeded 100 degrees during each day of the championship. In hot but gusty conditions, Armour opened with a 68 to take a five-shot lead – the largest 18-hole lead in U.S. Open history to that point. Goodman struggled with six bogeys and opened with a 75, tied for 16th with 12 others.

Like Armour the day before, Goodman was by far the class of the field during the second round. On a day when the scoring average was nearly 78, Goodman was a dozen strokes better. He opened with birdies on four of his first five holes, pitched in for eagle on the 15th and closed with a tap-in birdie to post a 66. His round equaled the lowest score in U.S. Open history and broke the course record at North Shore by two strokes. Goodman led Armour by two shots with 36 holes remaining in the championship.

On the morning of the final day, Goodman again was low man in the field. A 2-under-par 70 left him six strokes ahead of Ralph Guldahl with one round to play. Teeing off more than 40 minutes before Guldahl, Goodman started the final round par-eagle-birdie on the first three holes to extend his lead to a seemingly insurmountable nine strokes.

Then everything changed very quickly. Whether it was the pressure of leading a major championship or fatigue from playing 36 holes in scorching heat, Goodman's game began to unravel. Trying to protect the lead, he played defensively, later describing his own play as "gutless." Goodman bogeyed the fourth, double bogeyed the sixth and closed the outward nine with bogeys at holes seven, eight and nine. Guldahl played steady golf on the front side, posting a 35 that left him just two strokes behind – an unfathomable thought two hours earlier.

Goodman regained his composure on the back nine, but bogeys at 14 and 17 opened the door for Guldahl, who was on the 13th hole when Goodman finished. At that point, the two men were tied at one under par. Guldahl parred the next five holes, but his approach on the 72nd hole found a greenside bunker. With Goodman waiting nervously in the locker room, unable to watch, Guldahl blasted to 4 feet but missed the putt that would have forced a playoff. It was not pretty, but Johnny Goodman could breathe a sigh of relief. He was the 1933 U.S. Open champion.

On a personal level, the victory validated Goodman's regional successes and confirmed that his victory over Jones was no fluke. Jones, himself a spectator at North Shore, wrote, "Now people will quit asking me how Goodman beat me at Pebble Beach."

From his hardscrabble upbringing, Goodman had reached the top of the mountain. "Omaha made a gala holiday of the day when Johnny came marching home from the Chicago golf war," pronounced *The American Golfer* in July 1933. "It was fitting that they should. No champion ever traveled a rougher path to the heights than the blond, smiling young Johnny."

Goodman's win was also a boon to Omaha, a factory city ravaged by the Great Depression. Nebraska's capital was never a hub for professional sports, but as Don Lee of the *Omaha World-Herald* wrote, "Goodman brought the world to Omaha's doorstep as no other sports personality has done."

Goodman went on to win the 1937 U.S. Amateur and even appeared on the cover of the June 6, 1938, issue of *Time* magazine with a headline crowning him "The King of Swing." Shortly after, however, his stardom faded away. Goodman joined the U.S. Army at the peak of his career and was stationed in India during World War II. On his return to the United States, he shattered his left arm in a car accident and could never return to top competitive form.

In 1949, Goodman, his wife, Josephine, and their only child, 3-year-old Johnny Jr., moved to California. A decade later, the man who remained an amateur for nearly half a century turned professional at the age of 50 so he could teach golf lessons at California's nine-hole Bellflower Golf Center.

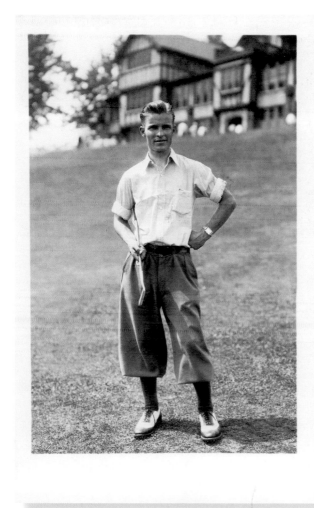

Johnny Goodman, seen here in this George Pietzcker portrait, won the U.S. Amateur Championship in 1937 before serving in India during World War II.

"Out-Hoganed" | Jack Fleck 1955

In U.S. Open competition from 1940 to 1960, Ben Hogan finished no worse than 10th while winning the championship a record-tying four times (1948, 1950, 1951, 1953). He had the ideal game for the toughest test in golf, and the golf world expected that Hogan would eventually capture a fifth title and become the greatest U.S. Open champion of all time. After Hogan finished his 72nd hole at The Olympic Club's Lake Course in 1955, it looked as if this prophecy had come to pass. But ultimately Hogan would be "out-Hoganed" by a little-known golf professional from Iowa.

Jack Fleck was born on November 8, 1921, in Bettendorf, Iowa, to a family of simple means. Like many children of the Great Depression, he came to rely on hard work, determination and grit. All five of the Fleck children – Jack was the middle child of three boys and two girls – contributed to the family's welfare by growing food and taking on odd jobs. One of the most profitable jobs Fleck had as a child was caddieing, during which he also discovered a passion for playing the game.

A member of America's "greatest generation," he served in the U.S. Navy during World War II and took part in the D-Day invasion from a British rocket ship off Normandy's Utah Beach. Following his discharge from the Navy, he took up a position as assistant professional at the Des Moines Golf and Country Club and eventually became the head professional at two municipal golf courses in Davenport. Like Hogan, Fleck was an incredibly accurate ball-striker. Although he was never a great putter nor a long hitter, he was a straight driver and a good shotmaker with his irons. Fleck took his skills to play the professional winter tour, where he had the game to compete, but struggled to control

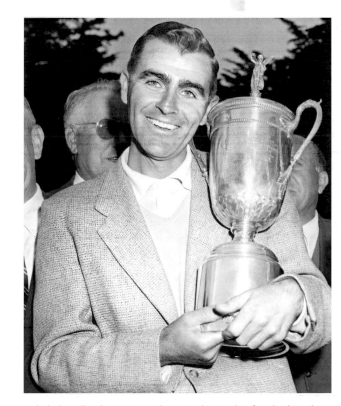

Jack Fleck cradles the U.S. Open Championship Trophy after shocking the golf world by beating Ben Hogan in an 18-hole playoff at The Olympic Club.

Facing page: Jack Fleck practices at Olympic for the 1955 U.S. Open, just over a decade after taking part in Normandy as part of the D-Day invasion during World War II.

Thousands of fans surround the 18th green at the 1955 U.S. Open at Olympic. Robert Trent Jones Sr. modified the Lake Course in 1953 in preparation for the 1955 championship.

his temper. For nearly a decade, it was his passion, rather than his tournament earnings, that provided his inspiration to play competitive golf.

The turning point for Fleck came in 1954. Three stokes off the lead after 36 holes at the Wayne Open in Texas, a personal dispute with a Rules official had him fuming. He lost his composure in the third round and walked off the course in frustration at the sixth green. Reflecting on his actions and what could have been had he controlled his temper, Fleck finally understood the value of learning to check his emotions. His game began to improve almost immediately, and this led to an unlikely encounter with Ben Hogan. Fleck idolized every aspect of Hogan's approach to the game. When he came across the newly designed Ben Hogan irons that winter, he wrote to his idol to request a set. The steely eyed Hawk was not known for his generosity to fellow professionals, but some kinship in their backgrounds stirred Hogan's response.

Hogan made a set of clubs for Fleck, invited him to the factory in Fort Worth, Texas, when they were ready and offered him a spot in his Colonial National Invitation Tournament, where Fleck finished in 24th place.

One month later, in early June, Fleck earned a spot in the 1955 U.S. Open, surviving the 36-hole qualifier near Chicago by two strokes. Before the championship began, Hogan, exempt from qualifying as the 1953 champion, met Fleck in Olympic's locker room and hand-delivered the pitching wedge and sand wedge that were omitted from the initial delivery, as the original clubs did not meet Hogan's exacting standards. Fleck put the clubs to immediate use in his marathon practice sessions. He played 44 holes on Sunday, Monday and Tuesday and 18 holes on Wednesday. Many professionals thought it foolish to practice so intensely, for fear that the punishing setup might have a demoralizing effect before play even began.

Hogan was widely respected for his ability to predict the winning score for a U.S. Open and then build a strategy for reaching his target score in a patient and comfortable fashion. Tommy Bolt's opening round of 3-under-par 67 did not concern Hogan, who had shot a 2-over-par 72. He knew that "the longest short course I ever played" was going to produce a winning score that was over par. The severely canted and narrow fairways bordered by thick rough and towering Monterey cypress trees punished poor shots. On a course that featured some of the smallest greens in the championship's history, accuracy and the ability to shape shots were critical to good scoring. Thus, it was not surprising that the average score in the first round was 79.8.

Jack Fleck admires the *San Francisco Examiner* headline while in his hotel room after winning the 1955 U.S. Open.

Fleck, who had not broken 80 in any of his numerous practice rounds, posted a respectable 76, but he knew he would have to play better in the second round to make the 36-hole cut. He made a solid start with pars on the first four holes, then hit a beautiful approach to 22 feet on the difficult, 457-yard, par-4 fifth. Of the ensuing birdie putt, he later recalled, "I had some kind of wonderful feeling in my hands over the ball. I didn't change my grip or stance. It was just a feeling in my hands." The birdie putt fell, as would many other putts, on his way to a second-round 69, matching Sam Snead and Julius Boros, the 1952 U.S. Open champion, for the low round of the day. More importantly, Fleck now had confidence in every aspect of his game.

As Hogan predicted, Olympic would not continue to surrender low scores to the early leaders. After two rounds, Bolt, with a second-round 77, and Harvie Ward led the championship at four over par, with Fleck, Boros, Hogan and Walker Inman one stroke back.

Heading into the final 36 holes, Fleck began his morning on Saturday just as he would any other. He awoke early, completed his yoga routine and showered.

The "Super Mex" | Lee Trevino 1971

Lee Trevino, the Mexican-American icon from Dallas, Texas, embodies the eclectic spirit of U.S. Open champions who have come from a myriad of backgrounds to claim the game's most coveted title. In relative obscurity, he had arrived at The Olympic Club in San Francisco in 1966 to compete in his first national championship. To that moment in time, he was known as little more than an accomplished hustler. Still, he finished tied for 54th at Olympic, and the following year he finished fifth in the U.S. Open at Baltusrol's famed Lower Course. In 1968, Trevino won the U.S. Open at Oak Hill, matching Jack Nicklaus' scoring record of 275 and defeating the Golden Bear by four strokes. Nicklaus, golf's greatest major champion, had a new rival – the self-proclaimed "Super Mex."

Trevino's path to become a champion golfer was anything but typical. Raised by his mother, Juanita, and a loving grandfather, he grew up knowing the constant pressure of what it took to pay the rent and put food on the table, but he never knew his father. His family's home stood 100 yards to the right of the seventh tee of the Dallas Athletic Club, where Trevino collected lost balls in the tall grass and sold them back to golfers to help support the family. Like many champions, he learned the game first as a caddie. He did not pursue the game with lofty aspirations of championship titles, instead he viewed it as the best chance he had to support his family.

Trevino served honorably in the U.S. Marine Corps for four years and played in numerous matches during his service in Asia. After returning to Texas in 1960, he turned his attention again to golf, securing a job from a friend, Hardy Greenwood, who owned a driving range in Dallas. Trevino played in local professional events while pursuing a Class A PGA card, which would allow him to

Lee Trevino, the self described "Super Mex," follows his shot during the 1971 U.S. Open.

Facing page: Lee Trevino, wearing a marshal's hat, pulls out a rubber snake and a hatchet in the rough at Merion during the 1971 U.S. Open.

Trevino was not a long player but was exceptionally accurate off the tee, an advantage at the relatively short Merion Golf Club.

qualify for the PGA Tour. "At that time, they did not have a qualifying school," Trevino later recalled. "If you weren't in their little group [Class A PGA], or if you weren't a hot-shot college player with a hell of an amateur record, they wouldn't invite you to play." As fate would have it, his fifth-place finish at the 1967 U.S. Open gained him access to the PGA Tour, and his victory in the 1968 U.S. Open earned him a lifetime exemption.

When Trevino arrived at Merion Golf Club's East Course for the 1971 U.S. Open, he had already won six PGA Tour events in his professional career, including two earlier that year. His meteoric rise to the top of the game made him an obvious contender, especially considering the venue. Designed by Hugh Wilson in 1912 and measuring 6,544 yards, Merion was one of the shortest courses in the recent history of the championship. Trevino was not a long player, but he was extremely accurate tee to green and had an excellent short game, which gave him an advantage on Merion's narrow fairways and small, well-protected greens.

After the first two rounds, Trevino's 142 placed him tied for third alongside Jim Simons, a young amateur from Wake Forest University who provided the surprise performance of the championship, posting a stunning 65 to take a two-stroke lead over Nicklaus heading into the final round.

Paired with Nicklaus in the fourth round, Simons' nerves held steady on the front nine, but he drove into a fairway bunker on the 10th hole en route to a bogey that dropped him into a tie with Nicklaus. Moments later, Trevino struck a beautiful approach to the long, elevated green of the 405-yard, par-4 12th hole with the ball spinning back from 20 feet to finish 15 inches from the hole. His ensuing birdie putt resulted in a three-way tie.

Trevino birdied the par-4 14th hole to take a one-stroke lead that he protected until he reached the 18th hole. He missed the green with his approach, and his chip left him with a 6-foot, uphill, left-to-right putt for par, a total of 279 and likely the championship. Just as Trevino was about to putt, a member of the gallery slipped and fell while trying to climb the 18th hole scoreboard and Trevino backed off. After gathering himself, his attempt at par slid past the right edge of the hole.

Simons also succumbed to the pressure on the final hole, missing the green with his approach and carding a double bogey to end his bid for the championship. No one had ever birdied the 72nd hole to win the U.S. Open, and so it would be for Nicklaus, whose 15-foot attempt rolled just past the left edge of the hole. He dropped his par putt to tie Trevino at 280. The two would meet the next day for an 18-hole playoff.

A spirited Trevino was quick to change the tense mood he encountered on the first tee of the playoff. Removing a rubber snake from his golf bag, he tossed it toward Nicklaus. A woman in the gallery shrieked as Nicklaus, laughing and seemingly unsurprised at Trevino's antics, returned the toy to its owner. With the serpent sheathed, their game faces returned as Nicklaus and Trevino played their opening tee shots.

Nicklaus took the early lead when Trevino bogeyed the first, but Jack quickly fell two strokes back after failing to escape greenside bunkers on the second and third holes. After hitting his approach to within 5 feet at the fifth hole, Nicklaus closed the gap to a single stroke with a birdie, but then Mother Nature intervened and play was suspended due to a thunderstorm.

Trevino felt an immediate advantage. "The greens were getting really hard and with my low trajectory ball, it was very difficult for me to get the ball close. When we got that downpour for about an hour, it softened the greens." Trevino recalls thinking, "Now, I can go in there and play my game. I can go in there low… and as soon as it hit the green it was going to stop."

Following the rain delay, on the 360-yard, par-4 eighth hole, Trevino's approach landed inches from the hole and, just as he predicted, the ball stopped dead. He holed the birdie putt to move two strokes ahead. Nicklaus answered at the 195-yard, par-3 ninth hole, playing his trademark high fade to within 10 feet for a birdie to pull within one stoke with nine holes left to play.

At the 12th hole, Trevino made an unlikely birdie, sinking a downhill, left-to-right breaking putt from 25 feet to pull two strokes ahead. Nicklaus countered on the 15th, hitting his approach to within 8 feet, only to see Trevino sink another 25-foot putt. Nicklaus sank his putt for birdie but did not gain any ground.

At the 18th hole, Nicklaus was three shots behind. Trevino remained relaxed even after his approach found the greenside bunker. Without hesitation, he played from the bunker, twirling his sand wedge on his follow through. His ball came to rest just a few feet below the hole. Approaching the green with his trademark smile, he blew an appreciative kiss to the gallery before sinking his putt for par to claim his second U.S. Open and beat one of the game's greatest champions.

Trevino would win six major championships in his career, four of which required him to defeat Nicklaus at his best, and he did it all with his trademark charismatic and fun-loving style. He had come a long way in the five short years since his first U.S. Open appearance. Although Trevino claims to have "never" experienced discrimination during his career, as the first person of Hispanic descent to claim the U.S. Open, his contribution to the game is undeniable. He overcame poverty and an unwelcoming professional game, proving that an ordinary American can achieve greatness through grit, determination and honest hard work. It is a legacy that continues to inspire the future of the game.

Lee Trevino jubilantly tosses his hat into the air after making a putt in his playoff against Jack Nicklaus at the 1971 U.S. Open.

Veteran Moxie | Hale Irwin 1990

Hale Irwin holds the U.S. Open Championship Trophy aloft after his historic victory at the 1990 U.S. Open at Medinah. At age 45 he became the oldest champion to date.

In early June of 1990, Hale Irwin drove through the gates of Chicago's Medinah Country Club as a two-time U.S. Open champion. For some fans, his national championship titles may have felt like ancient history. He hadn't won a tournament in more than five years, and his best finish on the PGA Tour money list during that stretch was 73rd in 1988. Irwin wasn't even automatically exempt into the U.S. Open – his 10-year exemption for winning in 1979 had expired the year before – but because the USGA's executive committee had extended a special exemption, he was in the field once again.

At age 45, Irwin was a part-time player on the PGA Tour. He had won 17 tournaments during a 14-year stretch beginning in 1971, but in 1985 he had started his own golf course design business and was constantly working on projects that took him away from competitive golf. Though he had finished in a tie for third in the Kemper Open just two weeks before, Irwin was not garnering many headlines coming into the 1990 U.S. Open.

Over the years, he had built a reputation for winning at difficult golf courses. In 1974, Irwin won his first U.S. Open title with a 7-over-par 287 in the championship often referred to as "The Massacre at Winged Foot." Five years later, he won at Inverness with an even-par total of 284. Over the course of his career, Irwin also won PGA tournaments at Harbour Town, Butler National and Pebble Beach – three of the most challenging venues on the PGA Tour's schedule. Each of these courses demand accurate driving, precise iron play and perseverance – all qualities that described Irwin's game. Par had not been bettered in the two previous U.S. Opens held at Medinah, Cary Middlecoff at two over in 1949 and Lou Graham at three over in 1975, which seemingly played to Irwin's strengths.

It appeared that the trend would continue in 1990, but a rainstorm on Wednesday took away much of Medinah's sting. Earlier in the week it seemed that par might be a good score, but in Thursday's opening round, an even-par 72 was good only for a tie for 40th. In all, 39 players broke par and 21 more matched it. Irwin birdied his final two holes to post 69.

The bigger story of the day, however, was that two-time defending champion Curtis Strange, who was attempting to join Willie Anderson as the second player in history to win three consecutive championships, had opened with a lackluster 73. He was so disappointed with his performance around the greens that he switched putters following the opening round. Three other men had been denied in their pursuit of the three-peat – Johnny McDermott in 1913, Ralph Guldahl in 1939 and Ben Hogan in 1952 – and one other, Bob Jones, had retired instead of defending his title in 1931. "I've been thinking about this week for a year," admitted Strange. "Not a day has gone by when it hasn't been on my mind. It has consumed me for the last couple of months."

Scoring conditions remained favorable during the middle rounds. Not only was the cut (1-over 145) the lowest in U.S. Open history, but four players – Mark Brooks and Tim Simpson in the second round and Jeff Sluman and Scott Simpson in the third round – reached nine under par, a score previously reached only by Ben Hogan in 1948. After posting a 2-under-par 70 on Friday, Irwin backed up with a 74 on Saturday that left him in a tie for 20th. Strange, meanwhile, had played himself back into the championship. "I'm fired up. I'm back in the U.S. Open," said Strange, whose 68 left him just two strokes behind co-leaders Mike Donald and Billy Ray Brown. The goal of the quest that had consumed him for the better part of a year now seemed within his grasp.

Though other big names like Nick Faldo, Fuzzy Zoeller and even 50-year-old Jack Nicklaus were lurking on a very crowded leader board, most eyes were on Strange to start the final day. But his charge never materialized. A fat 6-iron at the par-3 second led to a bogey, and, despite a birdie at the fifth, Strange dropped shots at the par-5 seventh and par-4 ninth to fall out of contention.

With 27 players starting the day within four strokes of the lead, Irwin teed off nearly two hours before the final group. An opening-nine 36 gave little indication that he would be a threat down the stretch. But with his playing competitor, Greg Norman, going out in 33, Irwin stepped up his game and reeled off four consecutive birdies starting at hole 11. "Greg is such a force that you have to feed off him a little," said Irwin. While Norman faded with bogeys at 14 and 17, Irwin was still in the thick of things with one hole to play.

After a good drive on the 18th, he played an indifferent 7-iron to the middle of the green, leaving a 50-foot putt with 5 feet of break. He struck the putt and

Hale Irwin salutes the crowd after sinking a remarkable 50-foot putt on the 18th green for birdie. The putt gave Irwin a four-day score of 280, which ended up being good enough to force a playoff for the title.

In an outburst of emotion that was years in the making, Hale Irwin ran around the green and high-fived members of the gallery after sinking his 50-foot birdie putt on the 18th green.

watched the ball intently as it rolled over a hump and began tracking. With Irwin crouching as he watched so he could follow its line, the ball kept turning as it lost speed and plunged into the hole for a birdie 3. Showing an explosion of emotion that he had rarely demonstrated in his 22-year pro career, Irwin ran toward the hole with his putter held high, then made an abrupt left turn for the gallery. "I don't know how you could remain stoic after doing something like that," recalled Irwin, whose inward nine 31 gave him a closing 67. Feeding off the energy from the crowd, he took a lap around the 18th green and traded high fives with gallery members along the ropes, who cheered and laughed as Irwin ran past.

"I probably have never done anything so spontaneous," said Irwin. "But to tell you the truth, that was years of emotion pouring out of me. I remember looking up after the putt dropped at some people in the gallery. They were so happy. I realized they were happy for me … for me! All I could think to do was to run and thank them."

As Irwin celebrated on 18, Donald and Brown were just making the turn. As the field fought its way to the finish, it became clear that no one was going to challenge Irwin's 280 except the two men in the final group. Donald, who had just one professional victory to his name, made dramatic par saves from 35 feet at 12 and from 15 feet at 14 to maintain his advantage, but a bogey on 16 dropped him into a tie with Irwin at eight under. Playing in his first U.S. Open, Brown pulled within one after a tap-in birdie at the par-3 17th, but he could not find the hole with his 15-foot birdie bid on the home hole. A routine par by Donald set up a playoff with Irwin.

On Monday, neither golfer had their best game. Irwin, who struggled off the tee for much of the day, was two behind Donald with three to play. The 426-yard, par-4 16th was the most difficult hole on the course through the first four rounds. It had yielded only 37 birdies due in part to the shallow, elevated green that was difficult to hold. After hitting his drive down the left side of the fairway, Irwin faced a 210-yard approach. He was one of the best long-iron players in the game, but this shot was especially challenging, as some overhanging branches blocked his direct line to the flagstick that was tucked on the left side of the green. He had a clear play to the center of the green, but, trailing by two, Irwin knew he needed to make something happen. He pulled a 2-iron – a club that was vital in his two previous U.S. Open victories – and delivered again. The shot started at the right side of the green, drew around the branches and settled 6 feet from the hole. He drained the putt to pull within one.

After both players parred the 17th, Donald, who had missed only one fairway all day, hooked his drive into the gallery on 18. From thick rough, he advanced his 5-iron approach to the greenside bunker and blasted out to 15 feet. After Irwin lagged his birdie effort to tap-in range, Donald settled over a putt to win the U.S. Open. It appeared to start on line but stayed too high, sliding by the right edge. The two players were deadlocked again – the first playoff to end in a tie since 1946 – setting up the first sudden-death playoff in U.S. Open history.

It ended quickly. Both players hit good drives that left wedges into the green. Donald played first, but his approach checked up on the front of the two-tiered green, 20 feet from the hole. Irwin played more aggressively to the back hole location, leaving himself 10 feet for birdie. After Donald missed his birdie putt, Irwin stepped up and again came through in the clutch. As the putt dropped, Irwin turned away from the green, leapt twice and ran to hug his wife and daughter, who had broken through the crowd. He had never once led the championship until he won outright on the 91st hole. Improbably, at age 45, Irwin was a U.S. Open champion for the third time.

"Experience is invaluable and having played well in U.S. Opens and having won a couple can't hurt you," explained Irwin, who remains the oldest player to claim the title. "I've always felt I had a certain kind of tenacity and never-give-up attitude. You can call it guts, confidence, experience, any number of things and I think they're all appropriate when you talk about winning a U.S. Open." The following week, Irwin won again at the Buick Classic at Westchester Country Club. How did he do it? Fittingly, he sank a birdie putt on the 72nd hole and raced around the green giving high-fives to adoring fans.

Winless in the previous five years, Hale Irwin hugs the U.S. Open Championship Trophy as he relishes his sudden-death playoff victory for the 1990 championship over Mike Donald – the first U.S. Open ever to go to sudden death.

The Ignominy of Being Second-Best

BY DAVID SHEFTER AND RON DRISCOLL

"There is no such thing as second place. Either you're first or you're nothing."
– Gabe Paul, longtime baseball executive

Everyone loves winners. We celebrate major champions with bold headlines, magazine covers and spots on cereal boxes. Streets are named after them, trophies and medals carry their names and late-night talk show hosts never seem to tire of them.

But what about those who finish second? What is it about being the runner-up, especially when the effort falls short of public or media expectations, that often leads to scrutiny and criticism? The objective truth is that you have beaten all but one person. But in the realm of the subjective, it is sometimes difficult to accept. There's something melancholic about it, and all the sympathy in the world proves little consolation.

The misfortunes of Hall-of-Famer Sam Snead are most often invoked in discussions of U.S. Open runners-up. For all of the Virginia native's greatness – he won seven major championships among his 82 PGA Tour titles – Snead is equally recalled for his four second-place finishes and zero victories in the National Open. "Sure, it bugs me that they make such a big deal of it because I never won the U.S. Open," Snead once said, "but I must have been playing pretty good and sinking putts when I won those three Masters, three PGAs and the British Open."

Of course, Snead is not alone. A number of great golfers – some of them Hall of Famers – never hoisted the U.S. Open Trophy. Players such as Macdonald Smith, Mike Brady, Tom McNamara, "Lighthorse" Harry Cooper, Jock Hutchison, Bobby Cruickshank, Bob Rosburg, Colin Montgomerie and Phil Mickelson all posted multiple runner-up finishes without having their names etched on the U.S. Open Trophy.

Other major champions such as Greg Norman, Seve Ballesteros, Nick Faldo and Tom Lehman were often in the hunt but somehow came up short. Norman, in fact, was the 54-hole leader in all four majors in 1986 but claimed only the British Open. Lehman played in the final pairing on the final day in four consecutive U.S. Opens (1995–98) and never won, with his best finish a tie for second in 1996.

The U.S. Open is golf's toughest test. It is played at a different venue each year, on demanding courses with thick rough and lightning-quick greens, and the mental pressure can be excruciating. This helps to explain why so many great golfers falter; some want the title so much that it affects the way they play. The immensely talented Mickelson had the 2006 U.S. Open in hand at Winged Foot Golf Club in Mamaroneck, New York. A par on the 72nd hole would have secured him a third consecutive major. But his wild tee shot caromed off a hospitality tent, and his aggressive recovery effort led to a disastrous double-bogey 6, leaving him one stroke behind winner Geoff Ogilvy of Australia.

Since the inaugural championship in 1895, the pressure to win the National Open has been part of the proceedings. Whether the advent of social media, the 24-hour sports news

Facing page: Sam Snead, the winner of 82 PGA Tour events and seven major championships, finished runner up at the U.S. Open four times. Of golf's major championships, the U.S. Open is the only one Snead did not win.

cycle and seemingly endless analysis have added to it is debatable. But of the many thousands of participants in the 112 championships that have been contested, just 82 golfers have had their names inscribed on the trophy.

In the early 1900s, a pair of New England natives not named Francis Ouimet both thought they might be crowned champion. Mike Brady and Tom McNamara were former caddies who went on to become outstanding professionals.

McNamara was born in Boston and caddied at the Warren's Farm Golf Club and The Country Club before becoming a professional at Bellows Falls in Vermont and later at three clubs in Massachusetts. While serving at Wollaston Golf Club outside Boston, McNamara became the first American-born golfer to break 70 in a U.S. Open, with a round of 69 at New Jersey's

Englewood Golf Club. He held the 36-hole lead by four strokes, but he wilted in the oppressive heat, recording a final-round 77 that led to a second-place finish, four strokes behind George Sargent.

Though he went on to win prestigious events such as the Western Open and the North and South Open, the missed opportunity would haunt McNamara his entire career. He finished fifth in the 1910 U.S. Open and made another run at the title in 1912 at The Country Club of Buffalo, New York, closing with then championship-record rounds of 73-69, only to come up two strokes behind winner Johnny McDermott, who had become the first American-born U.S. Open champion one year earlier. McDermott's 294 total made him the first golfer in U.S. Open history to better par, while McNamara earned the lesser distinction of being the first to *match* par.

Three years later, McNamara again came up short, losing by one stroke to amateur Jerry Travers at Baltusrol Golf Club in Springfield, New Jersey. McNamara went on to become the head pro at Siwanoy Country Club in Bronxville, New York, where he proposed the idea of a national professional tournament to his boss, Rodman Wanamaker. (That competition became the PGA Championship, with its trophy named the Wanamaker Trophy, and it was first played at Siwanoy in 1916.) McNamara never did win that trophy, either. His final appearance in the U.S. Open, in 1919, resulted in a tie for third place.

Brady was born in the Boston neighborhood of Brighton. After working and learning the game as a caddie, he took up positions as the professional at four Massachusetts clubs: Wollaston, Commonwealth, Hyannisport and Oakley. He won nine PGA events between 1916 and 1926, but the U.S. Open was not one of those titles. Like his cohort McNamara, Brady is remembered for his "seconds" rather than his wins.

At the 1911 U.S. Open at Chicago Golf Club, Brady lost by two strokes in a three-man playoff to McDermott, who birdied the 72nd hole to tie Brady and George Simpson, both of whom had finished their rounds. Brady tied for third place the following year behind McDermott and McNamara, and eight years later, he led the championship after three rounds in his backyard at Brae Burn Country Club in West Newton, Massachusetts. However, he shot a final-round 80, which allowed Walter Hagen to tie him, and Hagen prevailed by one stroke in the playoff, giving him his second U.S. Open title and Brady his second runner-up finish, among an eventual nine top-10 finishes.

After the 1919 U.S. Open, Hagen resigned from his position as club pro at Oakland Hills Country Club in suburban Detroit and the club promptly hired Brady, who would go on to win the 1922 Western Open. But the national championship forever eluded him.

Macdonald Smith, a Scottish professional from Carnoustie, is one of the greatest players from the pre-World War II era to have never won a major title. He registered 24 official victories, but it was his brothers who tasted U.S. Open glory, Willie in 1899 and Alex in 1906 and 1910. In fact, Macdonald lost a three-way playoff in 1910 to brother Alex (McDermott was the third participant). And in 1930, Smith fell two strokes short of Bob Jones, who holed a 40-foot putt on the 72nd hole at Interlachen Country Club in suburban Minneapolis to win the third leg of his impregnable quadrilateral. Earlier that summer, Smith had

Above: Macdonald Smith is one of the greatest pre–World War II players not to have won a major. His brothers fared much better; Willie won the U.S. Open in 1899, and Alex in 1906 and 1910. **Facing page:** Mike Brady and Walter Hagen putt during the 1919 U.S. Open. Brady nearly pulled off the upset, but his poor final round forced a playoff with Hagen, who ultimately triumphed.

also finished second to Jones at the British Open, conducted at Royal Liverpool (Hoylake).

When his career concluded in the mid-1930s, Macdonald Smith, who Bing Crosby once said had one of the finest swings in the game, had amassed 17 top-10 finishes in majors, but his legacy is one of near-misses and what-ifs.

Left: Sam Snead, in his familiar hat, and Lew Worsham await a ruling by USGA officials during the 1947 U.S. Open Championship at St. Louis Country Club.
Right: Lew Worsham and his wife accept the trophy at the 1947 U.S. Open. Sam Snead (right) was the runner-up.

The post-World War II era ushered in a new generation of great players. Snead, born in the same year as Ben Hogan and Byron Nelson (1912), never joined his two contemporaries in hoisting the U.S. Open Trophy. Instead, Snead lost the U.S. Open in every conceivable fashion.

While he is remembered most for a 72nd-hole debacle in 1939 at Philadelphia Country Club and a missed 18-inch par putt in the 1947 playoff with Lew Worsham, few remember that Snead nearly won the title in 1937 at Oakland Hills as a 25-year-old rookie. Most observers thought Snead, competing in his first U.S. Open, had secured the championship when he birdied the 72nd hole to leap-frog Bobby Cruickshank for a 5-under-par total of 283.

"I think people may have congratulated Snead after he finished because his [72-hole] score was only one stroke off the record and most people would have assumed he won," golf historian and former *Golf Journal* editor Robert Sommers wrote in *The U.S. Open: Golf's Ultimate Challenge*. Stellar play, and a key break, allowed Ralph Guldahl to pass Snead in the end. At the par-4 15th hole, Guldahl's approach was headed for some thick rough when it glanced off a spectator's heel and into a greenside bunker, leaving a much easier recovery shot. Guldahl managed

to get up and down for a par, when bogey or worse seemed imminent. The spectator later apologized to Snead for costing him the title. Snead preferred to credit his fellow competitor's play. Guldahl played the final holes in even par, a remarkable feat on such a demanding course, for a record 7-under 281 total. Snead took the disappointment in stride, firmly believing that he would win a future U.S. Open.

In 1939, he came to the 72nd hole needing only a par 5 to secure the championship. But thinking he needed a birdie 4 to win, he played the hole aggressively. One miscue led to another, and Snead ended with a triple-bogey 8, two strokes behind Nelson, Craig Wood and Denny Shute. Nelson would win the 18-hole playoff, and Snead was left with more U.S. Open heartache. Later Snead said, "Why didn't someone tell me I only needed to par? I'd have played this hole a lot different."

But the blowup didn't shatter Snead's confidence, and fans continued to flock to watch him play, particularly because of his natural flowing swing and the power it generated.

Following World War II, Snead would earn another chance to capture a U.S. Open, at St. Louis Country Club. After 72 holes, the 1947 championship went to an 18-hole playoff between

Snead and Worsham, who tied at 2-under-par 282. Snead held a one-stroke lead at the turn, and Worsham's birdie at number 12 deadlocked the contest. Snead picked up two strokes over the next three holes, thanks to his birdie on number 13 and a Worsham bogey on number 15. At the par-3 16th, Worsham holed a putt from the back of the green for a birdie 2, while Snead's birdie attempt lipped out. Worsham made a remarkable par after a wild drive on number 17, while Snead failed to get up and down for par, leaving the two tied again.

What happened on number 18 was one of the most talked-about incidents in U.S. Open history. Snead's approach finished 20 feet from the flag, while Worsham's second barely avoided the high greenside rough. His ensuing chip hit the edge of the hole and stopped a short distance away. Snead, putting downhill, misread the speed and left his ball short of the hole. Believing he had the right to putt out – it was a stroke-play competition, not match play – Snead began to line up his par attempt. Worsham had other intentions and called for a measurement to determine who was away. USGA Rules official Ike Grainger used a measuring tape to find that Snead was 30½ inches from the hole with Worsham's ball 1 inch closer.

Grainger, in a 1972 letter to Sommers, wrote that Worsham had contested Snead's right to continue, "whereupon I injected myself into the situation. Snead told me he wanted to putt first and, in effect, advised me that he had this right whether he was away or not. I advised him that he did not have this choice, and I called Eddie Miller [from the USGA] to bring in the tape to make the measurement. Snead was obviously upset over this procedure."

Perhaps flustered by the circumstances, Snead missed the short putt. Worsham holed his, and the championship was over. Nevertheless, Snead was a pure gentleman at the prize ceremony, according to Grainger. "Snead's attitude was completely changed," Grainger wrote, "and his comments were of the highest order, really some of the best I have heard on such an occasion."

Two years later, Snead again would play his way into contention over the final 36 holes, shooting 71-70 at Illinois' Medinah Country Club, only to come up one stroke short of Cary Middlecoff, who won despite a closing 75 for the first of his two U.S. Open titles. Snead had his chances in the final round, but he

Golf has a way of flummoxing the game's best players, especially on its grandest stages.

bogeyed the par-3 17th and failed to birdie the finishing hole to leave himself tied for second with Clayton Heafner. Four years later at Oakmont, Snead finished second for the fourth and final time, though the margin was not a thin one. Hogan shot a remarkable 5-under 283 to best Snead by six strokes. "So many times the river's gone over the bank," said Snead, discussing his string of U.S. Open disappointments for a 1996 story in *Golfweek*. "I sort of used predestination to explain it all. If it's my turn, I'll win, and if it's not, OK. No sense in going and hiding into a hole."

Golf has a way of flummoxing the game's best players, especially on its grandest stages. For example, Greg Norman, of Australia, was arguably the best player on the planet in the 1980s, but he experienced disappointment of every kind in his major-championship quest.

In the 1984 U.S. Open at Winged Foot, Norman played the final 54 holes in four under par. When he holed a 40-foot putt on the 72nd hole, Fuzzy Zoeller, who was standing in the fairway waiting to hit his approach shot, thought Norman had just birdied to take a one-stroke lead. Zoeller hadn't realized that Norman had fanned his 6-iron approach to the right of the green and that the 40-footer was for par. Zoeller famously waved a white towel from the fairway as a gesture of surrender, but he went on to make par to tie and then easily won the next day's playoff when Norman carded a 75 to Zoeller's 3-under 67. Two years later at Shinnecock Hills, Norman dominated the first three days of play, shooting 71-68-71, before a final-round 75 left him six strokes behind winner Raymond Floyd.

Colin Montgomerie would go on to mirror Norman's disappointments, though at least Norman collected a pair of British Open titles, while the Scotsman never won a major. In 1992, a fresh-faced Montgomerie shot a 2-under 70 for a total of 288 at

Colin Montgomerie examines his putter at the 1997 U.S. Open at Congressional Country Club. Including 1997, Montgomerie finished second three times in the U.S. Open.

Pebble Beach before fierce afternoon winds kicked up, wreaking havoc on the late starters. While the brutal conditions led some – including Jack Nicklaus on national television – to project Montgomerie as the eventual winner, Jeff Sluman (71–287) and Tom Kite (72–285) managed to beat his total, with Kite claiming his only major victory.

Monty, as he is known to his peers and the press, would get three more glorious opportunities to win the U.S. Open. In 1994 at Oakmont, he worked himself into a three-way playoff with the up-and-coming Ernie Els and the steady Loren Roberts. Montgomerie, however, shot a 78 in the playoff, and Els defeated Roberts on the second sudden-death hole after both shot 74.

At Congressional Country Club in 1997, Montgomerie led the way with an opening-round 65 only to follow it up with an inglorious 76. He worked his way back with a 67, the best third-round score in the field, and was deadlocked with Els in the final round when he famously paused and waited out the clamor on the nearby 18th green before attempting his 4-foot putt for par on number 17. He missed the putt and again wound up second to Els, who parred the last five holes to match Montgomerie's final-round 69 and post a one-stroke victory.

"It's getting me down, this major business," said Montgomerie in the aftermath, amid tears of disappointment. "I felt good out there today. I didn't feel I was under pressure. I just have to be patient."

It seemed his patience might be rewarded nine years later, at Winged Foot in the 2006 championship. Instead, it turned out to be perhaps the most gut-wrenching moment in Montgomerie's U.S. Open career. With seemingly every player in the field becoming unraveled on the 72nd hole, Monty stood in the middle of the fairway with a routine approach shot to the final green. However, he was indecisive on club selection, changing from a 6-iron to a 7-iron, then left his approach well short of the putting surface in heavy rough. He went on to make a double-bogey 6 that left him in a group of three players tied for second, one stroke behind Geoff Ogilvy.

That was also the U.S. Open that Phil Mickelson let slip through his hands. He was the hottest player in the game, having won the 2005 PGA Championship and the 2006 Masters. Fighting his driver all day, Mickelson still managed to reach the 72nd hole with a one-stroke lead. While many questioned Mickelson's tactics, saying he should have opted for a 3-wood, or even an iron from the tee, the go-for-broke left-hander hit driver and sliced it wildly, where it struck a hospitality tent. Instead of playing back to the fairway for a possible par and almost-certain bogey, Mickelson chose a bold route toward the green. His shot caught a tree, and, like Montgomerie, he went on to make a messy double-bogey 6 that left him one stroke out of a playoff with Ogilvy. It was Mickelson's fourth runner-up U.S. Open finish.

The first had come in 1999 at Pinehurst, when Payne Stewart's memorable 15-foot par putt at the 72nd hole lifted him to a one-shot victory. Mickelson's caddie had worn a pager all week because Phil's wife, Amy, was expected to go into labor at any time with the couple's first child. He weathered that distraction and retained a one-shot lead through most of the final nine holes, until his lone bogey of the round at the par-4 16th hole dropped him into a tie with Stewart. At the par-3 71st hole, Mickelson missed a birdie try from 8 feet, and Stewart holed his birdie from 5 feet for the lead. A poor drive at 18 forced Stewart to lay up, but he managed to hit his third to 15 feet and make the putt after Mickelson's birdie effort from 25 feet barely missed. Stewart, coming off his runner-up showing at The Olympic Club in 1998, had his second U.S. Open title. Certainly there would be more chances for Mickelson, the 1990 U.S. Amateur champion.

In 2002 at Bethpage State Park's Black Course, Mickelson was serenaded all week by the New York fans. He nearly chased down the front-running Tiger Woods, eventually falling by three strokes. In 2004 at Shinnecock Hills, Mickelson was victimized by a brilliant putting performance by South Africa's Retief Goosen and a putting misstep of his own. Goosen registered 11 one-putts in the final round to defeat Mickelson by two strokes. Though Goosen ended up as the only golfer among the final 16 groupings to better par, Mickelson actually held a one-stroke lead going to the 71st hole, thanks to a run of three birdies on the previous four holes. Mickelson's tee shot on the par-3 17th was bunkered, and he three-putted for a double-bogey 5, while Goosen managed a sand save for par. A two-putt par on number 18 sealed Goosen's second U.S. Open title and Mickelson's third second-place finish.

When the U.S. Open returned to Bethpage in 2009, Mickelson again put himself in the hunt. With weather forcing the first Monday regulation finish in 26 years, Mickelson was battling not only a stellar field and a difficult course but also his wife Amy's pending surgery for breast cancer. Just when it appeared Mickelson might finally etch his name on the U.S. Open Trophy, he slipped yet again with two costly late bogeys as Lucas Glover won by two strokes over Mickelson, Ricky Barnes and David Duval. "Certainly, I'm disappointed," Mickelson said, "but now that it's over, I've got more important things going on." His wife's surgery was successful, and the cancer went into remission.

Phil Mickelson on the 15th hole during the fourth round of the 2009 U.S. Open at Bethpage. Mickelson would again falter on the final day and would ultimately lose by two strokes to Lucas Glover.

As he approaches his mid-40s, Phil Mickelson's window for winning a U.S. Open is narrowing. A favorite among fans for his good nature, his generosity and his candor, Mickelson would undoubtedly be a popular U.S. Open champion. But for now, like McNamara, Snead, Montgomerie and other members of the "near-miss" fraternity, Mickelson has the dubious distinction of being best remembered for finishing second-best. And despite wanting to see a perennial runner-up finish atop the heap, it is that very stalemate with victory that helps foster the reputation of the U.S. Open as the toughest challenge in all of golf.

COMEBACKS

"I've always made a total effort, even when the odds seemed against me.
I never quit trying; I never felt I didn't have a chance to win."
– Arnold Palmer

From the impossibly low final round to the former champion who, after being written off, proves himself again, we love to root for the realization of improbable feats. Great comebacks in golf come in many forms and create legends that transcend time. Whether it is age, injury or a seemingly insurmountable deficit that confronts a player, we find ourselves united behind their effort to overcome any obstacle. The U.S. Open is not sentimental in deciding its champions, but when a compelling storyline is realized, the drama lifts our hearts and inspires us. The moments presented here illustrate the gritty determination, singular focus and occasional stroke of luck sometimes needed to overcome the odds and become the national champion.

Iron Byron | Byron Nelson 1939

Byron Nelson holds his finish. Introduced to golf as a caddie at Glen Garden Country Club in Fort Worth, Texas, Nelson became known for his legendary smooth swing.

Some championships are remembered for great shots or exciting duels, others because a promising athlete's potential was realized in the form of a major victory. And some championships are remembered best for the players who did not win.

The 1939 championship at Philadelphia Country Club had each of those elements, including a 36-hole playoff and a victory for one of the game's true gentlemen. Perhaps most significantly, though, it came to define Sam Snead's U.S. Open career better than any other championship. He stood on the 71st tee with a two-stroke lead over Byron Nelson, who had already finished at 284, with challengers Craig Wood and Denny Shute still on the course. As it would turn out, Snead only needed to play the final two holes in one over par to win, but a disastrous bogey-triple bogey finish left him two strokes out of a playoff and denied Snead what was perhaps his best chance at winning the U.S. Open.

Snead's collapse overshadowed a fine performance by Nelson, whose 68 was the low score of the final round. Nelson defeated Wood and Shute in a playoff the following day to win the only U.S. Open title of his career. The victory validated Nelson's 1937 Masters title and propelled a career that included just eight victories at the time.

Nelson and Snead, the two protagonists of the 1939 U.S. Open, were born months apart in 1912 and combined to win 12 major championships and more than 130 PGA Tour events in their careers. Along with Ben Hogan, Nelson and Snead became the face of golf during World War II and were instrumental in growing the game in the era before television.

A huge gallery watches Byron Nelson putt on the 18th green during the 1939 U.S. Open at Philadelphia Country Club.

Nelson – the humble, affable, smooth-swinging Texan – was introduced to golf as a caddie at Glen Garden Country Club in Fort Worth, Texas. It was the same course where Hogan had grown up caddieing. When the pair was 15 years old, Nelson beat Hogan in a playoff for the coveted caddie championship.

Nelson turned professional in 1932 and five years later won his first major, the 1937 Masters. Trailing Ralph Guldahl by two strokes with only nine holes to play, Nelson birdied the 10th and 12th holes and eagled the par-5 13th to surge ahead of Guldahl en route to victory.

Nelson won 32 tournaments between 1944 and 1946, including 11 consecutive victories (and 18 total) in 1945. Drained from the grind of competition and wanting to provide a home for his wife, Louise, Nelson retired from golf in 1946 at his competitive peak and used his winnings to buy a ranch in Roanoke, Texas, where he lived for more than 50 years.

It was nine years earlier that Snead had made his tour debut. Born in rural Virginia, the youngest of six children, he learned the game by watching his older brother, Homer, hit balls across the family's cow and chicken farm using clubs carved from tree limbs by their father.

Snead established himself as one of the game's young stars prior to World War II. He immediately took the professional ranks by storm, winning four times in 1937, his first season on Tour, and eight times the following year. His strength and natural athleticism contributed to one of the most admired swings in the history of golf, and with it he won a record 82 official PGA Tour tournaments, including seven major championships, and was selected to seven U.S. Ryder Cup teams.

Snead came to Philadelphia Country Club in 1939 as one of the favorites. He had set the record for PGA Tour earnings in 1938 and finished in the top 10 in each of the six tournaments he entered in 1939, including the Masters, where it appeared Snead was going to win the first major championship of his career. But an inward-nine 33 by Ralph Guldahl edged him by one stroke. Guldahl had also gotten the best of Snead two years earlier at the 1937 U.S. Open at Oakland Hills. Snead birdied the 72nd hole to post 283, but Guldahl, playing more than two hours behind Snead, recorded three birdies and an eagle over his final 11 holes to win by two strokes.

By June of 1939, however, Snead appeared poised for yet another major breakthrough. He opened the championship with a 1-under 68, the only sub-par round of the day, which gave him a one-stroke lead.

Nelson, who had recently taken the head professional job at Reading Country Club in Pennsylvania, only 44 miles from the course, started poorly, bogeying five of his first eight holes. He kept himself in the championship with steady play on the inward nine to salvage a 72 for the first round.

Despite a double bogey at the 12th, Snead shot a 71 in the second round and maintained his one-stroke lead. Fifteen players were within five strokes of the lead, but that group did not include Nelson, who three-putted five greens and sat six behind Snead heading into Saturday's final 36 holes.

In the third round, a 73 by Snead dropped him into a second-place tie with Shute and Wood, one stroke behind long-hitting Chicago native Johnny Bulla. Birdies at 16 and 17 saved Nelson's chances at the U.S. Open title. A 2-over-par 71 left him five strokes behind at 216.

Bulla faded quickly in the final round, with bogeys at his first two holes and a double bogey at the par-3 seventh. Nelson birdied the first, bogeyed the third and then ran off 13 consecutive pars before a birdie at the 17th. He sank an 8-foot par putt on the closing hole to post 284.

Snead played steady golf for the first 16 holes of the final round, and even a bogey at the 17th left him one stroke ahead of Nelson. Mistakenly thinking he needed a birdie to win, Snead played aggressively on the par-5 closing hole. He was in a bunker just short and right of the green in two, but he left his third

Craig Wood (left), Byron Nelson (right) and Denny Shute (not pictured) finished in a tie after regulation during the 1939 U.S. Open. The three would meet the following day to decide the national championship.

Facing page: Byron Nelson, shown here demonstrating his smooth swing, took on the head professional job at Reading Country Club in Pennsylvania just before the 1939 U.S. Open.

Byron Nelson's MacGregor Tourney golf ball, which he used during the 1939 U.S. Open.

Byron Nelson (left) shakes hands with Craig Wood (right) during the trophy presentation ceremony at the 1939 U.S. Open.

Facing page: The mechanical "Iron Byron," used by the USGA Research and Test Center for golf club and ball specification testing for three decades, holds its namesake's Spalding 1-iron, which Nelson used during the 1939 U.S. Open at Philadelphia Country Club.

shot in the bunker. His fourth sailed over the green and into the gallery. He pitched onto the green, but needing to sink the putt to join the playoff, Snead three-putted.

Wood birdied the 18th to join Nelson at 284, and Shute came in with the same total an hour later to force the first three-way playoff since Francis Ouimet defeated Ted Ray and Harry Vardon at s in Brookline, Massachusetts, in 1913.

Both Nelson and Wood shot 68 in the playoff to force another 18 holes, with Shute dropping out after a 76. In the second playoff, Nelson and Wood were tied through two holes when Nelson hit two of the greatest shots in U.S. Open playoff history. After hitting an 8-iron within 2 feet of the hole to set up a birdie at the par-4 third, Nelson holed out with a 1-iron from 215 yards for an eagle 2 on the par-4 fourth. In just two holes, Nelson gained four strokes on Wood, completely changing the complexion of the playoff. Despite bogeys from Nelson on holes 10, 12 and 13, Wood was never able to draw closer than two strokes. Nelson finished with a 70 to Wood's 73.

Nelson played in only five more U.S. Opens due to the suspension of the championship for World War II. He finished runner-up in 1946, losing a three-way playoff to Lloyd Mangrum. Nelson was in position to win the championship in regulation, but he was assessed a two-stroke penalty in the third round when his caddie inadvertently kicked his ball. Nelson retired from competitive golf two months after the championship.

Snead came painstakingly close to winning other U.S. Opens, including the following year in 1940, when he led after three rounds but shot a final-round 81 to finish 16th. In 1947, he missed a 30-inch putt on the final hole of an 18-hole playoff with Lew Worsham to lose by one stroke. He would finish runner-up again in 1949 and 1953. Snead finished second a total of four times in the U.S. Open, a total surpassed only by Phil Mickelson.

Snead remained a dominant force on the PGA Tour well into his 50s, winning the Greater Greensboro Open in 1965 and finishing tied for third in the 1974 PGA Championship at the age of 63, but the championship he coveted most – the U.S. Open – always eluded him.

A Triumph of Will | Ben Hogan 1950

Ben Hogan's victory in the 1950 U.S. Open was not simply the story of a man playing better than his competition or mastering every element of a difficult course. Just 16 months earlier, Hogan had survived a head-on collision with a Greyhound bus that had left him severely injured. When doctors assessed his condition, it became clear that he might never walk again, let alone play golf. But through sheer force of will, Hogan overcame the terrible odds and summoned a heroic performance at Merion, accomplishing one of the greatest and most inspiring feats in the history of sports.

By early 1949, Hogan's tenacity, perfected swing and devout practice regimen had made him one of the game's iconic figures. He had become a dominant force in professional golf in the years immediately following World War II and, at age 36, was arguably the greatest player in the game. Hogan was coming off a year in which he won 10 tournaments, including two major championships. It seemed as if nothing could slow him down.

But on February 2, 1949, Hogan and his wife, Valerie, were driving back to their home in Fort Worth, Texas, after the Phoenix Open. On a fog-shrouded Highway 80, just east of the small Texan town of Van Horn, the driver of a Greyhound bus was speeding in the opposite direction while attempting to pass a slow-moving truck. Unable to avoid the head-on collision, Hogan instinctively threw his body across the front seat of the car to protect Valerie, and the force of the impact with the 10-ton bus drove the steering column of his Cadillac into the rear seat.

Valerie escaped unharmed, but Hogan suffered a shattered left collarbone, a double ring fracture of the pelvis, a broken left ankle, a broken rib and several

Ben Hogan is presented the U.S. Open Championship Trophy with his wife, Valerie, at his side at Merion Golf Club.

Facing page: This Hy Peskin photograph of Ben Hogan making his approach to Merion's 458-yard, par-4 18th is one of golf's most famous images. Hogan hit a 1-iron to within 40 feet of the hole that set up a two-putt for par and a U.S. Open playoff.

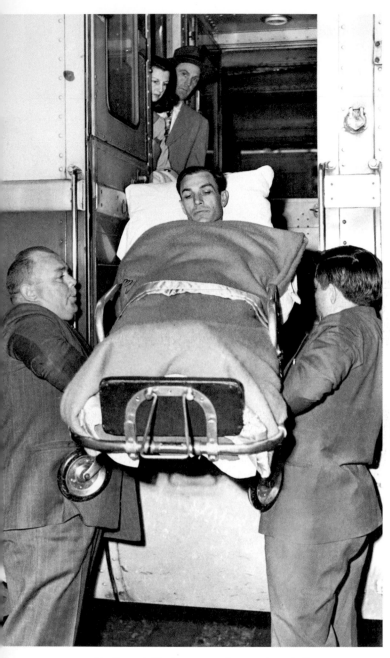

Ben Hogan is lifted on a gurney from a train on April 7, 1949, in Fort Worth, Texas. He was returning to his hometown to recuperate from a near-fatal car accident in February of that year.

deep cuts around his left eye. News of the accident broke across the national wire services, including some erroneous reports that Hogan had died. In the days that followed, blood clots developed in his legs and began to move toward his chest, threatening to take his life. They necessitated emergency surgery that kept him in the hospital until April. The question seemed to be whether Hogan would survive, not if he could play championship-caliber golf again.

In March of 1949, he told the *Fort Worth Star-Telegram*, "You work for perfection all your life, and then something like this happens. But you can bet I'll be back there swinging."

Amazingly, he was. He walked within months. Within one year, he returned to professional golf. In the 1950 Los Angeles Open, his first competition after the accident, Hogan walked Riviera Country Club with his legs bandaged from hip to ankle to control the swelling. Despite being in tremendous pain, Hogan played well and finished regulation tied for the lead with Sam Snead. Though Snead prevailed in the playoff, Hogan was lauded for his gritty performance. Sportswriter Grantland Rice wrote, "His legs weren't strong enough to carry his heart around."

Because of the pain, Hogan played a limited schedule in 1950, with his focus squarely on the U.S. Open at Merion. The U.S. Open always seemed to suit Hogan's game. With fast greens, narrow fairways and dense rough, the typical U.S. Open setup meshed with his emphasis on pure shotmaking and accuracy.

Hogan had won in his last U.S. Open appearance – in 1948 at Riviera Country Club – but due to his injuries was viewed as more of a sentimental favorite, while the press favored the likes of Snead, Jimmy Demaret and defending champion Cary Middlecoff. While there was some question whether Hogan could endure playing 72 holes over three days, including 36 on Saturday, Snead, for one, told the Associated Press that, "Hogan is the man who might make some trouble. He's the man I've got to beat."

The weather was cold and wet during the week leading up to the championship. Hogan didn't play a practice round until the day before the U.S. Open started, reasoning that he only wanted to play the course in championship-like conditions. He went so far as to say, "I think anybody who plays this course before Wednesday is crazy."

After 18 holes, many of the main contenders were still in the mix, but it was unheralded Lee Mackey who led the U.S. Open. In fact, Mackey was such a surprise leader that one Philadelphia newspaper headline proclaimed, "Jobless Unknown Shoots Record 64 To Lead Stars in National Open Golf." Mackey used 11 one-putts to shoot the lowest score in U.S. Open history to that point. Hogan, using a collapsible chair between shots to rest his legs, shot a 2-over 72 that left him in a tie for 18th.

While Mackey ballooned to an 81 on Friday, Hogan, off in the morning wave, started strongly, birdieing four of his first 10 holes to move into red figures. He was still at one under for the championship when he three-putted for bogey at the 16th and missed a 4-foot putt for another dropped shot at the 17th. Hogan's 69 left him in fifth place, two strokes behind the leader, E.J. (Dutch) Harrison.

In the third round, Hogan again surged to the top of the leaderboard with birdies at the 10th and 11th, but bogeys on three of his next four holes left him two behind Lloyd Mangrum, the 1946 U.S. Open champion, with just 18 holes to play on Saturday afternoon.

Playing an hour before Hogan in the final round, Mangrum faltered, shooting a 5-over 41 on the front nine to let several players back in the championship. One of the players who took advantage was George Fazio, who previously had never finished better than 25th in the U.S. Open. Fazio began the final round six strokes off Mangrum's pace, but an even-par 70 gave him a total of 7-over 287. Mangrum steadied his game on the back nine for a 76 to match Fazio's total of 287.

Hogan stood on the 15th green ahead by two strokes, seemingly in control of the championship. But he three-putted from 25 feet, missing a par attempt from 30 inches. Still, three pars would win him an improbable second U.S. Open. Hogan parred the 16th but found a bunker on the long, par-3 17th and failed to get up and down. Now he needed a par on Merion's uphill 458-yard, par-4 18th hole to force a playoff. After a perfect drive, Hogan hit a 1-iron on the green within 40 feet of the hole – a moment captured by photographer Hy Peskin that remains one of golf's iconic images. Hogan two-putted for par to force a playoff with Fazio and Mangrum.

Despite nearly winning the U.S. Open in regulation, Hogan had performed so poorly on the greens during the final round, needing 38 putts, that he considered changing putters for the playoff. His younger brother, Royal, who was still living in Texas, sent one of Hogan's old brass putters to New York. It made it to Merion on Sunday morning, but not in time for Hogan to practice with it. In the end he stuck with the putter he had and fared better on the greens during the playoff.

Through 13 extra holes Hogan held a one-stroke lead over both Fazio and Mangrum. Fazio faded down the stretch with four bogeys in his last five holes, but Mangrum hung tough, bouncing back from a bogey on the 14th with a birdie on the 15th to remain within one stroke.

On the 16th hole, Mangrum marked his ball so Fazio could finish out, but once he replaced his ball on the green, a bug landed on it. Mangrum then re-marked, blew the bug off and holed the putt for what he believed was a par to stay within one. As he was about to tee off on the 17th, USGA Rules official Ike Grainger informed Mangrum that he had incurred a two-stroke penalty for

Ben Hogan stands next to the wrecked Cadillac he and his wife, Valerie, were in when it was struck by a bus in February 1949.

										SCORING										

SCORING
After each hole the marker shall check the score with the competitor. On completion of the round the marker shall sign the card and hand it to the competitor.
The competitor shall check his score for each hole, settle any doubtful points with the USGA Committee, sign it, and return it to the USGA Committee immediately.

Official Score Card
Golden Anniversary
Open Championship
of the United States Golf Association
Questions as to the Rules of Golf shall be referred to the USGA Rules Committee

Ben Hogan — Round, Play-off June 11

HOLES	1	2	3	4	5	6	7	8	9	OUT	10	11	12	13	14	15	16	17	18	IN	TOTAL
YARDS	360	555	195	595	425	435	360	367	185	3,477	335	378	400	133	443	395	445	230	458	3,217	6,694
PAR	4	5	3	5	4	4	4	4	3	36	4	4	4	3	4	4	4	3	4	34	70
	4	6	3	5	4	4	3	5	3	36	4	4	4	3	4	4	4	2	4	33	69

Scorer's Signature _____ Competitor's Signature _____

incorrectly marking his ball a second time. In 1950, the PGA Tour allowed a player to mark his ball at any time while on the green, but in USGA championships, marking a ball on the green in stroke play was only permissible when it was in another player's line. Now three shots clear of Mangrum, Hogan made a 50-foot putt for birdie at the 17th and parred the 18th to seal his unlikely victory.

Interestingly, the 1-iron used for his approach to the 72nd hole was not in Hogan's bag for the playoff. That night, several items were stolen from his locker, including the club that had helped him reach Merion's final green. For more than three decades, the club's whereabouts remained a mystery. Finally, in 1982, the 1-iron was rediscovered. An anonymous man wandered into a golf collector's shop in Williamsburg, Virginia, owned by Bob Farino looking to sell a full set of Ben Hogan signature MacGregor clubs. Farino bought the clubs for $150, but he noticed the 1-iron was marked "personal model" and did not match the rest of the set. Through some friends, Farino was able to get the club to Hogan's Fort Worth office in 1983, and according to Doug McGrath, the former vice president of sales for the Ben Hogan Company, Hogan looked at the club, verified its authenticity and said, "Good to see my old friend back. Give it to the USGA." The club now resides in the USGA Museum in Far Hills, New Jersey.

In his career, Hogan amassed nine major championships, including four U.S. Opens, but it is this win at Merion in 1950, just 16 months after his near-fatal car accident, that best exemplifies his courage, tenacity and determination. Hogan's story had particular resonance to an entire generation of Americans – golfers and non-golfers alike – who were impacted by crippling injuries sustained in World War II. Everyone seemed to know someone, be it a relative, a friend or a neighbor, who was affected by the war. Against this backdrop, Hogan's personal battle and recovery from injury had even greater significance to the nation.

Ben Hogan's par on the 72nd hole of the 1950 U.S. Open got him into a three-way playoff against Lloyd Mangrum and Geroge Fazio; Hogan won the playoff. His scorecard is above.

Facing page: The 1-iron Ben Hogan used to reach the green at Merion's 18th hole during the final round of the 1950 U.S. Open is paired with his 1950 championship medal. The set are resting on one of Merion's signature wicker-basket flags.

A King's Coronation | Arnold Palmer 1960

On the afternoon of June 18, 1960, at Cherry Hills Country Club outside of Denver, the game's past, present and future collided in one of the most dramatic finishes in U.S. Open history. Over the course of the final round, the era of Ben Hogan ended, Arnold Palmer was crowned "The King," and a young Jack Nicklaus announced his arrival. When the final 36 holes began that morning, none of these men were in contention. But by the time the drama came to a close, the stage had been set for the next two decades of major championship golf.

After 36 holes of play, Mike Souchak had set a U.S. Open scoring record of 135 and was seven under par. He led Doug Sanders by three strokes, and the championship seemed to be his for the taking. Hogan and Nicklaus, paired together for the final 36 holes, were trailing Souchak by seven strokes, and Palmer was a distant nine strokes back. Souchak held a four-stroke lead as he approached the tee on the 54th hole, but, distracted by a camera shutter, he hit his drive into the water and finished his third round with a double bogey. His lead was now only two over Dow Finsterwald, Jerry Barber and Julius Boros, the 1952 U.S. Open champion. Hogan and Nicklaus both posted 2-under-par 69s to pull within three strokes, but Palmer's 1-over-par 72 left him seven strokes out of the lead.

In the locker room at lunch, Bob Rosburg and Ken Venturi, who would go on to win the 1964 U.S. Open, were discussing potential outcomes for the championship with reporters Bob Drum and Dan Jenkins. Palmer joined the group with his cheeseburger and asked Drum, a longtime friend from Pittsburgh, "If I drive the green [of the first hole] and get a birdie or an eagle, I might shoot 65. What'll that do?"

Arnold Palmer (left) receives the U.S. Open Championship Trophy from USGA President John G. Clock (right) after winning the 1960 U.S. Open, which featured a convergence of golf heroes. It was Ben Hogan's last hurrah, Jack Nicklaus emerged as a future star and Arnold Palmer solidified his position as the game's dominant force.

Facing page: Arnold Palmer's visor, which he famously tossed into the air at the conclusion of the 1960 U.S. Open at Cherry Hills.

Pictured here is the 18th hole at Cherry Hills Country Club. Designed by William Flynn and opened in 1922, the club has hosted five major championships and two U.S. Amateur Championships.

Drum replied, "Nothing. You are too far back."

"It would give me 280," Palmer said. "Doesn't 280 always win the U.S. Open?"

"Yeah, when Hogan shoots it." Drum said, laughing. "Go on, boy, get out of here. Go make your seven or eight birdies and shoot 73."

Palmer, furious with his friend's lack of support, left his half-eaten lunch behind and stormed out of the locker room for the practice tee. The charge had been primed. Fifteen minutes later, Palmer drove the first green and made birdie. Word found its way back to Drum and Jenkins, but they were unimpressed. Palmer chipped in for birdie on the par-4 second hole, and Drum and Jenkins remained seated. He almost drove the 348-yard, par-4 third hole and recorded another birdie after a delicate pitch from the heavy rough. Hearing the roar in the locker room, Drum looked at Jenkins and said, "Care to join me at the fourth hole?"

They arrived in time to see Palmer hole an 18-foot putt for birdie. Seeing Drum near the fifth tee, Palmer walked over and said wryly, "Fancy seeing you here." Palmer would go on to par the fifth and then birdie the sixth and seventh holes. Six under par for seven holes, the quintessential Palmer charge had been made. Although he would bogey the long and difficult par-3 eighth hole, his front-nine 30 sent a message to the field.

Souchak, playing behind Palmer, wilted under Palmer's charge and the hot summer sun, letting his lead slip away on the front nine. After Souchak's bogey at the ninth hole, the championship had a new leader, Nicklaus at five under par. Exempt from qualifying as the 1959 U.S. Amateur champion, Nicklaus was now in a position to become the first amateur to claim the U.S. Open title since Johnny Goodman in 1933. Hogan, at four under par, was also now in contention. With Palmer just one stroke back, three generations began their battle over the final nine holes.

Nicklaus would be the first to succumb to the pressure. After a 10-foot birdie attempt slid 20 inches past the hole on the par-4 13th hole, he noticed there was a raised ball mark between his ball and the hole. Nicklaus later said, "I was an inexperienced nervous kid. Of course you can fix a ball mark." But in his indecision about fixing the damage, he was overeager to finish and get out of Hogan's way. His ball deflected off the ball mark and missed the hole. A three-putt bogey, the result of a mental error, had brought doubt into his mind. Nicklaus lost his one-stroke lead almost as quickly as he had gained it and was now tied with Hogan.

Palmer and Paul Harney were playing behind Hogan and Nicklaus, separated by the twosome of Boros and Gary Player. Although not within sight of each other, Palmer's gallery was loud enough to inform Hogan and Nicklaus that he had birdied the par-5 11th hole and joined them at four under par. Nicklaus, who had lost focus on the 13th green, then three-putted the 14th hole for another bogey. It would prove to be the stroke that placed the championship out of the amateur's reach. Now tied with Hogan, Palmer would have to defeat the greatest U.S. Open competitor up to that time to claim his crown.

Hogan knew what it took to win the U.S. Open, having won the championship four times previously (1948, 1950, 1951, 1953). He had hit all 34 greens on Saturday when he arrived at the 17th hole, and he thought he would need to birdie this straightaway 548-yard par-5 to beat Palmer. With the hole cut just over a pond at the front of the green, the play that offered the best chance for birdie was a good drive and then a lay-up to a comfortable wedge distance. Hogan split the fairway and then played his second some 50 yards short of the green. Player and Boros watched from the 17th fairway and Palmer from the tee as Hogan hit his approach, which struck the front of the green near the hole and then shockingly spun back into the water. The steely-eyed Hogan had done the unthinkable – he had made a mistake with the U.S. Open within his grasp.

The gallery went silent. Hogan stared in disbelief then calmly removed one of his shoes to play his fourth shot from the water. Although he got the ball out and onto the green, he missed his 18-foot putt for par and made six. Palmer now

Arnold Palmer used this driver during the 1960 U.S. Open at Cherry Hills.

Above and facing page: Arnold Palmer had missed the green with his approach to the 72nd hole at Cherry Hills Country Club. He chipped to within 3 feet, carefully read his putt and, without hesitation, tapped in for a par 4, after which he jubilantly tossed his visor in the air. The visor was picked up by a young boy named Skip Manning, who donated it to the USGA Museum in 2008.

held the lead alone at four under par. And when Hogan hit his tee shot into the water on the 72nd hole, the championship was Palmer's to win.

As Palmer posted a par on the 17th, Nicklaus faced a short birdie putt on the 18th for a total of 281. Thinking that the championship was over, Nicklaus casually missed the putt that would have reduced Palmer's lead to a single stroke. Palmer hit his drive safely over the water on the difficult, 468-yard, par-4 18th hole but hooked his 4-iron approach just off the left edge of the green. He chipped up to about 3 feet and without hesitation stroked the putt into the hole.

Palmer sent the red visor he was wearing sailing into the air. True to his own prediction, he had shot 65. Although he would have to wait another 90 minutes as the groups behind him finished to see his 280 officially win him the U.S. Open, the coronation had already begun. Hogan commented after the round, "I guess they will say I lost it. But I'll tell you something. I played 36 holes today with a kid who should have won this U.S. Open by 10 shots." Nicklaus would learn from his mistakes at Cherry Hills and eventually go on to join Hogan as a four-time U.S. Open champion, along with Willie Anderson and Bob Jones. Although Hogan would play in another six U.S. Opens, the last in 1967, he would never again seriously contend for the title. The era of Hogan had ended, and by nightfall golf had crowed Palmer its new king as the U.S. Open champion.

A Round for the Ages | Johnny Miller 1973

Johnny Miller poses in 1973 with the U.S. Open Championship Trophy. Miller hit all 18 greens in regulation en route to a 63 in the final round of the 1973 U.S. Open for a one-shot victory over John Schlee.

Some numbers endure as the standard of excellence in a particular sport. Wilt Chamberlain's 100-point game. The 1972 Miami Dolphins' perfect season. Joe DiMaggio's 56-game hitting streak. Michael Phelps' eight gold medals in the 2008 Summer Olympic Games. In golf, we have Jack Nicklaus' record of 18 major championship victories. But for a single round, it is hard to overlook the brilliance of Johnny Miller's 63 in the final round of the 1973 U.S. Open at Oakmont Country Club.

Nicklaus and Tom Weiskopf equaled Miller's score in the first round of the 1980 U.S. Open at Baltusrol, and Vijay Singh did the same in the second round of the 2003 championship at Olympia Fields, but no one has surpassed his mark. If you factor in the circumstances under which Miller accomplished the feat – in the final round to win the championship by one stroke – and the way in which he did it – hitting all 18 greens in regulation – you have arguably the greatest round of golf played in the game's history.

Miller was no stranger to shooting low numbers. He broke course records at Phoenix Country Club during the 1970 Phoenix Open, where he shot 61, as well as at Tamarisk during the 1973 Bob Hope Desert Classic, where he shot 63. By mid-1973, Miller had gone low with single rounds of 65 or lower 11 times, with four of those rounds coming in the first half of 1973 alone.

Miller was born and raised in San Francisco and at age 5 was taught to play the game by his father, Laurence, who constructed a practice area in the family basement, where Johnny pounded balls with a cut-down club into a canvas tarp for hours each day. In 1963, as a teenager, he became a junior member at The Olympic Club, and he won the U.S. Junior Amateur the following year, before enrolling at Brigham Young University in 1965. In 1966, with the U.S. Open being held at his home course, the 19-year-old Miller made it into the field as an alternate and finished the four rounds at The Olympic Club tied for eighth.

Coming into the 1973 U.S. Open, Miller had claimed just two victories in four years on the PGA Tour, but he had performed well in major championships. He finished runner-up in the 1970 Masters and recorded top-10 finishes in the 1971 and 1972 U.S. Opens. In 1973 Miller had eight top 10s to his record, including a tie for sixth at the Masters. He came into the U.S. Open at Oakmont brimming with confidence.

"I had heard a lot about the fearsome greens and bunkers of Oakmont," said Miller, "but I thought the course suited me as much as anyone else. To win there, I believed you had to drive it straight, hit high iron shots and putt fast greens well. I considered these my three strongest suits."

Miller played his first two rounds with Arnold Palmer, who attracted massive galleries at any tournament. But "Arnie's Army" was especially large at Oakmont because the course was only 35 miles from The King's hometown, Latrobe, Pennsylvania. Palmer had not won a major championship since 1964, but he had led for a good portion of the previous U.S. Open held at Oakmont, in 1962, before being defeated by a 22-year-old Jack Nicklaus. And with Palmer's third-place finish at the 1972 U.S. Open fresh in everyone's memory, along with one tournament victory in 1973, Arnie's Army was hoping the 43-year-old could summon one last charge.

"In those days, in Pittsburgh, Arnold Palmer was a rock star," said Miller. "Everybody was following him and in some ways it was a difficult experience because if he made a putt, the gallery didn't exactly stick around to watch me putt. They liked me alright, but they *loved* Arnie. To be paired together and both play well – that's what I remember about the U.S. Open almost as much as the 63 in the final round."

The course itself played just 27 yards longer than in 1962; however, 33 bunkers had been added, bringing the total to 187. Despite a rainy spring that softened conditions, the course seemed primed to play as difficult as ever. In fact, the USGA asked Oakmont to *widen* two of its fairways from everyday play.

In the first round, Oakmont lived up to its billing. Gary Player led the field with a 4-under 67, but no one else broke 70 on Thursday. Though Player was one of the leading players in the game in the early 1970s, his position at the front of the field was somewhat surprising given that he had been hospitalized for 12 days in February for emergency bladder surgery. He had played in just three tournaments in the previous five months and was 14 pounds below his normal weight, yet he paced the field by three strokes over Lee Trevino, Jim Colbert and Raymond Floyd.

A 1973 U.S. Open Championship final-round ticket. While many in the crowd were part of Arnie's Army, Johnny Miller garnered plenty of attention as he marched to victory.

Then something happened overnight to make Oakmont a different course on Friday. Despite no rain, the greens that were firm and fast on Thursday had become soft and accessible. Players abandoned their conservative strategies in favor of firing at flagsticks. Gene Borek, a club professional from Long Island who got into the field as an alternate, shot 65 and broke the course record in the morning. Altogether, 19 players broke par, including reigning U.S. Amateur champion Vinny Giles, who holed a 6-iron for eagle at the 15th and converted short birdie putts at 17 and 18 for a 2-3-3-3 finish to shoot 69.

Exactly what happened was never made clear, but in all likelihood the overnight sprinklers were allowed to run longer than they should have, altering the track of the championship. "Let's just say the greens are softer than I would like to see them," said P.J. Boatwright, the executive director of the USGA. "They won't be watered tonight." Though scores had improved across the board, some players agreed with Boatwright. "I personally would like to see the greens as hard as a table and just as fast," said Nicklaus, the defending champion. "Then I don't think very many players could handle them." Player still led at 137 with Colbert one stroke behind. Miller and Nicklaus were tied for third with Bob Charles at 140.

After a rainstorm further saturated the course on Saturday morning, the leader board became bunched at the top. Player's game collapsed with a 77, but when the dust cleared after 54 holes, four shared the lead at 210: Palmer, Jerry Heard, John Schlee and 53-year-old Julius Boros, a two-time U.S. Open champion. Tom Weiskopf, who had won tournaments in three of the previous five weeks, was one stroke back.

Miller, meanwhile, fell into a tie for 13th, six strokes off the lead, after a 76. In his rush to get to the course on Saturday, Miller forgot his yardage book in his hotel room and made three bogeys and a double bogey over the first six holes. "My iron game was very precise and I could usually get within a couple feet of my yardage, but without my book I was just guessing out there and, psychologically, that really threw me for a loop," said Miller.

While taking out his frustration at the driving range after his round, Miller heard a voice tell him to alter his stance. "I was trying to figure out some little key and a pretty clear voice – it wasn't audible but I could hear it in my head – said, 'Open your stance way up.'" After hitting several shots, Miller found that the tactic helped him shorten his backswing and play a controlled fade. But even with his yardage book in hand and a revitalized swing, Miller still didn't like his chances on Sunday morning. "I was six shots out of the lead and all the greatest players were ahead of me: Nicklaus, Palmer, Player, Trevino and Weiskopf," said Miller. "I didn't think I had any chance to win when I teed off

Johnny Miller eyes a putt at the 1973 U.S. Open. Six shots out of the lead, Miller didn't like his chances going into the final round of the championship.

Facing page: Johnny Miller's wedge, golf ball and red, white and blue shoes, which he used during the 1973 U.S. Open at Oakmont.

Johnny Miller hits an approach shot at the 1973 U.S. Open. Ten of Miller's approach shots finished within 15 feet of the hole, with five of them finishing 6 feet or closer.

that final day." In fact, before he left for the course, Miller told his wife, Linda, to make sure their bags were packed so they could leave quickly after he finished his round.

Many people thought a historic comeback could be in store on Sunday, but most eyes were on another power hitter with long, blond hair. Two months earlier, Nicklaus had started the final round at Augusta eight strokes off the lead but closed with a 66 to challenge the leaders. He finished in a tie for third, two strokes behind Tommy Aaron. This time, however, his deficit was only four strokes. When he arrived at Oakmont on Sunday wearing a grim, determined look and started out par-birdie, it appeared the charge was on. Nicklaus, however, could not string together enough birdies. Though his 68 was the third-lowest round of the day, it was overshadowed by Miller's brilliance.

Teeing off an hour before the leaders in the eighth-to-last group, Miller birdied his first four holes to move into red figures. "For the first time it occurred to me that I could win," said Miller, after his fourth consecutive birdie. After three pars, he three-putted the eighth for bogey to go back to even. "I went from being nervous to semi-mad," said Miller. "That kind of got me focused again. I told myself, 'If you're going to win the U.S. Open, you can't be nervous, so let's put the hammer down.' " He proceeded to birdie the ninth, 11th, 12th and 13th holes to pull into a share of the lead at 4-under. As he played the 453-yard, par-4 15th, Miller was tied with Palmer, Boros and Weiskopf. He struck a 4-iron to 10 feet and sank the birdie putt to take the outright lead for the first time. He parred the final three holes for an 8-under 63.

Unaware of Miller's run, Palmer thought he was in control of the championship. He missed a 4-foot birdie putt on the 11th but hit what he thought was a perfect drive on the 12th. Walking down the fairway, he finally saw the leader board and noticed that Miller was 5 under. Instead of being ahead, as he thought he was, Palmer was in fact trailing by one stroke. To make matters worse, Palmer's ball had taken a bad kick to the left and settled in some heavy rough. He bogeyed the 12th, 13th and 14th holes and was never again in contention. Schlee was the only player on the course with a chance to tie Miller, but when his 40-foot birdie chip on the 72nd hole slid past to the left, Miller was the U.S. Open champion.

While it can be argued that Miller's 63 was not played under the most challenging conditions, the facts are clear. Only four of the other 65 players in the field broke 70 on Sunday. Miller hit all 18 greens in regulation and took only 29 putts, including a three-putt. Ten of his approach shots finished within 15 feet of the hole, with five of them finishing 6 feet or closer. His scorecard did not contain a single 5. Seven of the players that Miller passed on Sunday – Palmer,

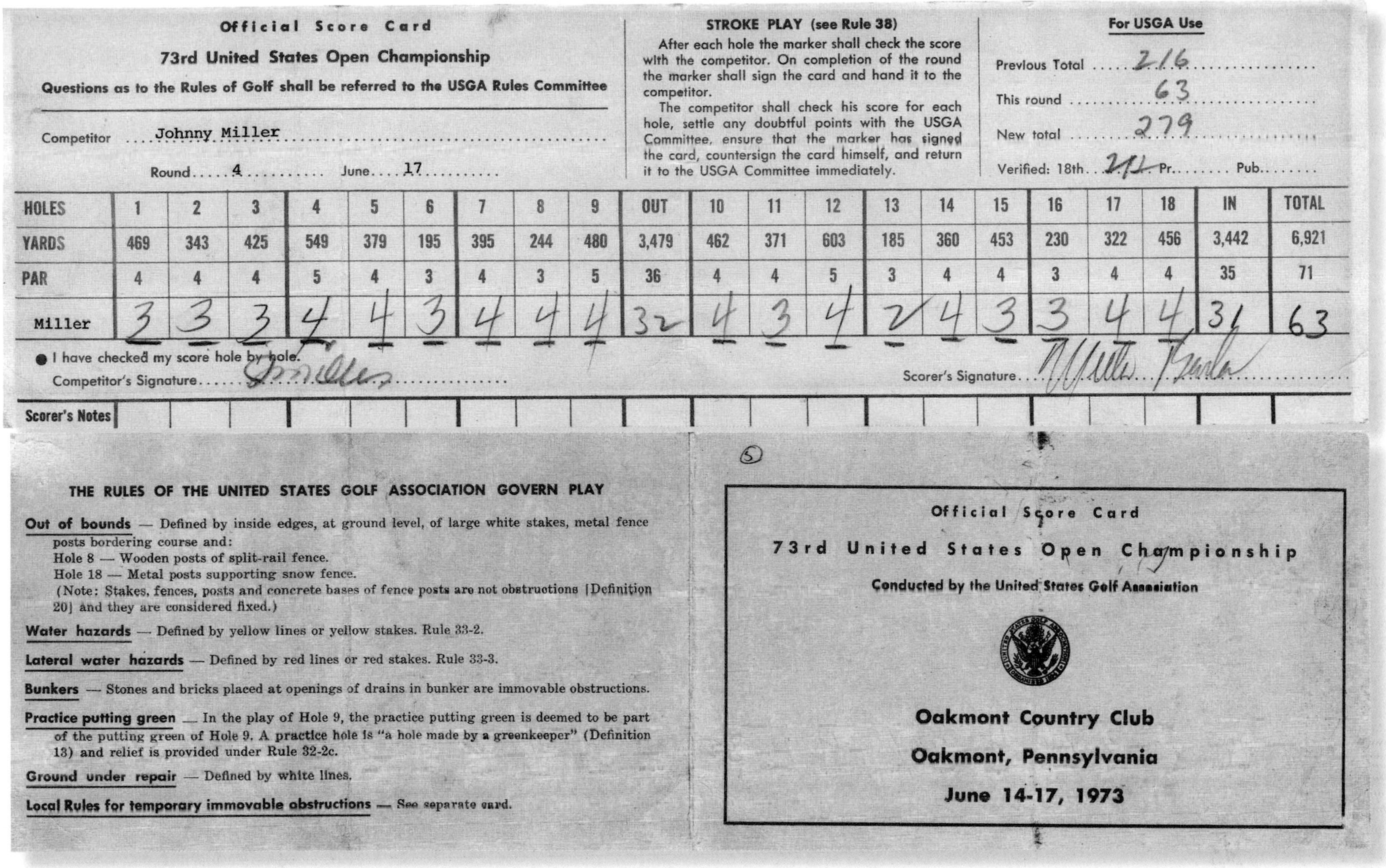

Official Score Card

73rd United States Open Championship

Questions as to the Rules of Golf shall be referred to the USGA Rules Committee

Competitor .....Johnny Miller...

Round.....4..... June....17..........

STROKE PLAY (see Rule 38)

After each hole the marker shall check the score with the competitor. On completion of the round the marker shall sign the card and hand it to the competitor.

The competitor shall check his score for each hole, settle any doubtful points with the USGA Committee, ensure that the marker has signed the card, countersign the card himself, and return it to the USGA Committee immediately.

For USGA Use

Previous Total ......216..............

This round ......63..........

New total ......279..........

Verified: 18th....2/2..Pr........ Pub........

HOLES	1	2	3	4	5	6	7	8	9	OUT	10	11	12	13	14	15	16	17	18	IN	TOTAL
YARDS	469	343	425	549	379	195	395	244	480	3,479	462	371	603	185	360	453	230	322	456	3,442	6,921
PAR	4	4	4	5	4	3	4	3	5	36	4	4	5	3	4	4	3	4	4	35	71
Miller	3	3	3	4	4	3	4	4	4	32	4	3	4	2	4	3	3	4	4	31	63

● I have checked my score hole by hole.
Competitor's Signature.....................................

Scorer's Signature.....................................

Scorer's Notes

THE RULES OF THE UNITED STATES GOLF ASSOCIATION GOVERN PLAY

Out of bounds — Defined by inside edges, at ground level, of large white stakes, metal fence posts bordering course and:
Hole 8 — Wooden posts of split-rail fence.
Hole 18 — Metal posts supporting snow fence.
(Note: Stakes, fences, posts and concrete bases of fence posts are not obstructions [Definition 20] and they are considered fixed.)

Water hazards — Defined by yellow lines or yellow stakes. Rule 33-2.

Lateral water hazards — Defined by red lines or red stakes. Rule 33-3.

Bunkers — Stones and bricks placed at openings of drains in bunker are immovable obstructions.

Practice putting green — In the play of Hole 9, the practice putting green is deemed to be part of the putting green of Hole 9. A practice hole is "a hole made by a greenkeeper" (Definition 13) and relief is provided under Rule 32-2c.

Ground under repair — Defined by white lines.

Local Rules for temporary immovable obstructions — See separate card.

Official Score Card

73rd United States Open Championship

Conducted by the United States Golf Association

Oakmont Country Club

Oakmont, Pennsylvania

June 14-17, 1973

Boros, Trevino, Nicklaus, Player, Littler and Charles – had combined for 35 major championships at that time.

"It was definitely no fluke," said Miller Barber, his playing partner during the round. "It was just an excellent round of golf. Everything he hit was right at the flag. He lipped out a few putts too. It very easily could have been a 60."

Miller's spectacular play in the early 1970s drew comparisons with Bob Jones and Jack Nicklaus. In 1975, *Newsweek* anointed him "Golf's New Golden Boy." He won 15 tournaments between 1974 and 1976, including his second major championship title at the 1976 British Open. While Miller struggled with his putter in the late 1970s, he won several more events in the early 1980s before capping off his competitive career with a victory in the 1994 AT&T Pebble Beach National Pro-Am at age 47 while in semi-retirement. As a broadcaster, Miller has watched several extraordinary finishes in the U.S. Open over the past two decades, but none quite as impressive as his 63 at Oakmont – a round still remembered as one of the greatest in major-championship history.

Pictured here is Johnny Miller's fourth-round scorecard. Though he was in the eighth-to-last group, nine birdies and one bogey helped Miller leapfrog Lee Trevino, Tom Weiskopf, Jack Nicklaus and Arnold Palmer on his way to winning the national championship.

Jack Is Back | Jack Nicklaus 1980

Jack Nicklaus is arguably the greatest U.S. Open champion of all time. His meticulous course management, unmatched skills and remarkable longevity – claiming his four titles over a span of 18 years – are just some of the reasons that Nicklaus remains in a class by himself. Each of Nicklaus' U.S. Open victories was distinctive, but 1980 was truly different – sweeter in some ways. Coming into 1980, Nicklaus hadn't won a tournament since 1978, and some critics claimed that he was over the hill. Traditionally, he had always been among the top PGA money-earners, never finishing lower than fourth on the money list since turning professional in 1962, but in 1979 he finished 71st. Rumors of his impending retirement circulated periodically, and Nicklaus was even beginning to doubt himself.

"I had just a horrible year in 1979 – the worst year I'd ever had on Tour," said Nicklaus. "I didn't win a tournament and because of that I made a lot of big adjustments to my golf swing."

He also called Phil Rodgers, an old friend and noted short-game expert, before the 1980 season and asked him for help around the greens. Rodgers agreed and stayed with Nicklaus at his home in North Palm Beach for two weeks. Each afternoon, the pair worked on chipping and putting on a green that Nicklaus had installed on his Florida property.

Though he did not win during the spring of 1980, Nicklaus' game showed signs of life. He posted only one top-10 finish, a playoff loss to Raymond Floyd at Doral, but placed inside the top 20 at Pebble Beach, Los Angeles, The Players Championship and the Memorial. But these accomplishments were marred by inconsistency. In his last tournament before the U.S. Open, Nicklaus shot rounds of 78 and 67 to miss the cut in Atlanta. Still, he was feeling better about

A victorious Jack Nicklaus gets a police escort through the crowd at the 1980 U.S. Open at Baltusrol.

Facing page: USGA officials and spectators applaud Jack Nicklaus as he hoists the U.S. Open Championship Trophy during the closing ceremony at the 1980 U.S. Open.

LEADERS

NICKLAUS	0	16	6
AOKI	2	16	4
HINKLE	0	18	4
WATSON	0	18	4
HAYES	4	8	0
FERGUS	0		
TREVINO	0		

THRU 18
NICKLAUS
AOKI

Jack Nicklaus, putting on the 17th green on the final day of the championship, felt confident about playing at Baltusrol. He had set the 72-hole scoring record there during his 1967 U.S. Open victory.

one part of his game. "I didn't play well in Atlanta," he professed, "but I accomplished something – I learned how to putt."

Another reason that Nicklaus felt confident was that the U.S. Open was returning to Baltusrol Golf Club, where he had set the 72-hole scoring record in his 1967 victory. The club, located less than 25 miles west of New York City, was founded in 1895 and was hosting its sixth U.S. Open. Nicklaus claimed that Baltusrol was an "extremely fair" course that "just fit my eye."

The spring of 1980 was unusually wet in northern New Jersey. More than 24 inches of rain had fallen in the region, and storms struck yet again on the Monday and Tuesday preceding the first round. The course was soft and vulnerable to low scores. At the time, *Golf Magazine* was offering a $50,000 prize to any player who broke either the 18- or 72-hole scoring records in any of the four major championships. In June 1980, Charles Price, of *Golf Magazine*, wrote, "While Johnny Miller's U.S. Open record of 63, set at Oakmont in 1973, is almost certain to remain unassailable, that four-round record could very well topple at Baltusrol given the ideal weather this year." It did not take long to realize that both records could be in jeopardy.

On a sunny and windless Thursday, Nicklaus' recent struggles surfaced again early in his round. He began with two wild tee shots and quickly found himself one over par through two holes. But with his wife, Barbara, and the couple's youngest child, 6-year-old Michael, in the gallery, Nicklaus then kicked things into gear. He struck a 7-iron to within a foot of the hole on the third and drained a 40-foot putt on the fifth to move into red figures. After turning in 32, Nicklaus added birdies at 11 and 12, finessed another 7-iron to within a foot on 13 for his third consecutive birdie and added two more birdies at 15 and 17 to reach seven under. Needing to birdie the par-5 18th to break the U.S. Open scoring record, Nicklaus hit a driver, 3-wood and pitch to within 3 feet of the hole, but he missed the short putt and settled for a 63. "I really wanted that 62 and I thought I had it," said Nicklaus. Despite the miss on 18, Nicklaus had put together one of his finest rounds in years. "The last time I putted this well might have been the last time I was here," said Nicklaus, referring to his 1967 victory at Baltusrol. Others also took advantage of the benign course conditions. Despite a bogey at the first hole, Tom Weiskopf also shot 63. In all, 19 players broke par on one of the easiest scoring days in championship history.

The second round got off to a strange start. Seve Ballesteros, the reigning British Open and Masters champion who had shot 75 in the first round, arrived late for his 9:45 a.m. starting time and was disqualified. Ballesteros mistakenly thought he was supposed to tee off at 10:45 a.m., and he discovered his error too late to make it to the course on time, due to heavy traffic.

Then, just when it appeared that Nicklaus and Weiskopf were poised to run away with the championship, they came back to the field. Weiskopf birdied the first hole by draining a 30-foot putt, but he three-putted the second to fall back to seven under. He doubled the sixth, three-putted the 12th and closed with three consecutive bogeys for a 75. He was never again a factor in the championship, shooting rounds of 76 and 75 over the weekend to finish in 37th place.

Nicklaus, meanwhile, birdied the first and third holes to move to nine under. Despite a three-putt bogey at the sixth, he seemed to be in full control of his game at the turn. Indeed, he was threatening to become the first player in U.S. Open history to move double-digits under par, but he made a bogey at the 11th and a disappointing double bogey at the par-3 12th. He reached the par-4 13th in regulation, but he rolled his first putt 6 feet past the hole and faced the possibility of dropping four strokes in three holes. But Nicklaus collected himself and coolly sank the putt that he later claimed was the key to salvaging his round.

Despite his struggles, Nicklaus' 36-hole total of 134 was still a U.S. Open record, and when he posted 32 on his first nine on Saturday, he was three shots clear of the field and appeared in control of the championship. But bogeys at

Jack Nicklaus and Isao Aoki played all four rounds together during the 1980 U.S. Open.

Jack Nicklaus tees off on the final day of the 1980 U.S. Open. Though he struggled in 1979, Nicklaus' game was rounding into form as the golf world turned its attention to the 1980 championship.

Facing page: An elated Jack Nicklaus raises his club after making a 22-foot birdie putt on the 17th hole in the final round of the 1980 U.S. Open.

14 and 15 and a par at 18, the easiest hole on the course, resulted in an even-par 70. "I'd love to have made this a very dull tournament," said Nicklaus, whose second-nine 38 allowed several players to remain in contention.

One of those players was Japan's Isao Aoki, who posted his third consecutive 68 to move into a tie for the lead with Nicklaus. Aoki was playing in just his second U.S. Open and was relatively unknown in the United States despite six appearances in the Masters. He had won 32 tournaments in his career, mostly in Japan, and was labeled "the best golfer in the world from inside 50 yards" by Gary Player. True to advertising, Aoki was among the championship's leaders in putting for the week. In fact, he needed just 10 putts over his final nine holes of the second round.

Aoki employed a unique style of putting – with the toe of the putter blade raised off the ground – that he stumbled upon while playing in an exhibition match at a U.S. Air Force base in Japan. The putter he borrowed for the match was a few inches longer than his normal putter, so he was forced to stand back from the ball with the toe elevated. Aoki made every putt he saw that day and continued to use that method of putting for the rest of his career.

Also in the mix was Tom Watson, who was arguably the best player in the world at the time, having won 20 PGA Tour events since 1977, including five already in 1980. Watson improved on an opening 71, that included an ace at the 194-yard fourth, with rounds of 68 and 67 to pull within two strokes of the leaders. But Watson was unable to make any critical putts on Sunday, missing all six of his chances between 4 and 10 feet over his final nine holes.

As Watson and the other contenders faded, Sunday fittingly developed into a duel between Nicklaus and Aoki, who were paired together for the fourth consecutive day. Nicklaus pulled ahead early when Aoki bogeyed the second and he made a five-foot birdie putt on the third. Both players bogeyed the fourth and, despite some wild drives on the sixth, seventh and eighth holes, Nicklaus still held a two-stroke lead at the turn. On the 10th, Nicklaus struck a 7-iron to within 3 feet of the flagstick, setting up an almost certain birdie. Staring squarely at a three-shot deficit, Aoki chipped in for birdie to match Nicklaus, who converted his putt. As they came down the stretch, Nicklaus later reflected, "I was feeling exceptional pressure. I had revamped my entire game, worked my tail off all season, but hadn't won in almost two years. As well as I'd played that week, it was hard not to wonder whether the wheels would stay on." With the television cameras focused solely on the final group, Nicklaus and Aoki matched one another stroke for stroke from the 11th to the 16th.

One of Baltusrol's unique characteristics is that it is the only course in U.S. Open history to finish with consecutive par 5s: the 630-yard 17th and 542-yard

18th. Because both were good scoring opportunities, Nicklaus wrote, "I was sure I needed at least a birdie and a par on the last two holes to avoid a play-off." On 17, Nicklaus hit a driver and 2-iron, leaving him 88 yards to a front-left hole location. After Aoki hit his approach to within 5 feet, Nicklaus hit his pitch safely out to the right of the hole, leaving an uphill 22-footer for birdie. "I played with Aoki all four rounds and the way he was putting I just knew he would make that one," said Nicklaus. Which meant that Nicklaus needed to make his putt to maintain his two-stroke advantage. And as he did so many times in his career, Nicklaus delivered when it mattered most. "That was probably as crucial a putt in a U.S. Open championship as I've ever made," said Nicklaus.

As Nicklaus predicted, Aoki made his putt. By maintaining his two-stroke lead, Nicklaus could afford to play conservatively on the final hole. He hit a 3-wood off the tee, laid up with a 3-iron and knocked a wedge to within 10 feet. He later said he was just trying to lag the putt close, but in true Nicklaus fashion it dropped in the center of the hole. His total of 272 broke by three strokes his own 72-hole scoring record from 1967 and gave him his fourth title, matching the mark of Willie Anderson, Bob Jones and Ben Hogan.

While the 40-year-old Nicklaus may not have been at his competitive peak, clearly he was still playing at an exceptionally high level. His victory in 1980 cemented his legacy as one of the greatest golfers of all time. But perhaps more than that, it represented the first championship in which the entire golf community finally embraced Nicklaus. For two decades he had been Arnold Palmer's foil, playing the villain who, in the eyes of the public, had denied The King several major championship titles. When he won the 1967 U.S. Open at Baltusrol, going head-to-head with Palmer, some fans printed signs that read, "Right Here Jack," with an arrow pointing down to a bunker. But by 1980, Nicklaus had won them over with his exceptional play and gracious sportsmanship. He showed this once again on the 72nd green, when he thrust his hand out to quiet the crowd long enough for Aoki to hole his final putt. But after the championship had been decided, Nicklaus was engulfed by adoring fans who chanted his name and climbed trees just to catch a glimpse of him. "It was really kind of neat, because I hadn't been part of what was going on for a long time," said Nicklaus. "It was just after the Olympic hockey team had won so there was a big American charge. The gallery was unbelievable and winning at Baltusrol again was something very, very special."

Despite his heroics on the course, the lasting image from this championship was a message spelled out by volunteers on the large leader board near the 18th green. It read: "Jack Is Back." And this time, the fans had embraced him with open arms.

The Global Game: The Rise of International Players

BY LEWINE MAIR

From its origins in 14th-century Scotland to its popular growth throughout Europe and North America, golf has constantly been captivating new audiences. Today, worldwide participation in golf has escalated so that, like the dimples that cover the sphere of a golf ball, the sport seemingly covers the globe and is played everywhere from the Maldives to Mongolia and from Tahiti to Tasmania. This global spread of the game makes up much of golf's glorious tapestry, and a glimpse of the game's shifting sands can be seen in the evolution of the U.S. Open since 1994.

As would be expected during the first years of a national championship in a country that was only recently bitten by the golf bug, the first 16 U.S. Opens, from 1895 to 1910, were won by Scottish or English professionals. But after Johnny McDermott became the first American-born player to win the U.S. Open, in 1911, the balance of power began to shift state side.

That shift became so pronounced that only three non-Americans – South Africa's Gary Player in 1965, England's Tony Jacklin in 1970 and Australia's David Graham in 1981 – won the U.S. Open between 1928 and 1993. Then came the seminal 1994 U.S. Open, which began an era of global parity for America's national championship. Including Ernie Els' victory at Oakmont Country Club that year, foreign players won 11 of the 19 subsequent U.S. Opens, through 2012.

This evolution has its roots in 1965, when Player became the first foreign-born U.S. Open champion since Tommy Armour's 1927 win, presaging golf's global growth in the decades to follow. Seve Ballesteros of Spain redrew golf's borders during the 1970s by helping to expand the Ryder Cup to include all of Europe in its biennial matches against the U.S., and Australia's Greg Norman became the world's top player during the 1980s. All the while, international competitors were making significant inroads at the Masters, winning 10 times at Augusta National between 1978 and 1994.

Even against this backdrop, Americans possessed a relatively dominant record in their national championship on the eve of the 1994 U.S. Open. But there were indications of the sea change to come, especially in the efforts of Ken Schofield, then CEO of the European Tour, who worked tirelessly to open additional playing opportunities on the PGA Tour for his charges. After making some progress, he achieved a breakthrough in 1994.

"In terms of real opportunity for European Tour members to play in majors," remembers Schofield, "the single biggest moment came in 1994, when the USGA agreed to exempt the top 15 from our Order of Merit into the U.S. Open."

Although the European contingent were eager to seize their chances in the States, these opportunities came hand in hand with the pressure of needing to prove themselves in an

Facing page: Rory McIlroy holds the U.S. Open Championship Trophy after the final round at the 2011 U.S. Open at Congressional. McIlroy rewrote the record books, tying or besting 12 U.S. Open records with his victory.

Australian David Graham won the 1981 U.S. Open at Merion.

environment where Americans had held the upper hand for so long. The weight fell most squarely on the shoulders of Colin Montgomerie, who nearly won the 1992 U.S. Open in his first appearance in the championship. Starting the final round six shots off the lead, the Scot posted a 2-under 70 at Pebble Beach in the wind while the leaders were playing in worsening conditions. Sitting inside, Montgomerie steadily climbed the leader board, and four-time U.S. Open champion Jack Nicklaus went so far as to congratulate him on television for his victory. Of course, it was Tom Kite and runner-up Jeff Sluman who upped their games in the worst of the weather to sneak in ahead of Montgomerie, but the writing was on the wall.

Montgomerie anticipated more chances to capture the U.S. Open. But even in his position as a perennial favorite, he was constantly reminded of the dominance displayed by U.S. players in their national championship.

"The fact that no one other than Australia's David Graham had won since Jacklin in 1970 was a big pressure on Nick Faldo and then on me," explained Montgomerie. "What would happen, is that you would be called to the media center as the leader

and, within a matter of minutes, the writers and TV people would be reminding you that no British player had won since Jacklin. It was almost as if they were saying that it wasn't possible for you to win, that it wasn't going to happen. By the time you left the room, you felt 10 times the amount of pressure on your shoulders than when you went in."

As Montgomerie discovered at Oakmont in 1994, the challenges of winning the U.S. Open come from all quarters, even those hardly anticipated prior to the championship. Even a player's clothing, which may seem like a trivial concern, can conspire against him. After playing well for four rounds, Montgomerie was sartorially ill-prepared for the 18-hole playoff on Monday against Els and Loren Roberts.

Mongomorie recalled:

"I was with Pringle at the time. Though they had given me six shirts at the start of the week, the sticky heat was such that I had none left by the Sunday night. Yes, I could have been sending them to the cleaners but, when you are playing in high temperatures and even higher humidity, you sweat a lot and a salt mark appears over the back of the shirt that nothing – at least

GREAT MOMENTS OF THE U.S. OPEN

Left Ernie Els, a promising young tennis player turned golfer, was the beneficiary of the strong South African junior golf programs that Gary Player helped establish. Els is seen here during his victory at the 1994 U.S. Open. **Right** Angel Cabrera became the first Argentinean to win the U.S. Open when he did so in 2007 at Oakmont Country Club in Oakmont, Pennsylvania.

in those days – would remove. The only acceptable shirt I could find for the Monday was one bearing a black-watch tartan.

I knew all about dark colors attracting heat, but I also had to consider Pringle. It was imperative that if I were not going to wear one of their shirts, I should wear one that was logo-free. The tartan number solved one problem but created another. The only trousers that went with it were navy blue, another wrong color for mid-summer America. By the time I had started par-double bogey-double bogey, I was not just hot but bothered. I had no chance. After that, I was trying to catch up with two great players and that was never going to happen."

Montgomerie shot 78, finishing four shots behind Els and Roberts, who were tied at 74 after 18 holes. The pair went to a sudden-death playoff, with Els prevailing after two extra holes. So instead of the likeliest candidate, Montgomerie, it was the 24-year-old South African who began the new era of international prominence in the U.S. Open.

"When you're in your early 20s," said Els following the play-off, "there's not too much fear around you. You haven't had too many disappointments. I felt it was my time and, when you've got that kind of confidence, you know you can do it."

Although Els had played in just one U.S. Open prior to his win, he had enjoyed success in America as a junior player. Ten years prior to his victory at Oakmont, Els had traveled halfway around the world, to San Diego, to win his age division in the Junior World Championship at Torrey Pines, defeating a local favorite named Phil Mickelson.

Els, a promising young tennis player turned golfer, was the beneficiary of the strong South African junior golf programs that Player had helped establish. Those programs also produced Retief Goosen, who was born just eight months before Els. Unlike Els, who won two U.S. Opens by the time he was 27, Goosen peaked later in his career, winning his two U.S. Opens in 2001 and 2004.

Els' second U.S. Open victory, at Congressional Country Club in 1997, again came at the expense of Montgomerie – as well as American Tom Lehman. In 2001, it was Goosen's turn as he came back to claim the championship at Southern Hills Country Club in Tulsa, Oklahoma, defeating Mark Brooks in

In 2010, Graeme McDowell, seen here driving on the 14th at Pebble Beach in the final round of the championship, became the first Northern Irishman to win the U.S. Open and the first European to win the championship since Tony Jacklin in 1970.

a playoff the day after missing a 2-foot putt on the 72nd hole. Three years later, Goosen redeemed the near-ignominy of his missed putt at Southern Hills with one of the finest putting displays in golf history. Over the final nine holes of the 2004 U.S. Open at Shinnecock Hills, Goosen had six one-putts on slick, firm putting surfaces that were confounding the best players in the world.

The U.S. Open torch lit by Els and Goosen was then seized by players from other countries. Goosen's 2004 victory began a string of four years of international U.S. Open winners. New Zealand's Michael Campbell captured the 2005 championship at Pinehurst Resort in North Carolina, and he was followed by Australia's Geoff Ogilvy, who was the only player among the

leaders who was able to safely negotiate the final hole of Winged Foot Golf Club to win the 2006 U.S. Open. The following year, Angel Cabrera, of Argentina, became the first player from South America to win the U.S. Open, having outlasted runners-up Jim Furyk and Tiger Woods at Oakmont.

Northern Ireland then took its turn in the spotlight as a pair of countrymen, Graeme McDowell in 2010 and Rory McIlroy in 2011, took the U.S. Open Trophy back to the Emerald Isle. In 2010, McDowell outlasted a number of big names, including Els, Mickelson and Woods, to win at firm, fast and windy Pebble Beach. McDowell, who was 30 at the time, took special meaning from defeating Els, whom he had idolized as a teen.

"I was only 14 at the time, but I was a big Ernie Els fan when he won at Oakmont," McDowell recalls. "I wanted the same Lynx clubs as he was using and the same Ashworth shirt that he was wearing."

Intriguingly, 1987 U.S. Women's Open winner Laura Davies, an Englishwoman, is one of many who feel that the advent of live television coverage of the U.S. Open around the world has greatly influenced today's international players. For Gary Player's 1965 victory at Bellerive Country Club in Missouri, only a few holes on the back nine were televised over the final two days of the championship. By 1994, two networks teamed up to provide more than 25 hours of coverage with cameras on all 18 holes. "I think Ernie probably did more than Gary Player in that regard," she says. "Great player that Gary was, golf fans couldn't follow his progress in the majors as they could Ernie's."

After inheriting the unofficial mantle as the face of international golf from Player and then Norman, Els has passed on the post to McIlroy, who put together one of the greatest performances in championship history at the 2011 U.S. Open at Congressional. The 21-year-old set or tied 12 U.S. Open scoring records, including the lowest 72-hole score (268) and lowest 72-score relative to par (16 under).

With nine international players winning 11 championships since 1994, the U.S. Open now reflects the current landscape of golf at the highest level. Today, top players from around the world play against each other much more frequently, thanks in large part to the World Golf Championships, which began when all of golf's major governing bodies from around the world joined forces in the late 1990s to have players from each tour participate together in tournaments.

As golf continues to expand globally, U.S. Open champions will surely emerge from countries that only recently began forging inroads into the game. No doubt, players from Asia will play a big role in the decades to come, led by potential stars such as 14-year-old Andy Zhang of China, who became the youngest contestant in U.S. Open history by qualifying for the 2012 championship at The Olympic Club in San Francisco. Although Zhang

Just as Gary Player and Ernie Els inspired subsequent generations, Andy Zhang and players like Y.E. Yang of South Korea are role models for the future of golf.

missed the cut, the golf audience would do well to heed his description of the game in his home country: "Golf hasn't developed as much as it has here. But people are starting to like the sport and it's becoming really popular."

Just as Player and Els inspired subsequent generations, Zhang and players like Y.E. Yang of South Korea, the first Asian player to win a major (the 2009 PGA Championship), are role models for the future of golf, especially in the world's largest continent. One of the great aspects of golf is its individuality, and a single player from even the most remote locations can develop and make an impact.

Perhaps that will be the fate of Ziwang Gurung, a teenager from Bhutan, a country with just nine holes and where Rick Lipsey, a visiting American, has introduced a junior program. Gurung, whose family lives in a nearby hut, was among the youngsters who signed up for lessons. In 2008, 16-year-old Gurung took his first trip abroad to play in a junior tournament in Vietnam. Incredibly, he finished second. Upon returning, Gurung found the prime minister of Bhutan waiting at the door of his home to proffer congratulations.

Now 19, Gurung is considering turning professional. But no matter which career he chooses, Gurung already has benefited greatly from his golf experiences. "It is helping to develop me and my overall education," he says. "I am meeting people from all over the world and, on top of all that, I get great pleasure from playing.

"Golf," he adds, "isn't just about golf."

As the increasingly global U.S. Open shows, that lesson is quickly being translated into different languages.

DOMINANCE

"The only way of finding the limits of the possible
is by going beyond them into the impossible."
– Arthur C. Clarke

The average margin of victory in the U.S. Open is less than three strokes. From 1895 to the present, nearly one-third of the championships have been decided by a playoff, and the title has been defended successfully only seven times. Golf's toughest test does not often lend itself to dominant performances. Their rare occurrence, however, makes these occasions all the more dramatic. Celebrated in the following pages are those few instances where an individual has humbled the field with a combination of power, precision and touch. Championships in which one player was in such command of his game, the course and the situation that he broke records and peers watched in awe – moments where excellence neared perfection.

Willie Anderson
TELLS ABOUT HIS GREAT RECORD MAKING VICTORY WITH A
HASKELL WHITE STREAK GOLF BALL
Time and time again in his match the perfectly balanced qualities of the WHITE STREAK overcame adverse conditions and carried true to the mark.

The First Four-Time Champion | Willie Anderson 1905

Willie Anderson, like many early American professionals, emigrated from Scotland and sought work at many of the new clubs springing up across the American landscape.

Facing page: Willie Anderson, perhaps one of golf's most tragic figures, was the first four-time U.S. Open champion. He capitalized on his notoriety by endorsing a line of golf balls manufactured by the Haskell Company.

On March 23, 1896, a 16-year-old aspiring golf professional from North Berwick, Scotland, named Willie Anderson arrived in New York Harbor on the SS *Pomeranian*. It is believed that his trip was sponsored by Frank Slazenger, the sporting goods entrepreneur who was looking to promote both the game and his products to a country that had only recently taken up golf. Anderson's eventual destination would be Rhode Island, where Slazenger had arranged for him to take up the position of assistant golf professional at Misquamicut Golf Club near Watch Hill.

Although Anderson's game had shown promise in Scotland, he was not considered an accomplished player. At the turn of the century, a club professional was expected to not only teach the game, but to oversee the upkeep of the course and to make and repair clubs. It was likely that his apprenticeships as a greenkeeper and club maker in Scotland were the primary reasons for his employment. Following his arrival, Anderson did not enter any significant competitions prior to the 1897 U.S. Open, which makes it all the more surprising that he finished second to Joe Lloyd by just one stroke at the Chicago Golf Club.

Anderson's runner-up finish in 1897 foreshadowed the arrival of one of the U.S. Open's greatest champions. Although he would not win the national championship until 1901, he would eventually go on to win the U.S. Open four times between 1901 and 1905, establishing records that remain to this day.

Many of Anderson's competitive traits would become synonymous with the qualities that make a player successful in the U.S. Open, even today. H.L. Fitzgerald outlined these characteristics in his article for *Everybody's Magazine* about the 1903 U.S. Open, writing that "the trait most pronounced

One of the first rivalries of American professional golf, Willie Anderson (left) and Alex Smith (right) won six of the first 10 U.S. Open Championships in the 20th century.

in Anderson's game is his resourcefulness. He is never dismayed and, no matter what the state of the match, Anderson is always capable of a great stroke that may turn the tide of victory in his favor." In a 1929 article for *The American Golfer,* Alexis J. Colman noted that Anderson's "imperturbability saved him many strokes under trying conditions."

Considered one of the premier courses in the United States at the turn of the century, Myopia Hunt Club in Massachusetts was the site of the 1905 U.S. Open. It was the third time in eight years that the prestigious club, located some 25 miles north of Boston, played host to the national championship. Anderson, who won the U.S. Open in 1901, 1903 and 1904, was the two-time defending champion. He opened with some mundane play over the first 36 holes, posting rounds of 80 and 81 that placed him well behind the leaders, including his rival, Alex Smith. Myopia was familiar ground for these two players, who had faced one another previously at the same club in a playoff for the 1901 U.S. Open title, when Anderson emerged the victor. The editors of *Golf,* the leading magazine on the sport at the turn of the century, detailed the setup for the 1905 U.S. Open, concluding that it was a course "where great golf is possible and where mediocre golf cannot win."

Although suffering from a recent bout with malaria, Smith was tied for the lead after 36 holes, a considerable testament to his determination, as well as his skill. At the start of the third round, he held a five-stroke advantage over Anderson but recorded an 80 to Anderson's 76, and his lead was cut to just one stroke. "It was evident to everybody that it was nothing but nerve and grit which upheld [Smith]" in the final round, but his courageous effort could only produce another 80, and he finished with a total of 316. Anderson now held a four-stroke lead as he came to the tee of the 380-yard, par-4 17th hole, but he scared the friendly gallery by slicing his drive badly into the deep rough, where it came to rest against the trunk of a tree. It took another four strokes for him to reach the green, where he one-putted for a double-bogey 6. Showing both resolve and composure on the final hole, "he drove a long, straight ball, pitched onto the green and ran down in two putts" to secure a par. The two-stroke victory secured his fourth U.S. Open title in five years. Alex Smith, who would go on to win the U.S. Open in 1906 and 1910, commented, "In my struggles to win the U.S. Open, Willie Anderson seemed to be my Nemesis."

"Anderson Wins Cup" and "Anderson Wins Title" were the headlines run by the *Washington Post* and *Chicago Daily Tribune* the following day. But these articles recounting his fourth victory in the national championship were written with little fanfare. It was too early in the championship's history for anyone to fully appreciate what Anderson had accomplished in winning four U.S. Open titles in just five years. Indeed, it would take some time. It was not until Bob Jones claimed his third U.S. Open in 1929 that Fred McLeod, a contemporary of Anderson's who won the 1908 U.S. Open (also played at Myopia) was able to put Anderson's record in perspective. When asked to compare Anderson's skill with that of Walter Hagen and Jones, McLeod replied simply, "as good as either one."

Tragically, Anderson's illustrious career was cut short at the age of 31. Complaining of bad headaches after playing three 36-hole matches, he died unexpectedly of an apparent epileptic fit in Philadelphia on October 25, 1910. Initially there were rumors that arteriosclerosis or alcoholism had caused his death, but his death certificate later confirmed the true cause.

Perhaps it was the Victorian distaste for the convivial habits of many Scottish golf professionals or Anderson's dour on-course demeanor that kept him from attracting widespread popularity. He complained to friends just before his death that "they don't know me," referring to the lack of public appreciation for his accomplishments. He was certainly not as celebrated by the American press as Harry Vardon, but off the course he was well liked by his fellow professionals, as well as by the members of the 10 clubs he served from 1896 to his death. Following his death, the members of the Apawamis Club in Rye, New York – where Anderson served as head professional from 1903 to 1905, when he won three of his four U.S. Open titles – held a fundraiser for his widow and young children.

Whatever the reasons, his dominance in the U.S. Open has often been overshadowed by the likes of fellow four-time champions Jones, Ben Hogan and Jack Nicklaus. As H.L. Fitzgerald wrote in the *New York Sun* at the time of Anderson's death, he "was the first pro of the highest class to be developed in this country." In 1905, Anderson set the standard that has come to define the greatest U.S. Open champions. And while the other members of this elite group – Jones (1923, 1926, 1929, 1930), Hogan (1948, 1950, 1951, 1953) and Nicklaus (1962, 1967, 1972, 1980) – are better known, no other player in history can lay claim to three consecutive U.S. Opens titles. From 1897 to 1910, Anderson finished in the top five 11 times and won the championship in 1901, 1903, 1904 and 1905, emerging as the first truly dominant player in U.S. Open history.

Willie Anderson used this mashie, equivalent to a modern-day 5-iron, in several U.S. Opens.

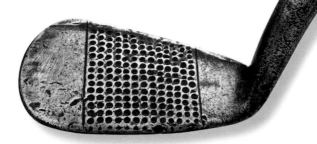

A British Breakthrough | Tony Jacklin 1970

Tony Jacklin is congratulated after winning the 1970 U.S. Open at Hazeltine National; it was only his second appearance in the championship.

Sports, like many other forms of cultural expression, including food, music and religion, represent the portable culture that immigrants brought with them and that helped shape the United States. Golf is no exception. The game came across the Atlantic from the British Isles at various points during the 18th and early 19th centuries and finally took hold in America in the last decade before the 20th century.

Through 1910, British golfers dominated the golf landscape worldwide. Even in the United States, the first 16 U.S. Open championships were won by men born in the United Kingdom. But by the 1910s, things had begun to change. Philadelphia's Johnny McDermott won the U.S. Open in 1911 and 1912, and Francis Ouimet became America's first golf hero the following year, when he defeated Harry Vardon and Ted Ray in a playoff at The Country Club in Brookline, Massachusetts. Inspired by Ouimet's victory, a new generation of homegrown talent emerged in the United States, led by Bob Jones, Walter Hagen and Gene Sarazen. The center of the golf world had shifted from Britain to the United States by the third decade of the 20th century. In fact, between 1928 and 2009, a stretch of 78 championships, only one European won the U.S. Open – Tony Jacklin in 1970.

Jacklin was playing in just his second U.S. Open, having finished in a tie for 25th, eight strokes behind Orville Moody, the previous year at Champions Golf Club in Houston. Later that summer, he won the British Open at Royal Lytham and St. Annes, becoming the first homebred champion since Max Faulkner in 1951. For the accomplishment, he was awarded the Order of the British Empire by Queen Elizabeth.

Jacklin became acquainted with the game at age nine, while caddieing for his father at a club in Scunthorpe, England, about 150 miles north of London. He left school at age 15 to work in a steel plant as an apprentice, but tired of working indoors, he answered a newspaper advertisement for an assistant professional position at Potters Bar Golf Club outside London. "The hours were long," said Jacklin, "but there was a putting green next to the shop and I spent a great deal of time practicing."

He honed his skills and turned professional at age 17. After some moderate success playing in Europe and South Africa in the mid-1960s, Jacklin won four tournaments and finished fifth in the Order of Merit in 1967. The following April, Jacklin won the Greater Jacksonville Open and briefly led during the third round of the Masters before finishing in a share of 22nd. In the spring of 1970, however, Jacklin gave little indication of what he would accomplish at Hazeltine National Golf Club. He had finished runner-up in the Tournament of Champions in April, but over the four weeks preceding the U.S. Open, Jacklin missed a cut and finished no better than 24th in three other events.

The 1970 championship marked the first time the U.S. Open returned to the Twin Cities area since Bob Jones had captured the third leg of his Grand Slam with a victory at Interlachen in 1930. Forty years had brought plenty of change to the golf landscape. The number of entries for the national championship had more than tripled, from 1,177 to 3,605. The total prize money of the event had grown from $5,000 to $200,000, and the course was now lined by more than 10 miles of gallery rope and patrolled by 360 marshals and 1,000 volunteers.

Due to his recent lackluster play, Jacklin consulted Jim Yancey, the brother of seven-time PGA Tour winner Bert Yancey, for a putting lesson on the Tuesday before the championship. "Jim told me that I wasn't standing over the ball as I should," said Jacklin. "The advice made me feel a lot more comfortable and enabled my hands to feel freer. It felt so natural during a practice round that afternoon that I didn't even play on Wednesday. I just took the day off."

Confidence on the greens was only a fraction of the battle in the opening round, however, as a 40-mile-per-hour wind swept across Hazeltine, wreaking havoc on the field. The wind was so strong that it nearly overturned a large scoreboard, ripped tents covering television towers and brought down large tree branches. After the dust settled, only 81 of the 150 competitors broke 80. The first-round scoring average of 79.1 was the highest in 12 years. Some of the game's best players struggled mightily. Arnold Palmer shot 79. Gary Player posted an 80. Jack Nicklaus turned in 43 and needed to rally for an 81, the highest score in his U.S. Open career until he posted 82 as a 60-year-old in 2000.

Tony Jacklin tees off at the seventh hole during the 1970 U.S. Open. Competitors struggled in 40-mile-per-hour winds during the first round of the championship.

A Tiger Stands Alone | Tiger Woods 2000

As he began his final round in the 2000 U.S. Open at Pebble Beach, the stage was set for Tiger Woods to claim his first U.S. Open championship. With a 10-stroke lead over Ernie Els, he stood on the first tee ready to fulfill the promise he had demonstrated as one of the most celebrated amateurs in the game's history. After winning USGA national championships in six consecutive years from 1991, to 1996 (three U.S. Junior Amateurs followed by three U.S. Amateurs), Woods' claim on the U.S. Open title seemed predestined.

His arrival on the professional tour was greatly anticipated, and he did not disappoint, as he won the 1997 Masters Tournament by 12 strokes in his first attempt as a professional. That same year, he finished 19th in his first professional appearance in the U.S. Open. In 1998, he bettered his finish by one position, before truly contending in 1999 and finishing third. By the start of Sunday's final round at Pebble Beach the following year, there was little doubt that Woods would claim his seventh and most significant national championship. How he won golf's toughest test would change the course of the professional game.

The 100th edition of the U.S. Open was staged at the site that had created many memorable moments in the championship's history. In the first U.S. Open played at Pebble Beach, Jack Nicklaus claimed the 1972 title after rattling the 17th-hole flagstick with his 1-iron tee shot in the final round. The 2000 U.S. Open marked Nicklaus' record-setting 44th consecutive, and final, appearance. As the Golden Bear said goodbye to the national championship following his second-round exit, Woods struck a drive on the first tee to begin his. It was a fitting changing of the guard from the greatest major champion of all time to the man who many suspected had the potential to surpass him.

Tiger Woods, seen holding the U.S. Open Championship Trophy, captured his first U.S. Open at Pebble Beach, the same venue where Jack Nicklaus, Tom Watson and Tom Kite recorded brilliant victories.

Facing page: Tiger Woods tees off alongside the Pacific Ocean on the final hole of the 2000 U.S. Open at Pebble Beach.

When faced with trouble, Tiger Woods was able to use his physical strength and superior course management skills to recover from even the most daunting of situations.

Woods finished his second round at eight under par and held a six-stroke lead over Spain's Miguel Angel Jiménez and Denmark's Thomas Bjørn. Strong winds off the ocean on Saturday afternoon created more challenging conditions than the players had faced in the first two rounds. Ernie Els, benefiting from an early start, avoided the windy conditions and posted a 68, the only sub-par round of the day, to finish at two over par through 54 holes. Woods, playing in the final group of the day, faced the worst of the wind and quickly dropped to six under par after finding the deep rough around the third green. Knowing that other players in contention would also struggle, he remained calm and reassured by the physical advantage he held over his fellow competitors.

Not only was Woods the longest player in the field, but his strength and sheer athleticism allowed him to play for the green even when he found trouble, as he did in the second round, when his tee shot found the deep rough to the right of the fairway of the par-5 sixth hole. Seemingly with no option but to pitch back to the fairway, Woods powered a 6-iron through the rough and propelled the ball onto the green en route to an unlikely birdie. This shot – from the deep rough, over a tree, a steep cliff and the ocean – was one only Woods would dare to play. Witnessing the shot, NBC commentator Roger Maltbie marveled, "It's just not a fair fight." So it was not a surprise that when Woods again found the deep rough on the eighth and 10th holes in the third round that he played imaginative and miraculous recovery shots, maintaining his momentum and keeping his competitors in awe.

After reaching the green in two with an iron from 245 yards at the uphill 573-yard, par-5 14th hole, Woods posted a birdie to get back to even par for the day and eight under par overall. He was now the only competitor under par for the championship. In the difficult conditions, the scoring average for the third round soared to 77.12. A routine par at the home hole gave Woods an even-par 71 and a 10-stroke lead over a distant Els.

On Sunday, June 18 at 12:40 in the afternoon, Woods stood on the first tee prepared to make history. The outcome of the championship may have been obvious to those outside the ropes, but Woods did not allow himself the luxury of that thought. His objectives were simply to increase his lead and not make a bogey in the final round. As a great champion, he had set a higher standard. It was not enough to win; he wanted to win his way. He later recalled that he wanted to "bury" the competition and "cruise coming in."

Missing only one fairway and one green in his first nine holes, Woods recorded nine consecutive pars to begin his final round. Reaching the 446-yard, par-4 10th hole with a wedge approach, he made his first birdie of the day. He went on to birdie the 12th, 13th and 14th holes to reach 12 under par and

increase his lead to 13 strokes, the largest in U.S. Open history. With his goal of a bogey-free round within reach, Woods' tee shot on the 16th hole finished in the intermediate cut of rough to the right of the fairway. Unable to control the spin of the ball, his approach landed at the back of the green and bounded into the deep rough beyond the green. His chip required a delicate touch to keep his ball from rolling off the front of the green. He played a bunker-like explosion shot, and the ball landed softly but rolled 15 feet past the hole. Woods did not change his routine. After carefully studying the uphill, right-to-left putt, he stroked it and then willed the ball into the hole. After the putt fell, Woods unleashed a steely-eyed look of determination at his caddie, Steve Williams. It gave the world a glimpse of the inner fire that consumes a great professional in pursuit of perfection. He later recalled, "that putt was huge for me," even

Tiger Woods escapes the sand on his way to his historic 15-stroke victory that shattered the U.S. Open record, which was held by Willie Smith for more than 100 years.

Spectators surround the 18th green at Pebble Beach to witness Tiger Woods complete his record-setting championship performance on June 18, 2000.

Facing page: Tiger Woods' sand wedge (notice the contradictory 58° and 56° markings) and final-round scorecard from the 2000 U.S. Open.

if it was not so for the gallery, the media or the record book. In the drama that unfolded that Sunday afternoon, Woods had already conquered man-versus-man and man-versus-nature. Only man-versus-himself remained relevant.

Woods went on to par the 17th and 18th holes to finish at 12 under par with a record-tying final score of 272, matching Jack Nicklaus (1980) and Lee Janzen (1993). His winning margin of 15 strokes shattered the record of 11 storkes set by Willie Smith in 1899. Tom Watson, who won the U.S. Open at Pebble Beach in 1982, put Woods' victory in perspective, noting, "He's the best player in the world right now. I think it is obvious, everyone else in the world is playing for second place and I think they know it." "Unbelievable," confessed the awe-struck Els following the final round. "I played the last 18 holes with Tiger, but we weren't playing the same game."

It was fitting that one of the most dominant performances in the history of sport marked the U.S. Open's 100th anniversary. At the end of the millennium, Woods ushered in a new era, where a professional golfer was not only required to be a skilled practitioner of the game, but also needed to have the physical conditioning and mental attitude of an athlete to succeed at the highest level. More than a decade later, Woods' influence is clear – what many in the 20th century considered just a "game" is now celebrated as a true athletic contest.

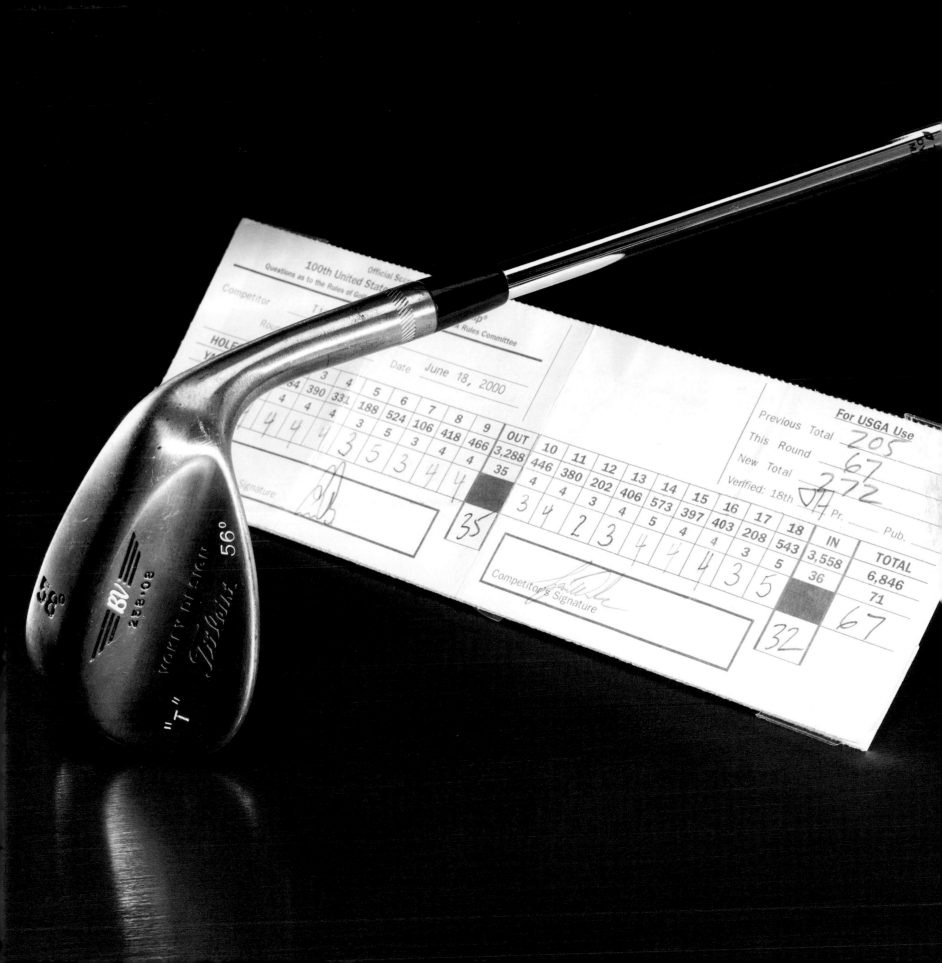

Sheer Brilliance | Rory McIlroy 2011

Rory McIlroy celebrates on the 18th green with his father after the final round of the 2011 U.S. Open at Congressional.

Earning a second chance to win a major championship in golf is rare. Players can wait years to atone for a title that slipped away. For some, the opportunity never comes again. Or, as in the case of Rory McIlroy, it could take just 10 weeks. Coming off a near-historic collapse at the Masters, McIlroy scorched the field at the 2011 U.S. Open at Congressional Country Club, winning by eight strokes and setting a dozen records in the process. In the span of a few days, the perception of the 22-year-old McIlroy shifted from a player with great potential who had trouble closing out tournaments to one of the game's most dominant players.

Because of his young age, the expectations heaped upon him and the manner in which he won, the inevitable comparisons to Tiger Woods began immediately after McIlroy's victory. "It was Tiger Woods of 11 years ago," said England's Ian Poulter, comparing McIlroy's dominance at Congressional to Woods' 15-stroke triumph at Pebble Beach in 2000. In many ways, the victories by Woods and McIlroy created excitement without drama. Their brilliance, exhibited by a rare separation from the field that left no doubt about the final result, left us wondering what heights they could reach.

Congressional Country Club, located just 11 miles outside of the nation's capital in Bethesda, Maryland, was hosting its third U.S. Open. The club had an undeniable connection to American politics. Designed by Devereux Emmet, Congressional was established in 1924 "to provide an informal common ground where politicians and businessmen could meet as peers, unconstrained by red tape." During World War II, Congressional formed a relationship with the Office of Strategic Services, which renamed the grounds "Area F" and used

Rory McIlroy plays from the rough on the third hole during the third round of the 2011 U.S. Open.

the property for training, missile testing and target range facilities to support the war effort. It is the only club to have five former U.S. presidents – William Howard Taft, Woodrow Wilson, Warren G. Harding, Calvin Coolidge and Herbert Hoover – as founding life members.

Only four players had bettered par in the first two U.S. Opens contested on the Blue Course at Congressional Country Club, which were won by Ken Venturi in 1964 (2-under-par 278) and Ernie Els in 1997 (4-under-par 276), but a perfect storm of circumstances left the course defenseless against McIlroy's historic assault in 2011. A heat wave had lingered in the Washington, D.C., metropolitan area the week prior to the championship, preventing the USGA from growing thick rough or cutting the greens to standard U.S. Open specifications for fear of losing them. When the temperatures dropped and rain moved in during U.S. Open week, the saturated course conditions allowed players to fire directly at hole locations that had been thought inaccessible just a week before. "This set-up [seems] a little more scorable than the previous two U.S. Opens I've played," said McIlroy before the start of the championship. He didn't take long to prove his point.

Starting on the 10th hole, McIlroy made six birdies while hitting 17 greens in regulation in an opening round of 65. He was the only player in the field without a bogey and held a three-stroke advantage over Y.E. Yang and reigning Masters champion Charl Schwartzel. The impressive day continued a trend of McIlroy starting well at major championships. He had opened with a 63 at the 2010 British Open and a 65 at the 2011 Masters. The question at Congressional, however, was if McIlroy could sustain his high level of play over four days – something he had not been able to do at St. Andrews, where he posted a second-round 80, or at Augusta, where he closed with an 80. "I don't know if it says I've got a short memory," said McIlroy, of his quick start. "You're going into the U.S. Open; you can't be thinking about what's happened before."

McIlroy's focus seemed only to intensify in the second round. The 2011 U.S. Open marked the fourth consecutive major in which he held at least a share of the lead at some juncture of the event. This time, he vowed to project a more confident demeanor on the course in an effort to avoid fading down the stretch. It worked. Out in the morning wave, the Ulsterman made six birdies and holed out a wedge from 114 yards for an eagle at the par-4 eighth en route to a 66. Not even a double bogey on the 18th hole could dampen his spirits as he opened a six-stroke lead at the midway point of the championship.

"I really don't know what to say," said McIlroy, whose 131 total was the lowest in U.S. Open history. "It's been two very, very good days of golf. To me, it really feels quite simple. I'm hitting fairways. I'm hitting greens. I'm holing my fair share of putts…. It's very nearly the best I can play."

But when we thought we had seen his best, McIlroy continued to improve upon his performance as scoring records fell by the wayside. A third-round 68 left him with a total of 14-under-par 199, the lowest 54-hole total in the championship's history. His eight-stroke lead at Congressional – double what it was at the Masters – seemed all but insurmountable, if not for the demons of Augusta. "[The Masters] was a great experience for me," said McIlroy. "It's hard, the first time in that situation. You're going to be feeling the pressure a little bit and I certainly did…. When you get yourself into that position again, you try and put those things that you want to do better into practice."

Putting to rest any doubts of a second consecutive collapse, McIlroy came out in the fourth round and continued his brilliant play. Using a "killer instinct" learned from Woods, McIlroy birdied the first and fourth holes to extend his lead to 10 strokes. There was never a serious challenge to his lead in the final round, but if there was a defining moment, it was at the 10th hole. Two months earlier at Augusta, McIlroy's four-stroke final-round lead had been cut to one through nine holes. At the 10th, he hooked his drive so far left it ended up near

The 6-iron used by Rory McIlroy during the 2011 U.S. Open Championship.

Facing page: Rory McIlroy plays his tee shot on the 10th hole during the final round at the 2011 U.S. Open at Congressional.

some of the club members' cabins, leading to a triple bogey and a second-nine 43. This time, at the same point in the championship, McIlroy selected a 6-iron at Congressional's 214-yard par 3 and took dead aim. His high-lofting shot cleared the fronting pond, landed on the top of a slope behind the hole and trickled down to within 6 inches, setting up a tap-in birdie.

"Walking off the 10th green today and walking off the 10th green at Augusta was a little different," said McIlroy, with a smile.

By the time the dust had settled at the end of the day, McIlroy had broken or tied 12 U.S. Open records. His 268 total bested the 72-hole scoring record by four strokes. His 16-under-par total was four better than Woods' from 2000. At 22 years, 1 month and 15 days, he was the youngest champion since Bob Jones in 1923. His 62 of 72 greens in regulation are the most since the record was formally tracked starting in 1980. Perhaps most telling is that runner-up Jason Day's 8-under-par total would have won 109 of the previous 110 U.S. Opens contested. In this championship, however, it was still eight shots behind McIlroy.

In the post-championship press conference, McIlroy discussed his respect for Woods' achievements and how, in trying to become an elite player, he had tried to emulate the man who has become a measuring stick for greatness on the course. "Growing up and watching him dominate at the Masters in '97 [and] at Pebble in 2000 ... [I'm] just trying to go out there with the same intensity he has." Woods, who was absent from the championship due to a knee injury, even sent McIlroy a message after the victory – "What a performance from start to finish. Enjoy the win. Well done."

As McIlroy had discovered in previous defeats, being destined for greatness can come with a heavy burden. There will be disappointments, struggles and doubts throughout every player's career, but it is how you respond to these setbacks that defines your character. Throughout the week at Congressional, McIlroy put it all together in spectacular, dominating fashion, leaving the memories of Augusta behind him for good. It was a spectacular display of shot-making that had his peers piling on the accolades. "I think he has probably the most talent I've ever seen from a golfer," said Luke Donald, at the time the world's top-ranked player. "Nothing this kid does surprises me," said Graeme McDowell, the 2010 U.S. Open champion, adding, "He's the best player I've ever seen.... He's great for golf. He's a breath of fresh air for the game and perhaps we're ready for golf's next superstar. Maybe Rory is it."

A few years earlier, Woods spoke about breaking through for his first major championship title as a 21-year-old at Augusta in 1997. "It's not easy to gain that experience," said Woods, who had amassed 14 major championship titles through 2012. "But once you're able to get one, then it becomes easier to get the

Rory McIlroy walks past the monster board near the 10th green during the final round at Congressional Country Club.

others.... It's a matter of getting that experience and building on it from there."

McIlroy validated his win at Congressional by blowing away the field with another eight-stroke victory at the 2012 PGA Championship at Kiawah Island's Ocean Course. His accomplishments and seemingly unlimited potential have the golf world wondering if Rory McIlroy, like Nicklaus and Woods before him, will be the defining player of his generation.

Rory McIlroy holds the U.S. Open Championship Trophy after the final round of the 2011 championship at Congressional.

Champions and Records | 1895 to 2012

CHAMPIONSHIP RESULTS				
YEAR	**DATES**	**CHAMPION, SCORE**	**RUNNER(S)-UP, SCORE**	**COURSE**	**ENTRIES**
1895	Oct. 4	Horace Rawlins, 173	Willie Dunn, 175	Newport G.C., R.I.	11
1896	July 18	James Foulis, 152	Horace Rawlins, 155	Shinnecock Hills G.C., Southampton, N.Y.	35
1897	Sept. 17	Joe Lloyd, 162	Willie Anderson, 163	Chicago G.C., Wheaton, Ill.	35
1898: EXPANDED TO 72 HOLES					
1898	June 17–18	Fred Herd, 328	Alex Smith, 335	Myopia Hunt Club, S. Hamilton, Mass.	49
1899	Sept. 14–15	Willie Smith, 315	George Low, Val Fitzjohn, W.H. Way, 326	Baltimore C.C. (Roland Park Course), Md.	81
1900	Oct. 4–5	Harry Vardon, 313	J.H. Taylor, 315	Chicago G.C., Wheaton, Ill.	60
1901	June 14–16	Willie Anderson, 331-85	Alex Smith, 331-86	Myopia Hunt Club, S. Hamilton, Mass.	60
1902	Oct. 10–11	Laurence Auchterlonie, 307	Stewart Gardner, Walter J. Travis (a), 313	Garden City G.C., N.Y.	90
1903	June 26–29	Willie Anderson, 307-82	David Brown, 307-84	Baltusrol G.C. (Original Course), Springfield, N.J.	89
1904	July 8–9	Willie Anderson, 303	Gilbert Nicholls, 308	Glen View Club, Golf, Ill.	71
1905	Sept. 21–22	Willie Anderson, 314	Alex Smith, 316	Myopia Hunt Club, S. Hamilton, Mass.	83
1906	June 28–29	Alex Smith, 295	Willie Smith, 302	Onwentsia Club, Lake Forest, Ill.	68
1907	June 20–21	Alex Ross, 302	Gilbert Nicholls, 304	Philadelphia Cricket Club (St. Martin's Course), Chestnut Hill, Pa.	82
1908	Aug. 27–29	Fred McLeod, 322-77	Willie Smith, 322-83	Myopia Hunt Club, S. Hamilton, Mass.	88
1909	June 24–25	George Sargent, 290	Tom McNamara, 294	Englewood G.C., N.J.	84
1910	June 17–20	Alex Smith, 298-71	John J. McDermott, 298-75; Macdonald Smith, 298-77	Philadelphia Cricket Club (St. Martin's Course), Chestnut Hill, Pa.	75
1911	June 23–26	John J. McDermott, 307-80	Michael J. Brady, 307-82; George O. Simpson, 307-85	Chicago G.C., Wheaton, Ill.	79
1912	Aug. 1–2	John J. McDermott, 294 (-2)	Tom McNamara, 296	Country Club of Buffalo, N.Y.	131
1913	Sept. 18–20	Francis Ouimet (a), 304 (+20)-72	Harry Vardon, 304-77; Edward Ray, 304-78	The Country Club (Original Course), Brookline, Mass.	165
1914	Aug. 20–21	Walter Hagen, 290 (+2)	Charles Evans Jr., 291	Midlothian C.C., Blue Island, Ill.	129
1915	June 17–18	Jerome D. Travers (a), 297 (+9)	Tom McNamara, 298	Baltusrol G.C. (Revised Course), Springfield, N.J.	141
1916	June 29–30	Charles Evans Jr. (a), 286 (-2)	Jock Hutchison, 288	Minikahda Club, Minneapolis, Minn.	94
1917–18: NO CHAMPIONSHIPS: WORLD WAR I					
1919	June 9–12	Walter Hagen, 301 (+17)-77	Michael J. Brady, 301-78	Brae Burn C.C., West Newton, Mass.	142
1920	Aug. 12–13	Edward Ray, 295 (+7)	Harry Vardon, Jack Burke Sr., Leo Diegel, Jock Hutchison, 296	Inverness Club, Toledo, Ohio	265
1921	July 21–22	James M. Barnes, 289 (+9)	Walter Hagen, Fred McLeod, 298	Columbia C.C., Chevy Chase, Md.	262
1922: FIRST YEAR TICKETS WERE SOLD					
1922	July 14–15	Gene Sarazen, 288 (+8)	Robert T. Jones Jr. (a), John L. Black, 289	Skokie C.C., Glencoe, Ill.	323
1923	July 13–15	Robert T. Jones Jr. (a), 296 (+8)-76	Bobby Cruickshank, 296-78	Inwood C.C., N.Y.	360
1924: FIRST YEAR OF SECTIONAL QUALIFYING					
1924	June 5–6	Cyril Walker, 297 (+9)	Robert T. Jones Jr. (a), 300	Oakland Hills C.C. (South Course), Birmingham, Mich.	319
1925	June 3–5	William Macfarlane, 291 (+7)-75-72	Robert T. Jones Jr. (a), 291-75-73	Worcester C.C., Mass.	445
1926: 36 HOLES ON LAST DAY INITIATED					
1926	July 8–10	Robert T. Jones Jr. (a), 293 (+5)	Joe Turnesa, 294	Scioto C.C., Columbus, Ohio	694
1927	June 14–17	Tommy Armour, 301 (+13)-76	Harry Cooper, 301-79	Oakmont C.C., Pa.	898
1928	June 21–24	Johnny Farrell, 294 (+10)-143	Robert T. Jones Jr. (a), 294-144	Olympia Fields C.C. (No. 4 Course), Matteson, Ill.	1,064
1929	June 27–30	Robert T. Jones Jr. (a), 294 (+6)-141	Al Espinosa, 294-164	Winged Foot G.C. (West Course), Mamaroneck, N.Y.	1,000
1930	July 10–12	Robert T. Jones Jr. (a), 287 (-1)	Macdonald Smith, 289	Interlachen C.C., Minneapolis, Minn.	1,177
1931	July 2–6	Billy Burke, 292 (+8)-149-148	George Von Elm, 292-149-149	Inverness Club, Toledo, Ohio	1,141
1932	June 23–25	Gene Sarazen, 286 (+6)	Bobby Cruickshank, T. Philip Perkins, 289	Fresh Meadow C.C., Flushing, N.Y.	1,011
1933	June 8–10	John Goodman (a), 287 (-1)	Ralph Guldahl, 288	North Shore G.C., Glenview, Ill.	915
1934	June 7–9	Olin Dutra, 293 (+13)	Gene Sarazen, 294	Merion Cricket Club (East Course), Ardmore, Pa.	1,063
1935	June 6–8	Sam Parks Jr., 299 (+11)	Jimmy Thomson, 301	Oakmont C.C., Pa.	1,125
1936	June 4–6	Tony Manero, 282 (-6)	Harry Cooper, 284	Baltusrol G.C. (Upper Course), Springfield, N.J.	1,277
1937	June 10–12	Ralph Guldahl, 281 (-7)	Sam Snead, 283	Oakland Hills C.C. (South Course), Birmingham, Mich.	1,402
1938	June 9–11	Ralph Guldahl, 284 (E)	Dick Metz, 290	Cherry Hills C.C., Englewood, Colo.	1,223
1939	June 8–12	Byron Nelson, 284 (+8)-68-70	Craig Wood, 284-68-73; Denny Shute, 284-76	Philadelphia C.C. (Spring Mill Course), West Conshohocken, Pa.	1,193
1940	June 6–8	Lawson Little, 287 (-1)-70	Gene Sarazen, 287-73	Canterbury G.C., Cleveland, Ohio	1,161
1941	June 5–7	Craig Wood, 284 (+4)	Denny Shute, 287	Colonial C.C., Fort Worth, Texas	1,048
1942–45: NO CHAMPIONSHIPS: WORLD WAR II					
1946	June 13–16	Lloyd Mangrum, 284 (-4)-72-72	Byron Nelson, 284-72-73; Victor Ghezzi, 284-72-73	Canterbury G.C., Cleveland, Ohio	1,175
1947	June 12–15	Lew Worsham, 282 (-2)-69	Sam Snead, 282-70	St. Louis C.C., Clayton, Mo.	1,356
1948	June 10–12	Ben Hogan, 276 (-8)	Jimmy Demaret, 278	Riviera C.C., Los Angeles, Calif.	1,411
1949	June 9–11	Cary Middlecoff, 286 (+2)	Sam Snead, Clayton Heafner, 287	Medinah C.C. (No. 3 Course), Ill.	1,348

Continued ↗   All tables (a): Amateur

YEAR	DATES	CHAMPION, SCORE	RUNNER(S)-UP, SCORE	COURSE	ENTRIES
1950	June 8–11	Ben Hogan, 287 (+7)-69	Lloyd Mangrum, 287-73; George Fazio, 287-75	Merion G.C. (East Course), Ardmore, Pa.	1,379
1951	June 14–16	Ben Hogan, 287 (+7)	Clayton Heafner, 289	Oakland Hills C.C. (South Course), Birmingham, Mich.	1,511
1952	June 12–14	Julius Boros, 281 (+1)	Ed S. Oliver, 285	Northwood Club, Dallas, Texas	1,688
1953	June 11–13	Ben Hogan, 283 (-5)	Sam Snead, 289	Oakmont C.C., Pa.	1,669
1954	June 17–19	Ed Furgol, 284 (+4)	Gene Littler, 285	Baltusrol G.C. (Lower Course), Springfield, N.J.	1,928
1955	June 16–19	Jack Fleck, 287 (+7)-69	Ben Hogan, 287-72	The Olympic Club (Lake Course), San Francisco, Calif.	1,522
1956	June 14–16	Cary Middlecoff, 281 (+1)	Julius Boros, Ben Hogan, 282	Oak Hill C.C. (East Course), Rochester, N.Y.	1,921
1957	June 13–16	Dick Mayer, 282 (+2)-72	Cary Middlecoff, 282-79	Inverness Club, Toledo, Ohio	1,907
1958	June 12–14	Tommy Bolt, 283 (+3)	Gary Player, 287	Southern Hills C.C., Tulsa, Okla.	2,132
1959	June 11–13	Billy Casper, 282 (+2)	Bob Rosburg, 283	Winged Foot G.C. (West Course), Mamaroneck, N.Y.	2,385
1960	June 16–18	Arnold Palmer, 280 (-4)	Jack Nicklaus (a), 282	Cherry Hills C.C., Englewood, Colo.	2,453
1961	June 15–17	Gene Littler, 281 (+1)	Doug Sanders, Bob Goalby, 282	Oakland Hills C.C. (South Course), Birmingham, Mich.	2,449
1962	June 14–17	Jack Nicklaus, 283 (-1)-71	Arnold Palmer, 283-74	Oakmont C.C., Pa.	2,475
1963	June 20–23	Julius Boros, 293 (+9)-70	Jacky Cupit, 293-73; Arnold Palmer, 293-76	The Country Club (Championship Course), Brookline, Mass.	2,392
1964	June 18–20	Ken Venturi, 278 (-2)	Tommy Jacobs, 282	Congressional C.C. (Composite Course), Bethesda, Md.	2,341
1965: FIRST YEAR OF 18 HOLES FOR FOUR CONSECUTIVE DAYS					
1965	June 17–21	Gary Player, 282 (+2)-71	Kel Nagle, 282-74	Bellerive C.C., St. Louis, Mo.	2,271
1966	June 16–20	Billy Casper, 278 (-2)-69	Arnold Palmer, 278-73	The Olympic Club (Lake Course), San Francisco, Calif.	2,475
1967	June 15–18	Jack Nicklaus, 275 (-5)	Arnold Palmer, 279	Baltusrol G.C. (Lower Course), Springfield, N.J.	2,651
1968	June 13–16	Lee Trevino, 275 (-5)	Jack Nicklaus, 279	Oak Hill C.C. (East Course), Rochester, N.Y.	3,007
1969	June 12–15	Orville Moody, 281 (+1)	Deane Beman, Al Geiberger, Bob Rosburg, 282	Champions G.C. (Cypress Creek Course), Houston, Texas	3,397
1970	June 18–21	Tony Jacklin, 281 (-7)	Dave Hill, 288	Hazeltine National G.C., Chaska, Minn.	3,605
1971	June 17–21	Lee Trevino, 280 (E)-68	Jack Nicklaus, 280-71	Merion G.C. (East Course), Ardmore, Pa.	4,279
1972	June 15–18	Jack Nicklaus, 290 (+2)	Bruce Crampton, 293	Pebble Beach G.L., Calif.	4,196
1973	June 14–17	Johnny Miller, 279 (-5)	John Schlee, 280	Oakmont C.C., Pa.	3,580
1974	June 13–16	Hale Irwin, 287 (+7)	Forrest Fezler, 289	Winged Foot G.C. (West Course), Mamaroneck, N.Y	3,914
1975	June 19–23	Lou Graham, 287 (+3)-71	John Mahaffey, 287-73	Medinah C.C. (No. 3 Course), Ill.	4,214
1976	June 17–20	Jerry Pate, 277 (-3)	Tom Weiskopf, Al Geiberger, 279	Atlanta Athletic Club (Highlands Course), Duluth, Ga.	4,436
1977	June 16–19	Hubert Green, 278 (-2)	Lou Graham, 279	Southern Hills C.C., Tulsa, Okla.	4,608
1978	June 15–18	Andy North, 285 (+1)	J.C. Snead, Dave Stockton, 286	Cherry Hills C.C., Englewood, Colo.	4,897
1979	June 14–17	Hale Irwin, 284 (E)	Gary Player, Jerry Pate, 286	Inverness Club, Toledo, Ohio	4,853
1980	June 12–15	Jack Nicklaus, 272 (-8)	Isao Aoki, 274	Baltusrol G.C. (Lower Course), Springfield, N.J.	4,812
1981	June 18–21	David Graham, 273 (-7)	Bill Rogers, George Burns, 276	Merion G.C. (East Course), Ardmore, Pa.	4,946
1982	June 17–20	Tom Watson, 282 (-6)	Jack Nicklaus, 284	Pebble Beach G.L., Calif.	5,255
1983	June 16–20	Larry Nelson, 280 (-4)	Tom Watson, 281	Oakmont C.C., Pa.	5,039
1984	June 14–18	Fuzzy Zoeller, 276 (-4)-67	Greg Norman, 276-75	Winged Foot G.C. (West Course), Mamaroneck, N.Y.	5,195
1985	June 13–16	Andy North, 279 (-1)	Denis Watson, Dave Barr, Tze-Chung Chen, 280	Oakland Hills C.C. (South Course), Birmingham, Mich.	5,274
1986	June 12–15	Raymond Floyd, 279 (-1)	Lanny Wadkins, Chip Beck, 281	Shinnecock Hills G.C., Southampton, N.Y.	5,410
1987	June 18–21	Scott Simpson, 277 (-3)	Tom Watson, 278	The Olympic Club (Lake Course), San Francisco, Calif.	5,696
1988	June 16–20	Curtis Strange, 278 (-6)-71	Nick Faldo, 278-75	The Country Club (Championship Course), Brookline, Mass.	5,775
1989	June 15–18	Curtis Strange, 278 (-2)	Ian Woosnam, Chip Beck, Mark McCumber, 279	Oak Hill C.C. (East Course), Rochester, N.Y.	5,786
1990	June 14–18	Hale Irwin, 280 (-8)-74-3	Mike Donald, 280-74-4	Medinah C.C. (No. 3 Course), Ill.	6,198
1991	June 13–17	Payne Stewart, 282 (-6)-75	Scott Simpson, 282-77	Hazeltine National G.C., Chaska, Minn.	6,063
1992	June 18–21	Tom Kite, 285 (-3)	Jeff Sluman, 287	Pebble Beach G.L., Calif.	6,244
1993	June 17–20	Lee Janzen, 272 (-8)	Payne Stewart, 274	Baltusrol G.C. (Lower Course), Springfield, N.J.	5,905
1994	June 16–20	Ernie Els, 279 (-5)-74-4-4	Loren Roberts, 279-74-4-5; Colin Montgomerie, 279-78	Oakmont C.C., Pa.	6,010
1995	June 15–18	Corey Pavin, 280 (E)	Greg Norman, 282	Shinnecock Hills G.C., Southampton, N.Y.	6,001
1996	June 13–16	Steve Jones, 278 (-2)	Davis Love III, Tom Lehman, 279	Oakland Hills C.C. (South Course), Bloomfield Hills, Mich.	5,925
1997	June 12–15	Ernie Els, 276 (-4)	Colin Montgomerie, 277	Congressional C.C. (Blue Course), Bethesda, Md.	7,013
1998	June 18–21	Lee Janzen, 280 (E)	Payne Stewart, 281	The Olympic Club (Lake Course), San Francisco, Calif.	7,117
1999	June 17–20	Payne Stewart, 279 (-1)	Phil Mickelson, 280	Pinehurst Resort (No. 2 Course), Village of Pinehurst, N.C.	7,889
2000	June 15–18	Tiger Woods, 272 (-12),	Ernie Els, Miguel Angel Jimenez, 287	Pebble Beach G.L., Calif.	8,455
2001	June 14–18	Retief Goosen, 276 (-4)-70	Mark Brooks, 276-72	Southern Hills C.C., Tulsa, Okla.	8,398
2002: FIRST YEAR OF TWO-TEE STARTS					
2002	June 13–16	Tiger Woods, 277 (-3)	Phil Mickelson, 280	Bethpage State Park (Black Course), Farmingdale, N.Y.	8,648
2003	June 12–15	Jim Furyk, 272 (-8)	Stephen Leaney, 275	Olympia Fields C.C. (North Course), Ill.	7,820
2004	June 17–20	Retief Goosen, 276 (-4)	Phil Mickelson, 278	Shinnecock Hills G.C., Southampton, N.Y.	8,726
2005: FIRST YEAR OF INTERNATIONAL QUALIFYING					
2005	June 16–19	Michael Campbell, 280 (E)	Tiger Woods, 282	Pinehurst Resort (No. 2 Course), Village of Pinehurst, N.C.	9,048
2006	June 15–18	Geoff Ogilvy, 285 (+5)	Jim Furyk, Colin Montgomerie, Phil Mickelson, 286	Winged Foot G.C. (West Course), Mamaroneck, N.Y.	8,584
2007	June 14–17	Angel Cabrera, 285 (+5)	Jim Furyk, Tiger Woods, 286	Oakmont C.C., Pa.	8,544
2008	June 12–16	Tiger Woods, 283 (-1)-71-4	Rocco Mediate, 283-71-5	Torrey Pines G.C. (South Course), San Diego, Calif.	8,390
2009	June 18–22	Lucas Glover, 276 (-4)	Phil Mickelson, David Duval, Ricky Barnes, 278	Bethpage State Park (Black Course), Farmingdale, N.Y.	9,086
2010	June 17–20	Graeme McDowell, 284 (E)	Gregory Havret, 285	Pebble Beach G.L., Calif.	9,052
2011	June 16–19	Rory McIlroy, 268 (-16)	Jason Day, 276	Congressional C.C. (Blue Course), Bethesda, Md.	8,300
2012	June 14–17	Webb Simpson, 281 (+1)	Michael Thompson, Graeme McDowell, 282	The Olympic Club (Lake Course), San Francisco, Calif.	9,006

SCORING

Evolution of U.S. Open Scoring Records

36 HOLES

173	Horace Rawlins (91-82), 1895
152	James Foulis (78-74), 1896

72 HOLES

328	Fred Herd (84-85-75-84), 1898
315	Willie Smith (77-82-79-77), 1899
313	Harry Vardon (79-78-76-80), 1900
307	Laurie Auchterlonie (78-78-74-77), 1902
303	Willie Anderson (75-78-78-72), 1904
295	Alex Smith (73-74-73-75), 1906
290	George Sargent (75-72-72-71), 1909
286	Charles Evans Jr. (70-69-74-73), 1916
282	Tony Manero (73-69-73-67), 1936
281	Ralph Guldahl (71-69-72-69), 1937
276	Ben Hogan (67-72-68-69), 1948
275	Jack Nicklaus (71-67-72-65), 1967
272	Jack Nicklaus (63-71-70-68), 1980
272	Lee Janzen (67-67-69-69), 1993
272	Tiger Woods (65-69-71-67), 2000
272	Jim Furyk (67-66-67-72), 2003
268	Rory McIlroy (65-66-68-69), 2011

Additional Scoring Records

LOWEST SCORE, 72 HOLES

268	Rory McIlroy (65-66-68-69), Congressional C.C. (Blue Course), Bethesda, Md., 2011
272	Jack Nicklaus (63-71-70-68), Baltusrol G.C. (Lower Course), Springfield, N.J., 1980
272	Lee Janzen (67-67-69-69), Baltusrol G.C. (Lower Course), Springfield, N.J., 1993
272	Tiger Woods (65-69-71-67), Pebble Beach G.L., Calif., 2000
272	Jim Furyk (67-66-67-72), Olympia Fields C.C. (North Course), Ill., 2003
273	David Graham (68-68-70-67), Merion G.C. (East Course), Ardmore, Pa., 1981

MOST STROKES UNDER PAR, 72 HOLES

16 under (268)	Rory McIlroy, Congressional C.C. (Blue Course), Bethesda, Md., 2011
12 under (272)	Tiger Woods, Pebble Beach G.L., Calif., 2000
8 under (272)	Jack Nicklaus, Baltusrol G.C., (Lower Course) Springfield, N.J., 1980
8 under (272)	Lee Janzen, Baltusrol G.C. (Lower Course), Springfield, N.J., 1993
8 under (272)	Jim Furyk, Olympia Fields C.C. (North Course), Ill., 2003
8 under (276)	Ben Hogan, Riviera C.C., Los Angeles, Calif., 1948
8 under (280)	Mike Donald, Medinah C.C. (No. 3 Course), Ill., 1990
8 under (280)	Hale Irwin, Medinah C.C. (No. 3 Course), Ill., 1990

LOWEST SCORE, ANY ROUND

63 (-8)	Johnny Miller, final round, Oakmont C.C., Pa., 1973
63 (-7)	Tom Weiskopf, first round, Baltusrol G.C. (Lower Course), Springfield, N.J., 1980
63 (-7)	Jack Nicklaus, first round, Baltusrol G.C. (Lower Course), Springfield, N.J., 1980
63 (-7)	Vijay Singh, second round, Olympia Fields C.C. (North Course), Ill., 2003

LARGEST 54-HOLE LEAD

10	Tiger Woods (205), Pebble Beach G.L., Calif., 2000
8	Rory McIlroy (199), Congressional C.C. (Blue Course), Bethesda, Md., 2011
7	James Barnes (217), Columbia C.C., Chevy Chase, Md., 1921

LARGEST 36-HOLE LEAD

6	Tiger Woods (134), Pebble Beach G.L., Calif., 2000
6	Rory McIlroy (131), Congressional C.C. (Blue Course), Bethesda, Md., 2011
5	Willie Anderson (149), Baltusrol G.C. (Original Course), Springfield, N.J., 1903
4	Tom McNamara (142), Englewood G.C., N.J., 1909
4	James Barnes (144), Columbia C.C., Chevy Chase, Md., 1921

LARGEST 18-HOLE LEAD

5	Tommy Armour (68), North Shore C.C., Glenview, Ill., 1933
4	Olin Dutra (69), Fresh Meadow C.C., Flushing, N.Y., 1932

BEST COMEBACK BY WINNER, FINAL ROUND

7 strokes	Arnold Palmer (72-71-72-65), Cherry Hills C.C., Englewood, Colo., 1960
6 strokes	Johnny Miller (71-69-76-63), Oakmont C.C., Pa, 1973
5 strokes	Johnny Farrell (77-74-71-72), Olympia Fields C.C. (No. 4 Course), Matteson, Ill., 1928
5 strokes	Byron Nelson (72-73-71-68), Philadelphia C.C. (Spring Mill Course), West Conshohocken, Pa., 1939
5 strokes	Lee Janzen (73-66-73-68), The Olympic Club (Lake Course), San Francisco, Calif., 1998

BEST COMEBACK BY WINNER, FINAL 36 HOLES

11 strokes	Lou Graham, Medinah C.C. (No. 3 Course), Ill., 1975

BEST COMEBACK BY WINNER, FINAL 54 HOLES

9 strokes	Jack Fleck, The Olympic Club (Lake Course), San Francisco, Calif., 1955

LARGEST WINNING MARGIN

15 strokes	Tiger Woods (272), Pebble Beach G.L., Calif., 2000 (largest winning margin in all majors)
11 strokes	Willie Smith (315), Baltimore C.C., Md., 1899

Continued ↗

HIGHEST WINNING SCORE

331	Willie Anderson, Myopia Hunt Club, South Hamilton, Mass., 1901 (won in playoff)

HIGHEST WINNING SCORE SINCE WORLD WAR II

293	Julius Boros, The Country Club (Championship Course), Brookline, Mass., 1963 (won in playoff)
290	Jack Nicklaus, Pebble Beach G.L., Calif., 1972

HIGHEST 36-HOLE CUT SINCE WORLD WAR II

155 (+15)	The Olympic Club (Lake Course), San Francisco, Calif., 1955
154 (+14)	Southern Hills C.C., Tulsa, Okla., 1958
154 (+10)	Pebble Beach G.L., Calif., 1972

LOWEST 36-HOLE CUT

143 (+3)	Olympia Fields C.C. (North Course), Ill., 2003
144 (+4)	Baltusrol G.C. (Lower Course), Springfield, N.J., 1993
144 (+4)	Bethpage State Park (Black Course), Farmingdale, N.Y., 2009
145 (+1)	Medinah C.C. (No. 3 Course), Ill., 1990
145 (+5)	Oakland Hills C.C. (South Course), Birmingham, Mich., 1985
145 (+5)	Oak Hill C.C. (East Course), Rochester, N.Y., 1989
145 (+5)	Shinnecock Hills G.C., Southampton, N.Y., 2004

MOST SUB-PAR ROUNDS BY ONE PLAYER IN ONE CHAMPIONSHIP

4	Sam Snead, St. Louis C.C., Mo., 1947 (one round in playoff)
4	Billy Casper, The Olympic Club (Lake Course), San Francisco, Calif., 1966 (one round in playoff)
4	Lee Trevino, Oak Hill C.C. (East Course), Rochester, N.Y., 1968
4	Tony Jacklin, Hazeltine National G.C., Chaska, Minn., 1970
4	Lee Janzen, Baltusrol G.C. (Lower Course), Springfield, N.J., 1993
4	Curtis Strange, Oakmont C.C., Pa., 1994
4	Rory McIlroy, Congressional C.C. (Blue Course), Bethesda, Md., 2011
4	Robert Garrigus, Congressional C.C. (Blue Course), Bethesda, Md., 2011

U.S. OPEN PLAYOFFS

YEAR	CHAMPION	SCORE	RUNNER(S)-UP	SCORE
18 HOLES				
1901	Willie Anderson	85	Alex Smith	86
1903	Willie Anderson	82	David Brown	84
1908	Fred McLeod	77	Willie Smith	83
1910	Alex Smith	71	John J. McDermott	75
			Macdonald Smith	77
1911	John J. McDermott	80	Michael J. Brady	82
			George Simpson	85
1913	Francis Ouimet (a)	72	Harry Vardon	77
			Edward Ray	78
1919	Walter Hagen	77	Michael J. Brady	78
1923	Robert T. Jones Jr. (a)	76	Bobby Cruickshank	78
1925	William Macfarlane	75-72	Robert T. Jones Jr. (a)	75-73
1927	Tommy Armour	76	Harry Cooper	79
1939	Byron Nelson	68-70	Craig Wood	68-73
			Denny Shute	76
1940	Lawson Little	70	Gene Sarazen	73
1946	Lloyd Mangrum	72-72	Byron Nelson, Victor Ghezzi	72-73
1947	Lew Worsham	69	Sam Snead	70
1950	Ben Hogan	69	Lloyd Mangrum	73
			George Fazio	75
1955	Jack Fleck	69	Ben Hogan	72
1957	Dick Mayer	72	Cary Middlecoff	79
1962	Jack Nicklaus	71	Arnold Palmer	74
1963	Julius Boros	70	Jacky Cupit	73
			Arnold Palmer	76
1965	Gary Player	71	Kel Nagle	74
1966	Billy Casper	69	Arnold Palmer	73
1971	Lee Trevino	68	Jack Nicklaus	71
1975	Lou Graham	71	John Mahaffey	73
1984	Fuzzy Zoeller	67	Greg Norman	75
1988	Curtis Strange	71	Nick Faldo	75
1990	Hale Irwin	74-3	Mike Donald	74-4
1991	Payne Stewart	75	Scott Simpson	77
1994	Ernie Els	74-4-4	Loren Roberts	74-4-5
			Colin Montgomerie	78
2001	Retief Goosen	70	Mark Brooks	72
2008	Tiger Woods	71-4	Rocco Mediate	71-5
36 HOLES				
1928	Johnny Farrell	143	Robert T. Jones Jr. (a)	144
1929	Robert T. Jones Jr. (a)	141	Al Espinosa	164
1931	Billy Burke	149-148	George Von Elm	149-149

CHAMPIONS

MOST VICTORIES

4	Willie Anderson (1901, 1903, 1904, 1905)
4	Robert T. Jones Jr. (a) (1923, 1926, 1929, 1930)
4	Ben Hogan (1948, 1950, 1951, 1953)
4	Jack Nicklaus (1962, 1967, 1972, 1980)
3	Hale Irwin (1974, 1979, 1990)
3	Tiger Woods (2000, 2002, 2008)

CONSECUTIVE VICTORIES

3	Willie Anderson (1903, 1904, 1905)
2	John J. McDermott (1911, 1912)
2	Robert T. Jones Jr. (a) (1929, 1930)
2	Ralph Guldahl (1937, 1938)
2	Ben Hogan (1950, 1951)
2	Curtis Strange (1988, 1989)

OTHER MULTIPLE CHAMPIONS

2	Alex Smith (1906, 1910)
2	Walter Hagen (1914, 1919)
2	Gene Sarazen (1922, 1932)
2	Cary Middlecoff (1949, 1956)
2	Julius Boros (1952, 1963)
2	Billy Casper (1959, 1966)
2	Lee Trevino (1968, 1971)
2	Andy North (1978, 1985)
2	Payne Stewart (1991, 1999)
2	Ernie Els (1994, 1997)
2	Lee Janzen (1993, 1998)
2	Retief Goosen (2001, 2004)

OLDEST CHAMPION (YEARS/MONTHS/DAYS)

45/0/15	Hale Irwin 1990
43/9/11	Raymond Floyd, 1986
43/4/16	Ted Ray, 1920

YOUNGEST CHAMPION (YEARS/MONTHS/DAYS)

19/10/14	John J. McDermott, 1911

LONGEST SPAN BETWEEN FIRST AND LAST VICTORY

18 years	Jack Nicklaus (1962–80)

LONGEST SPAN BETWEEN VICTORIES

11 years	Julius Boros (1952–63); Hale Irwin (1979–90)

AMATEUR CHAMPIONS

Francis Ouimet (1913)

Jerome D. Travers (1915)

Charles Evans Jr. (1916)

Robert T. Jones Jr. (1923, 1926, 1929, 1930)

John Goodman (1933)

START-TO-FINISH WINNERS (NO TIES)

Walter Hagen (1914)

James Barnes (1921)

Ben Hogan (1953)

Tony Jacklin (1970)

Tiger Woods (2000, 2002)

Rory McIlroy (2011)

START-TO-FINISH WINNERS (WITH TIES)

Willie Anderson (1903)

Alex Smith (1906)

Charles Evans Jr. (a) (1916)

Tommy Bolt (1958)

Jack Nicklaus (1972, 1980)

Hubert Green (1977)

Payne Stewart (1991)

Retief Goosen (2001)

WINNERS OF U.S. OPEN, BRITISH OPEN, MASTERS AND PGA CHAMPIONSHIP

Gene Sarazen (1922, 1932 Open; 1932 British; 1935 Masters; 1922, 1923, 1933 PGA)

Ben Hogan (1948, 1950, 1951, 1953 Open; 1953 British; 1951, 1953 Masters; 1946, 1948 PGA)

Gary Player (1965 Open; 1959, 1968, 1974 British; 1961, 1974, 1978 Masters; 1962, 1972 PGA)

Jack Nicklaus (1962, 1967, 1972, 1980 Open; 1966, 1970, 1978 British; 1963, 1965, 1966, 1972, 1975, 1986 Masters; 1963, 1971, 1973, 1975, 1980 PGA)

Tiger Woods (2000, 2002, 2008 Open; 2000, 2005, 2006 British; 1997, 2001, 2002, 2005 Masters; 1999, 2000, 2006, 2007 PGA)

WINNERS OF U.S. OPEN AND U.S. AMATEUR

Francis Ouimet (1913 Open; 1914, 1931 Amateur)

Jerome D. Travers (1915 Open; 1907, 1908, 1912, 1913 Amateur)

Charles Evans Jr. (1916 Open; 1916, 1920 Amateur)

Continued ↗

Robert T. Jones Jr. (a) (1923, 1926, 1929, 1930 Open; 1924, 1925, 1927, 1928, 1930 Amateur)

John Goodman (1933 Open; 1937 Amateur)

Lawson Little (1940 Open; 1934, 1935 Amateur)

Arnold Palmer (1960 Open; 1954 Amateur)

Gene Littler (1961 Open; 1953 Amateur)

Jack Nicklaus (1962, 1967, 1972, 1980 Open; 1959, 1961 Amateur)

Jerry Pate (1976 Open; 1974 Amateur)

Tiger Woods (2000, 2002, 2008 Open; 1994, 1995, 1996 Amateur)

BROTHER CHAMPIONS

Willie Smith (1899) and Alex Smith (1906, 1910)

MISCELLANEOUS

MOST U.S. OPENS COMPLETED, 72 HOLES

35	Jack Nicklaus
27	Sam Snead
27	Hale Irwin
26	Gene Sarazen
26	Raymond Floyd

MOST TIMES RUNNER-UP

5	Phil Mickelson (1999, 2002, 2004, 2006, 2009)
4	Robert T. Jones Jr. (a) (1922, 1924, 1925, 1928)
4	Sam Snead (1937, 1947, 1949, 1953)
4	Jack Nicklaus (1960, 1968, 1971, 1982)
4	Arnold Palmer (1962, 1963, 1966, 1967)
3	Alex Smith (1898, 1901, 1905)
3	Tom McNamara (1909, 1912, 1915)
3	Colin Montgomerie (1994, 1997, 2006)

MOST TOP-5 FINISHES

11	Willie Anderson
11	Jack Nicklaus
10	Walter Hagen
10	Alex Smith
10	Ben Hogan
10	Arnold Palmer
9	Robert T. Jones Jr. (a)
9	Gene Sarazen
9	Julius Boros

MOST TOP-10 FINISHES

18	Jack Nicklaus
16	Walter Hagen
15	Ben Hogan

MOST TOP-25 FINISHES

22	Jack Nicklaus
21	Sam Snead
20	Walter Hagen

NUMBER OF TIMES A LEADER WENT ON TO WIN

After 18 Holes	19 times
After 36 Holes	37 times
After 54 Holes	48 times

MOST TIMES HOST SITE

8	Oakmont C.C., Pa. (1927, 1935, 1953, 1962, 1973, 1983, 1994, 2007)

WON FIRST TIME PLAYED IN U.S. OPEN

Horace Rawlins (1895)

Fred Herd (1898)

Harry Vardon (1900)

George Sargent (1909)

Francis Ouimet (a) (1913)

Acknowledgments | About the USGA

Many individuals contributed to the making of this special book. Without their participation, creativity and enthusiasm, this project would not have been possible. In particular, we would like to thank Ron Driscoll, Rhonda Glenn, Lewine Mair, David Shefter and Hunki Yun for their tireless dedication to this book.

We would also like to extend our gratitude to the staff of the USGA Museum: Robert Alvarez, Nicole Ciaramella, Shannon Doody, Susan Wasser and especially to Nancy Stulack for her diligent research. We'd also like to give special thanks to Kim Barney, Katie Bynum, Joe Goode, Dan Hubbard, Mary Lopuszynski and Amanda Weiner for their support, as well as to Kristen Williams for her editing skills that she inherited from her father, Mark Mulvoy. Thanks also to Nancy Foran for copyediting and Peter Ross of Counterpunch for his terrific design.

We extend a special thank you to Jack Nicklaus for contributing the Foreword to this book and to Andy O'Brien and Scott Tolley from the Nicklaus Companies in facilitating our research. In addition, we would like to acknowledge the patience, vision and creative genius of Steve Cameron, who spearheaded the project with our publisher, Firefly Books.

None of this would have been possible without the support of the USGA Members Program. We appreciate the supportive vision of Sarah Hirshland and the valuable contributions of Fiona Dolan and Amy Gianetti in making this book available to our Members.

We would also like to extend our appreciation to the members of the USGA executive committee, as well as Mike Davis and Glen Nager, for their support of this important project.

Finally, we would like to thank our fathers: Alan Jerris, Kenneth Mummert, Paul Trostel and Malcolm Williams – the first golfers we ever knew – for their love and support over the years.

Since its formation in 1894, the United States Golf Association (USGA) has served as the national governing body of golf with a working jurisdiction that comprises the United States, its territories and Mexico. Headquartered in Far Hills, N.J., the USGA conducts the U.S. Open, U.S. Women's Open and U.S. Senior Open, as well as 10 national amateur championships, two state team championships and international competitions. Together with The R&A, the USGA governs the game worldwide, jointly administering the Rules of Golf, Rules of Amateur Status, Equipment Standards and World Amateur Golf Rankings.

The USGA is a recognized global leader in the development and support of sustainable golf course management practices, while its USGA Course Rating and Handicap systems are used on six continents in more than 50 countries. Additionally, the USGA serves as a primary steward for the game's history through the USGA Museum and Arnold Palmer Center for Golf History and funds an ongoing "For the Good of the Game" charitable giving program.

For more information, please contact:
United States Golf Association
77 Liberty Corner Rd.
P.O. Box 708
Far Hills, NJ 07931
(908) 234-2300
www.usga.org

Photo Credits

All images courtesy of USGA Archives unless otherwise mentioned.

Photo Editing: John Mummert, Porter Binks, Nicole Ciaramella,
    Jolie Dobson

Photo Styling: Janice Engelke

T=top, B=bottom, M=middle, R=right and L=left.

USGA ARCHIVES

Jason Bridge: 183R

Darren Carroll: 206

Michael Cohen: 143, 202

J.D. Cuban: 88, 93, 142, 197, 198

Steven Gibbons: 94, 95

Russell Kirk: 160

Jonathan Kolbe: 79, 161, 169, 191, 205

L.C. Lambrecht: 62, 68

Jim Mandeville: 7

John Mummert: 2, 8, 9, 11, 12, 16, 25, 26, 31, 34, 41, 44T, 53, 60, 63, 64, 65,
    66, 67, 69, 70, 81, 84, 89, 92 all images, 96, 97, 98 all images, 99, 100,
    109, 112, 117, 150T, 151, 156, 158, 170, 180, 184, 186, 196, 199, 200, 201, 203,
    204, 207

Larry Petrillo: 133, 134

George S. Pietzcker: 28, 108, 121, 139

Kelly&Russell: 176, 179

Robert Walker: 183L

OTHER PHOTO SOURCES

Richard Mackson/Sports Illustrated/Getty Images: 58L, 59L

Hy Peskin, Photographer. Courtesy of Hy Peskin's Sports Legends
    & World Heroes. All Copyrights Reserved, www.HyPeskin.com: 152

© Corbis. All Rights Reserved: 154

Index